AF431423

Also by James Wood
Speaking Effectively (Book)
The Odd One (Book)
Broken Options (Book)
The System Eliminator (Book)

LIVING BY
TRIAL AND ERROR

True Life Novel

JAMES WOOD

DEDICATION

To My Family

To Those who Seek the Truth in Life,
To Those who Start Their Life Journey with Nothing,
To Those who are not Stoppable Despite Lack of Fairness,
Lack of Blueprint in Life, and Lack of Defined Path

LIVING BY TRIAL AND ERROR

True Life Novel

CHAPTER ONE

My mother and I stood alone on a plank platform along the railroad tracks. In the warm fall afternoon, Mom had decided we should move outside, where no one would overhear our conversation.

It was 1945. Two soldiers in uniform and a few parents and friends who had come down to see them off took no notice when we left the waiting room.

We watched for the approach of the one daily westbound passenger train. Trains were key for moving people and freight across the vast plains of Eastern Montana. Malta, population 2,000, was not a regular stop, even though it was the largest town for fifty or sixty miles in any direction. If passengers were to board, the elderly stationmaster would shuffle out and flag the train down.

Mom clung by her fingernails to a desperate decision. She didn't want a careless station manager to mess her up, though it hardly seemed likely he'd fail to stop the train for the service men.

She looked away from the tracks, "Are we doing the right thing?" She watched me closely. "Are you okay with going to Oregon?"

If I were a few years older, I'd probably say something like. "How should I know? He's your husband." She'd been at crunch points before, but she rarely asked my opinion. Now, barely thirteen, I truly wanted to help her make the decision. He was my father.

Later, on the train, I thought about the decision I'd accepted. For one year, Malta, the Milk River, and the low hills I'd hiked constituted my world. One year in one place and with a few friends seemed as good as it was likely to get. The next year, ninth grade, looked comfortably predictable, at least once I got beyond being caught in town and depantsed by upper-classmen. I felt no urge to leave it behind. So why had I said, "Yeah, we might as well go to Oregon."

I didn't know.

I felt kind of numb about my parents. Somewhere deep down, I hoped this time things would turn out well. Not too likely! We hadn't seen my father all year. About every week I'd hear Mom provide her sister with another example showing him to be an irresponsible bastard. Which made me wonder why she was on this train rolling along hour after hour to answer his summons. She was hardly the summons-answering type.

Maybe she was getting away from her sister and my three cousins. Their house was crowded, and when my uncle was in town between train tours as a military policeman, it got claustrophobic. I slept with my cousin Everett in the basement. My aunt had one room upstairs and cousins Doris and Ruth got the other bedroom. My mother slept on a rollaway in the living room. Space was tight, not really unusual for Malta. When uncle Newton was in town, I could see Mom tense up. I never saw any reason for her to be afraid of him.

Actually, with Mom, it was likely to be the other way around. In a hostile confrontation, people usually were afraid of her. She had a violent Irish temper and when she was at a full charge, nothing inhibited her. Once, she threw all the tableware in a kitchen drawer at me, hand-full by hand-full, and when she ran out of that, she went for the carving set. I was nimble, so I'll never know what damage she'd have done if she'd managed to plant that carving knife in me. Mom was paranoid, especially with men. She must have been a bit of a trial for my father.

At times we'd lived together like a regular family. Maybe remembering those times made me okay with going to Oregon. If that were the case, I didn't know it. At thirteen, on the way to an unpredictable reception in Oregon, I didn't consciously yearn for a normal family life.

- - - -

My earliest memories of being a family—mother, father, and me—were in a white stucco house in Durango, Colorado. The house overlooked a grassy park guarded on its perimeter by stately elm trees. My parents gave me an Easter egg hunt in part of the park closest to our house. It's one of the few family events I remember, maybe because it was so cheerful, with both Mom and Dad urging me on, hinting at hiding places, and laughing.

Another memory was less cheerful. In the stucco house, I remember sleeping on a couch in the living room, but I was there only a few weeks before I was moved to an upstairs bedroom. My parents—at least, my mother—wanted to check me frequently for signs of nerve damage and to change bandages. I'd sat in a bucket of near-boiling water left in the kitchen. Years later, a scar of varying smoothness and whiteness covered much of my butt.

My mother, I think, wanted to be a good parent, and that year in the stucco house she had about her best chance. I had a lot of freedom, however, for a four-year-old. Long afterwards, Mom would tell the story of when I came into the house carrying a rattlesnake. That made the papers as far away as Chicago. How did she deal with the rattlesnake? Apparently, she grabbed it and threw it out an open door. Then in seconds she stripped me and searched for fang marks. She was doing her best.

Durango, in the southwest corner of Colorado, was a tough town, but my unavoidable meeting with this fact came a few years later. For now, however, when I was three or four, my mother tried to shield me from some unpleasant family realities. Before I was born, a man named Rod Day had shot Dad's brother William Lyon twice in the back of the neck. With a small crowd wringing their hands, uncle Lyon bled to death on Main Street in Durango. Day pleaded self-defense (hard to prove when my uncle was shot from behind). He beat the rap, but it cost him his considerable fortune for lawyers and bribes. He was reduced to working as a skilled tradesman—in this case as a plumber in Durango. So, years later, when the hot water heater in the stucco house needed attention, Day showed up to handle the service call. My mother, of course, recognized him and advised him to leave immediately before my father came home. She was sure that my father would likely kill him. This is the story Mom told. A few details made it improbable. The murder of my uncle occurred years earlier, so why was Day still alive? At any rate, Day cut and ran that day, at least out of our house. I don't know how the water heater got fixed.

Assuming Mom's story was valid, the question, to me, is would my father have killed Day? Even now, many years later, given a direct encounter, I suspect Dad would have. He was much attached to a .44-Special revolver, and he was skilled in its use.

That year, Mom was a housewife. It's hard to imagine her in that role, though it might have been the one she wished for all her life. My father ran a farmers' co-op. Mom explained he'd taken the job agreeing to take as his pay a certain percentage of the profits. When he built the job up to where he was earning a lot of money, the board of owners decided they were paying him too much. They welched on their deal.

Dad quit in disgust.

Mom called him self-indulgent and irresponsible. The Great Depression was in full swing, and good jobs were hard come by. She was at least as angry with him as he was with the co-op board.

Mom and Dad didn't "just work things out" as most couples would have. They split, not for the first time, and not for the last time. I was only four. The split seemed normal.

Dad got a job managing advertising for a newspaper in Telluride. Mom got a teaching job in a country school, one room for twelve grades, several miles outside Durango. This was not a plum job. The kids were from farm families in a several-mile radius; some came to school on horseback. A shed and a small pasture were provided for their horses. For most of them, life was very physical. Discipline was enforced, on the infrequent instances it was required, by a father with a belt or razor strap. My mother was, of course, no match in strength for even one of the older kids, and they took it as an annual challenge to run off their teacher within the school year.

Mom knew two things about her students. They were, though hard-edged, basically good people, and they didn't like to look stupid. She put the older kids to working with the younger ones. She assumed they would learn most doing that.

One day, a crop-duster flew low overhead and most of the students rushed outside to look at it. As Mom told it, she waited for them to return to their seats. Then she explained she had no idea they had never seen an airplane before, and the next time one came near she'd certainly excuse them to go watch such a wonder. The problem of sudden exoduses from the classroom ceased.

As did many country schoolteachers, Mom boarded with a farming family. Nice people, but they had no inclination to take care of me while she was at school. This did pose a problem for Mom. I didn't understand the desperation of her dilemma until later. She was still working toward a teaching certificate, so she was very much a provisional teacher. She got teaching gigs because she was persuasive and experienced, but, in the middle of the depression, fully certified teachers were looking for jobs. In a couple of years, I'd be six years old and could legally, as a student, accompany Mom to her teaching job. Until then, what was she to do with me?

The fall I turned four, she tried a day-care school. I have only vague memories of that experiment, except for two incidents. As a child, I hated eating peas, and the staff couldn't abide insubordination. One day, peas were served as part of lunch. I wouldn't eat them, and I wouldn't fake it. The staff was unrelenting: I'd sit at the table until I ate my peas. It was a Mexican standoff that lasted well into the afternoon. I don't remember how it was resolved. Maybe by the school bus coming to take us home.

The second incident was more a matter of bad luck. In case of fire at the building, the day-care center rented a slide that started at a third-floor window. The slide was enclosed for the top five or six feet, I supposed to keep some panicked kid from over-leaping and going splat on the cement pad thirty feet below. My challenge was to go up the slide, partly by gripping the sides, until I reached the enclosed top. A greater challenge than the slide's slickness was timing the ascent when playground monitors were occupied elsewhere. I'd nearly reached the top about the time a monitor spotted me. This seemed to be the final straw with the staff, though I was not sure what the earlier straws were. So just short of my fifth birthday, I was expelled from day-care with no clear place to land.

My mother had another year to go before my existence would cease to be an awkward problem for her. She parked me with an unpleasant couple in Durango while she stayed with a rural family near her school. Every couple of weeks she'd come into town with the farm family. While they were in church, she'd take me out to lunch and see if I was doing okay. I consistently ordered hot dogs and sauerkraut. I didn't like change.

This arrangement would probably have worked for the year, except the man where I stayed played a trombone— and not well. Being hypersensitive to noise, I was not happy, and I yowled. The couple thrust me outside in the dark, so his musical career could continue. I yowled louder. The couple welcomed the pittance my mother paid them, so they faced a hard choice. Finally, I suppose you could say I won. They cancelled the deal, and the trombone nightmare was over.

But my mother's dilemma wasn't over. Several months of the school year remained. She knew the owner of a cheap motel on the edge of Durango and prevailed on her to manage me in return for us renting a room at a modest rate. For the most part, I was entrusted to the care of a large collie, one of the two smartest dogs I ever met. The collie and I got along fine. The motel owner agreed to make sure I didn't starve.

This arrangement worked until I got a severe case of measles. Mom, the motel manager, and a fly-by-night doctor agreed to confine me to the motel room and not make a fuss about my being contagious. My fever rose to a level that caused hallucinations. Like most young boys, I'd wanted small toy cars to play with, but our financial circumstance meant I rarely got one. Now, in my delirium, I imagined a dozen to drive and park on the bed cover. A few days later, the high fever subsided, and my toy cars vanished.

By failing to report, much less quarantine me, the motel manager probably violated the law. She apparently figured she'd pushed her luck far enough and asked Mom to take me off her hands.

I was still too young to go to school, and Mom was running out of places to stash me. She got desperate. That fall, she'd divorced my father, abruptly. A lot of things seemed to happen abruptly those days.

In December, she quit her job and married a rancher from the high country above Ridgeway. I'd never met Herb Porter before the wedding. Afterwards, we moved onto his ranch. Porter was a wiry, decisive guy who ran a big spread. We lived in a two-story ranch house presided over by Porter's mother. On the ranch, saddle horses were the standard means for getting around, but I preferred my feet. I wandered over the spread, sometimes stopping to watch a skilled blacksmith use a heavy hammer to pound white-hot iron into a needed shape or sharpen a plow sheer. Sheds and shelters were used for livestock. In a separate cabin lived the chief hired hand, who took a bath once a year whether he needed it or not.

For several months, I had a good life on Porter's ranch. Then Mom left suddenly, and we ended up in Durango.

Years later, in my teens, I asked Mom about Porter. At first, her response was "Porter?" I remembered too much to be put off that easily: the noisy shivaree, the night of their wedding, playing in the ranch-house's huge yard, the cap pistol Herb gave me—memorable because it took a six-shot round of caps, rather than the usual fifty-shot roll.

When I pressed my inquiry, she dismissed the marriage as unimportant. After several months of marriage, she'd obtained a divorce, or maybe an annulment. She said Porter was abusing me. I asked how. She didn't explain. I couldn't remember any abuse then. I still can't. Much later, I concluded she married Porter to provide a roof over my head. She manipulated him—and gave up her teaching job—in order to take care of me. I don't judge her.

The train click-clacked through endless high desert. I was a passive thirteen-year-old. At the edge of consciousness one question lurked: when we get to Oregon, would we again be a happy family, as we had been in the white stucco house in Durango?

Night settled in. We traveled coach, and the train was filled. It was hard to sleep sitting up. Occasional lights in the distance from remote ranch houses punctuated the inky dark outside the window. I listened to train wheels on the tracks and stole glances at my mother sitting bolt upright and staring resolutely ahead. She was worried.

I asked her, "What is Oregon like?"

"I don't know. I'm sure we'll get along fine."

"That isn't what I meant. I mean, does it get cold there, for instance?"

"You're worrying about cold, after a winter in Malta?"

"Okay, I want to know what I can expect from Dad. For years he hasn't been in the picture. You'd go off on tirades about how he'd abandoned us. But you sort of burned your own bridges in Malta, leaving after the school year started, to go to him now. How come?"

"You're the one wanted to go to Oregon. Remember, on the train platform?"

"That's not fair," I said. That was my naïve response. Several years later, I realized that strict honesty and fairness faded into irrelevance in the harsh light of her struggle to believe in herself. For her, tweaking reality was necessary for survival.

She seemed to think a couple of minutes before she responded.

"Years ago, we made a fresh start on the ranch. We can do it again." She turned to fix her gaze out the train window at the passing darkness.

True, when I was eight, we had tried another stint of family life. Dad gathered us up, and we moved to our primitive house a couple of miles outside Ridgeway, Colorado, where he took direct control of the family ranch. He bought a tractor and other equipment and asserted our family's legal rights to most of the water diverted from a year-around creek to farms for irrigation. Several nights, he or a hired man, rifle at hand, would mount guard on a diversion box to enforce his water rights. Despite his heavy-handed, but fair, methods, he and the other farmers cooperated to harvest wheat and alfalfa in the late summer and fall.

Mom and he remarried. She matched his purchases of new farm equipment with new furniture, curtains, and other wifely touches for the run-down house. Since all water for use in the house came from rainwater or a spring thirty or forty yards away and, at first, neither electricity nor phone lines reached that far into the country, life wasn't easy. This created no strain for me, but it must have been uncomfortable for my Mother. She gave it a fair try, and for a year and a half we lived as a family.

Dad took over as the breadwinner, as he had four or five years earlier in Durango. The farm sections of the ranch were only about a hundred and sixty acres. Power equipment was in short supply, and Dad would hire out to other small farmers in order to earn cash. He'd load the tractor and attached mower or other equipment onto a flatbed trailer and pull the trailer with a big Buick. He'd head up into high mesas, frequently on narrow, rocky roads most sane people would hesitate to navigate in a car even without a heavy trailer behind it. Sometimes Mom went along to help him drive. I went unless I was in school.

Some farmhouses in the high country made ours look good. Those farmers were what people meant by "dirt poor." During the school year, I got to know one of the kids well enough to stay overnight with his family once in a while. Now I'm not sure why I did that. I'd get blazing stress headaches, and the trail from the school bus stop up the face of Log Hill to their shack seemed to me seriously dangerous. They were Greek immigrants and lived at a survival level. They gathered pinion nuts, not for fun, but by the gunnysack-full as provisions and to sell. Fried chicken included the head, not as a delicacy, but because it was food. My friend's older sister, Effie, had remarkable artistic talent, at least my mother thought so from the girl's drawings she'd seen. Effie sometimes ran into the woods to stay away from home, apparently afraid of her father. I didn't understand why until much later, and my mother never explained. Even now, it's hard to figure why Mom let me go overnight to this place. But she did.

Running our own ranch was near a full-time job. Dad did piecemeal work on other farms on days he could have taken off or on evenings. Sometimes, with lights on the tractor, he'd work late into the night. To me, it was a big adventure. I could lie on the trailer watching him cut a swath smaller and smaller in an alfalfa field or sleep in the car into the wee hours after midnight while he plowed stubble under. He pursued a brutal work schedule. My mother supported him every step of the way; her criticism of his work habits ceased.

Dad got a boil on his arm, a bad one I guess, about the size of a half-dollar. Mom knew that a doctor was not an option, nor could Dad slow down and indulge the pain. She decided to take action the first evening he could quit work early enough.

She had him sit at the kitchen table with his lower arm in a basin of very hot water laced with Epsom salts. When the water began to cool, she poured in more from a pan heating on the stove. The soaking lasted more than an hour. She got out her sharpest paring knife and sharpened it further with a whetstone. She set aside a bottle of grain alcohol to use as disinfectant. They both focused on the task. My mother asked him a couple of times if he was doing okay, and he asked her if she was up to doing the job. It seemed odd to see them concerned for each other.

I'd seen chickens and hogs butchered, but this was as close to a surgical procedure as I'd been. Curious, I watched from a few feet away. I suppose Dad was grimly keeping control of a fair amount of pain and expecting more to come.

Finally, he said, "I think it's ready as it's gonna get. So, do it."

She made a firm, deep cut half an inch long in his arm. His head jerked back, but he held his arm steady, even when she squeezed the pus out and sloshed alcohol in and around the incision. She bandaged it with a square of gauze and tape.

"Let's eat," he said.

She smiled. She admired him.

As did I, at that moment.

Mom's cautious feeling of the bandaged arm next morning revealed no returning lump and little discomfort.

On the ranch, outside of school, I had few other kids to play with—mainly the Bentons who lived a half-mile below us along the river. Further away, a mile or two, another family had a boy near my age. The Benton boy died about a year after we moved to the ranch, so I had only his two sexually precocious older sisters as nearby playmates. That was okay. They filled in much of my education.

Mom stayed on the ranch while I rode the school bus and did fourth grade in public school in Ridgeway. The school had three rooms for grades one through eight and two or three rooms for high school plus a gym.

The next year, my father was gone most of the time, I guess to raise cash. Mom and I stuck it out on the ranch until about Christmas.

The Bentons had a small coal mine somewhere back in the mountains. They'd contracted with my father to keep us supplied with fuel during the winter.

On a wintry morning, we were down to our last bucket of coal. Mom didn't have many options. Dad, somewhere, had our only car. With snow flurries building, leaving the house to walk to the Bentons, who might or might not be home, risked serious frostbite or worse. Mom was considering how to bundle me so I'd have the best chance of surviving while she went for help.

Then, finally, old man Benton and one of his sons drove a beat-up truck into our yard, and started shoveling a load of coal into the shed. Mom watched from the kitchen window until they were almost done. Then she went out and explained the worry they'd caused.

Old man Benton listened politely while she said her piece. But the younger man interrupted to dismiss her criticism as "kind of dumb" since they'd arrived with coal before harm was done.

The old man watched, scratched the stubble on his chin, smiled and waited. He was not disappointed. Without shouting or profanity, and with barely bottled up anger, Mom dissected the young guy's lack of concern for neighbors in need and his lack of a grownup sense of responsibility. She didn't get an apology, but we never again ran dangerously short of coal.

Being down to less than a day's fuel when outside it's below zero seemed tangible proof that my dad lacked concern for his wife and son. You tend, even as a kid, to remember facing a strong chance of freezing to death.

For Christmas that year, Dad drove in from wherever he was working. We went to his parents' large house in Montrose, about twenty miles down the valley from the ranch. Getting the family together for Christmas seemed a jolly idea, full of love and so forth. If I sensed tension, it didn't register as something serious. Mom and Dad had seemed to get along on the ranch whenever he was there.

What I wasn't cued into is that my mother hated her mother-in-law, and the feeling was mutual. My mother faced not only her but my dad's three older, and very protective, sisters. Mom was outnumbered four to one, and the battleground was my father.

Two days after Christmas dinner, Mom and Dad got into a furious argument. They stood at the bottom of the stairway to the second floor. The rest of the family, including me, stayed back a respectful several feet. Emotional intensity ramped up between my parents. No one else tried to enter the fray. And no one—not my grandmother, not any of my three aunts, and certainly not my parents—tried to shield me from the charges and countercharges.

As we rumble toward Oregon, I try to remember what that argument was about. Even in a family given to crafty or violent persuasion, it stands out as a decisive encounter. Three and a half years have passed since, and I'm trying to anticipate what my mother and I are walking into. The issues at the bottom of the stairs? I can only remember the usual: accusations of abandonment on both sides, and my father's womanizing.

That Christmas Mom packed a couple of suitcases, all we'd brought to Montrose. She demanded to be taken to the bus station. One of my aunts obliged. Once again, my parents split.

Earlier, on the ranch, my father and I had developed a tenuous partnership. It was far from the ideal close bond, but I'd already decided, from what I'd seen among my cousins and friends, that ideal was pretty much crap. But still. . . .

The summer I turned nine, while we still lived on the ranch, Dad got me a single-shot .410 long gun. Mom tolerated his choice of present, but with misgivings. I don't know why she would object. Whenever she and Dad went with friends to shoot prairie dogs, someone would usually remark he could really see why Dad stayed in line. She was that good a shot with a .22, rifle or pistol.

Dad took me out to teach me how to handle my new shotgun. He was strong on safety. Always check the chamber and magazine when encountering a gun, no matter how many people tell you it's not loaded. Never point a gun at another person. Keep the gun unloaded or on safety until you intend to use it. Always know what's in your line of fire. And so forth. One kid in Ridgway a couple of years older than me served as an object lesson. He shot himself in the foot when climbing through a barbed wire fence. For a few days he was afraid to tell his dad, until he couldn't avoid limping.

After knocking over a few tin cans, I was due for an animal—not necessarily a moving target, but something alive, so I'd get the feel of killing. I didn't see Dad as cruel. Killing animals was part of life on the ranches and in the tiny mountain towns. You were defective if you hesitated when it was time to kill. I understood that.

We were on a slight mesa overlooking the farmhouse. The mesa was mostly a wheat field, now stubble. Both Dad and I scanned for prairie dogs. Saw none. On our way back to the path off the mesa, we spotted a large magpie on a fencepost. Dad touched me on the shoulder. We stopped and he nodded toward the bird, now fifteen or twenty feet away. Slowly I eased the safety off and raised the gun to my shoulder. Once my sights were set, I fired.

The magpie half rose in the air, then crashed to the ground. It fluttered feebly for a few seconds. I ejected the spent cartridge and replaced it. The bird now lay still. I flipped on the safety and breathed a sigh of relief. I had little stomach for shooting a bird point blank to end its futile efforts to live.

We walked back to the edge of the field. Dad set his jaw, in preparation for what he saw coming. I didn't see anything coming, until, with some pride, I told Mom about shooting at and hitting the bird.

She stared stonily at both of us. "So, you're proud of killing a helpless bird? And to what purpose?"

I started to tell her I needed the target practice, then thought better of it and said nothing.

She focused on Dad. "So you're teaching him? To do what? To be a callous killer of harmless animals? Perhaps he can graduate to people. How stupid can you get."

I expected my Dad to argue his case, to point out, for example, her proficiency in killing prairie dogs. He did not. He took my gun and walked past her to the bedroom to put it in a gun cabinet. As he reached the door, he turned and said, "I intend to teach the boy how to handle a gun."

That fall, Dad and I went duck hunting a couple of times before winter closed in. Then came Christmas in Montrose and the big argument. I didn't see him much for the next three and a half years.

As we clicked along on the rails, I tried to remember if I missed him. I must have, but I couldn't recapture the feeling. Images of talking with him, hunting together, watching him on the tractor seemed more and more smudged by a fog of gray anger. My mother had a near monopoly on memories of him. I heard her talk to her friends about his irresponsibility, his womanizing, his willingness to sacrifice wife and child for whatever his mother and sisters demanded. She admitted, in a rare generous moment, that he was the smartest man she ever met. He had unusual charismatic power, but to Mom this was not necessarily praise since he often used it to seduce other women. His talents and motives got mixed in her mind. I guess now on a train bound for Oregon, she thinks he's changed his ways. I don't know why she's thinking that.

CHAPTER TWO

I was glad the big blowup between my parents didn't happen until after Christmas Day that year. At least, I had some happier memories of opening presents and a festive dinner. It would be a long time before I'd see this family again.

Two days after Christmas, the streets in Montrose were slushy. Aunt Dorothy was elected to take Mom and me to the bus station. My father's sister drove in silence. She pulled the Buick into a covered boarding garage next to the terminal waiting room. With the motor running, she looked at me, it seemed with regret.

As Mom got out of the car, Dorothy turned to her. "You're sure you want to do this, Marie?"

My mother didn't answer her. She opened the rear door and pulled out her suitcase and then mine. "Let's go Ken."

I had to move fast to keep up. My aunt shouted after me, "Be good, Ken. And come back."

Inside the terminal, Mom left me with the suitcases while she went to the ticket window. Passengers would carry their luggage to the bus, and the driver would stow the bigger pieces. Suitcases ranged from fancy leather to cardboard boxes tied with twine or clothesline rope. Buses were about the only choice for people without cars or who preferred not to navigate the gravel, single-lane Million Dollar Highway eighty miles to Durango.

I shared my mother's hostility toward my grandmother, but I liked my three aunts. Dorothy was the youngest, but Frances seemed warmer and more interested in me, a better friend. Ruth, the oldest, was a kind person, behind an iron façade. They were the most of what family I knew. I felt droopy, almost scared to leave them.

I didn't know where Dad went after their last fight in Montrose. Now, it was just Mom and me. That's the way it would be for three more years. We'd see Dad a couple of times in the next year and a half, but he'd be always on the move. Then, when I was in the sixth grade, he went to Alaska on some army job.

In the bus, I got over worrying or even wondering what was happening to us as a family. I just felt empty.

By the time we got to Silverton, the driver was clearly trying to beat the onset of darkness. He had to go slow. When two cars or trucks had to pass in opposite directions, one would take the closest pullout while the other went by. Sometimes a driver would have to back up a few hundred yards. Drop-offs were spectacular, often starting within three or four feet off the edge of the highway and plunging almost straight down a sheer rock face for a long, long way.

On some occasions, in better days, my mother and father came up behind people who'd lost their nerve and simply stopped in the road. Dad would drive their car and Mom would drive ours to the next town.

Driving a bus or truck down off a pass was especially tricky. Staying in low gear could wreck a transmission, but constant braking burned out brake shoes. A driver needed to perform a fairly skillful balancing act. A few years earlier, Mom was in a bus that lost its brakes. The driver warned passengers to brace or hang on, then he drove at a slant into a snowbank. No one got seriously injured.

Our driver made it to Durango at dusk. Mom went into the terminal and phoned friends who ran a florist shop. The florists knew my parents as a married couple. In the back of their shop they had a small apartment to use when they worked overnight in town. They invited us to stay there until we got settled. Mom did not like to impose on friends, but sometimes it couldn't be helped. I think she was embarrassed because they'd blame her for the split. I couldn't see that they did. They didn't even seem surprised.

Mom had to find work, teaching she hoped, and a place to live. A few phone calls to people she knew from earlier jobs put her in contact with the superintendent of a six-room school a few miles out of town.

Yes, he could use an experienced teacher who could handle two grades. Rural schools always seemed in need of teachers like Mom. Inexperienced teachers often didn't last long. No, he thought it unlikely that a farming family near the school would provide room and board and certainly not for her son. Most of the teachers at the school lived in Durango and commuted. He gave her a couple of names.

Next she located an apartment, modest but sufficient, in a building with four units, one unit occupied by the owner-manager. Mom made sure I met her.

Then she arranged to pay part of the gas for another teacher who sounded pleasant, except she insisted they leave school on her schedule, and she usually put in an hour or two at the end of the day finishing up.

So now Mom's problems were solved—except what to do with me. I think she was afraid I'd mess up her commute. She arranged for me to do the last half of my fifth grade in the Durango public schools, one of which was only seven blocks away, an easy walk from our apartment, and I'd have a key.

This was not to be the happiest five months in my life.

With two or three rooms per grade, this Durango school was bigger by far than any I'd ever been in. Starting in the middle of the year, totally without friends and lost in a sea of students, I pulled in on myself.

Mom arrived home usually at least two hours after I did. What can you do day after day in a small apartment? Not enough! I'd drift around town, usually on or near Main Street. And it was the main street, with the huge, old Strater Hotel, J.C. Penny and Montgomery Ward, other department stores, the Gun and Sport Shop, and a couple of real estate offices. Ritchy's ice cream and soda fountain, took up maybe a sixth of a store that also sold all sorts of paper goods, from comic and coloring books to office forms. Four or five blocks of Main Street and two streets which ran parallel right above Main and below alongside the railroad tracks formed the heart of Durango. Car dealers and farm equipment stores were further out with gas stations and motels. While the streets above Main had classier homes and specialized shops, River Front, below the railroad tracks, seemed to me to have more intriguing possibilities.

An old guy, fat and shifty-eyed, ran a candy and magazine shop near the train depot. One cold afternoon, I stopped in to buy a dime's worth of candy. I preferred strips of licorice, both red and black. The cluttered store was warm. I didn't want to rush my decision.

"Hey, kid, you want to make some money?" the fat guy asked.

"Doing what?" I might have been new to the big city, but I was smart enough not to trust anyone.

"Peddling newspapers up on Main Street."

I waited.

"You buy the papers from me at three cents each and sell them for five. Every sale you make two cents."

"And if I don't sell my papers?"

"You turn them back in, and for every return I take three cents off what you owe me. At the end of the week we settle up. You can't lose."

"I don't have money, other than this dime, to buy the papers to begin with."

"Don't worry about that." This guy had several days of stubble on his face, and I don't think he'd had a bath recently. "I advance you, say, twenty papers, and charge you when we settle up."

"How do you know I won't sell the papers and forget to pay for them at the end of the week?" I asked.

"You look like an honest kid." His eyes narrowed. "And a smart one. You turn in your money to me every day or two."

"The three cents a paper, right?"

"You turn in your unsold papers along with five cents cash for every one you sell." He smiled like he was offering me diamonds dirt cheap. "I keep the accounts."

He could see I was suspicious of the deal, but tempted by the idea of money.

"It works like this. Say you sell a hundred papers in a week—and that's not hard. You've turned in unsold papers and given me five bucks. I take out my three, three times one hundred, and hand you two dollars." His hand swept toward the front of the store. "You could buy five comic books and a big bag of candy, and still have a dollar."

"Okay, I'll give it a try." So at the age of nine, I was in the newspaper business.

I was pretty good, two hours or so six days a week. Saturday evening was payday. I'd sold forty-eight papers. Generous guy, he rounded my profit up to an even dollar.

One comic book and a fair-sized bag of candy, I figured, would leave me with fifty cents. I was pondering a tough choice between Captain America and Superman when, out of the corner of my eye, I see a man in a suit and tie enter. He moves briskly toward the rear of the store, and, nervously, it seems to me, checks me out. I put back the Superman and riff through some other comic books on the rack. But I listen.

The fat guy mutters something like, "The usual?"

"Yes," the suit says, taking out two or three bills. I see this at a glance. On my next glance, I see the fat guy pull something from under the counter and hand it over. It's a flat sack, a little larger than what you'd need for comic books. In less than a minute, the customer is gone.

I really feel some urgency to see what's stored under that counter. The fat guy has a row of girlie magazines across the top of a rack, but those girls aren't fully naked.

I agree to continue my career in newspaper sales and depart. Someday I'm going to drop off my returns when the store is absent its owner.

I never got to see behind the counter. The fat man shorted me fifty cents, charged me for papers I never took. I could do nothing against him, but I didn't have to sell his papers.

"Ken, you say you're leaving the crew?" He frowned with deep disapproval. "That's too bad. You're about my best seller."

I nodded and walked out before he could bring up any objections.

I'd kept up a brave front, but I was scared. Being alone too much can do that to you, make you worry about things you can't nail down. I never tangled with the fat guy, but soon I had something specific and real to worry about, a lot.

A week or so after I stopped selling papers, a sixth grader approached me at morning recess. "Hey, kid, what's your name?" Having a sixth grader want to be friends should be a good thing, but his tone put me on guard, like he offered me no choice but to answer his question.

"Ken," I said. "What's yours?"

"Lawrence Cooper." I'd soon hate that name. And when I remember this, on the train three years later, I wonder if I'd kill him if I had a clean chance.

But for now, I see a boy a grade ahead of me, tall and spare, dressed in slacks, a cut above the cords most of us wore.

"You don't bring your lunch to school very often, do you?"

"No, not usually," I answered. "My mom has to leave for work early."

"How do you get lunch?"

"Mom gives me money for the cafeteria."

"Maybe you don't eat lunch at all." He smiled, but not like a friend would, and he seemed to be calling me a liar.

"Yeah, I eat lunch in the cafeteria a lot." I tried not to sound like I wanted to argue about it.

I figured he was maybe moving into some sort of facedown. I was tall for my age, but he was probably a couple of years older and an inch or two taller. I looked around for a recess monitor. They were expected to discourage serious fights and not do much else. I saw a male teacher a hundred yards or so away watching a pack of fourth graders harassing two girls.

So far I was okay. Maybe the situation was not the way I saw it.

"If you really have lunch money, show it to me," Cooper said. The teacher was a long way from us. I was nervous, but not scared enough to bolt. How much damage could he do before the monitor saw him?

"Why?" I asked.

"Then I'll know you're not lying to me."

I decided to just walk away. I turned, and now faced two guys, probably sixth grade friends of Lawrence. One looked beefy, like he'd be playing on the line for a football team in a few years. The other was smaller, looked wiry and quick, with a smirk like he'd enjoy beating the crap out of me.

The two of them said nothing, but their purpose was clear. Between them, they could do a lot of damage to me before the teacher could even reach us.

I turned back to Cooper and showed him two quarters in my palm.

He reached for them. I snapped my fist closed before his hand got to mine.

I glanced at the recess monitor, who was now strolling in our direction. It flashed through my mind that he knew Lawrence Cooper already.

"Show me those two quarters. I want to see them."

A person can make a decision as a reaction, without thinking through pluses and minuses or what happens next. Sometimes it's a good decision, sometimes not.

"Go to hell." I started to walk away.

Cooper's big friend moved directly in front of me. I dodged around him and kept walking.

"That's not nice!" Cooper shouted behind me.

No one followed me. But in the pit of my stomach, I knew this wasn't over.

Years later, on the train, I wondered if this whole affair would have gone better if I'd had a father to stand by me, at least give me some advice. Mom had enough problems of her own, and anyway there was nothing she could do.

Even if Dad were around he might not have been interested enough to give me advice.

The next day, I set off on the seven blocks from our apartment to school. I should have enjoyed the dry, cool weather, but I didn't. I was scared sick.

I didn't see them on the way to school.

During morning recess I spotted Cooper talking to a kid, maybe a fifth grader, probably shaking him down for his lunch money. They seemed to chat a couple of minutes, then I saw the kid, tears glistening in his eyes, hand over something to the bully and walk away. I got the feeling this happened often for this kid.

I hoped Lawrence and his two friends had moved on to easier hits and would leave me alone. I hoped that, but I didn't believe it. I'd stiffed the gang. Bad for business to let that go unpunished.

They'd most likely try to get me on the way home. I had all day to look forward to that. During afternoon recess, the three of them made sure I knew they were watching me.

After school was out for the day, I hung around in the halls. After a half hour or so, some teachers began to look curiously at me like they suspected I was waiting around for a chance to steal something.

With teeth gritted and breathing in quick, deep gulps, I crossed the schoolyard to the street. I searched for danger among the tree trunks lining the street and the yards and alley entrances on both sides of the street. Nothing seemed amiss in the two blocks or so ahead. A dozen people, some bundled up against a return of winter, were scattered along neat squares of a cement sidewalk. That was good. Though I doubted many people would try to prevent a gang of hoodlums beating up some kid, it would probably only take one person to save my hide. And then what? I tried not to think beyond today.

Lamar's Flower Shop, down a side street just off my route, would be my last safe haven before home. I passed that side street and kept walking, breathing easier. Only one long block to go.

A thick hedge shielded an alley entrance a hundred yards or so before my apartment. I didn't think about it. The alley was short and led to a path down a steep slope to Main Street a block below the street I was on. To avoid blocking traffic on Main Street trucks could back into the alley and offload to workers who carried electrical cable and other materials down to the rear of a big commercial building under construction on Main Street. On more than one boring afternoon after school and before Mom got home, I'd hung around the construction site. The workers tolerated me, when they were there, maybe because I kept out of their way.

When they weren't on the job, a watchman would be. We'd talk sometimes. His life sounded boring.

Thinking back three years later, safely on a train, I guess I should have seen this coming the way it did. I was a few feet past the alley entrance. Cooper stepped out first, crossed the sidewalk, and leaned against a tree, nonchalant and smiling in a fake-friendly way.

My choices ran rapidly through my mind. I could run back to Lamar's flower shop, but my enemy was trim and long-legged. I was pretty sure he could catch me. If the fight was going to happen, it might as well be here. I could keep walking toward my apartment building, maybe even say, "Hi, Lawrence." Or maybe not, better to ignore him.

I'd stopped when he came out. Too bad. I started walking again. That's when that wiry little bastard thug of his stepped out onto the sidewalk ahead of me. I kept moving. He backed up a few steps, but just to better separate me from my apartment. He took a stance, clearly ready to fight if I didn't stop. Lawrence was a few feet from him, loosely blocking me away from the street. This would be two on one.

I was about to get the crap beaten out of me. I hoped to avoid severe or permanent damage, but I didn't know what rules these guys played by. I was sure my face would be messed up for a while.

Expecting to see the other thug behind me, cutting off my escape the way I'd come, I looked back. He was nowhere in sight.

What was in sight was the short alley. I was practically at the entrance. Yeah, these guys could outrun me, on the street. But I knew that alley, the path that led from it and the construction site below like the back of my hand. I doubted they did.

I bolted at full speed through the alley and down the path to the construction site. I could have taken a bad fall, but I knew the worst spots and how to get by them.

At the bottom of the path, a few yards from the back of the new building, I looked back. They'd just started down the path, taking their time and grinning. They thought they had me cornered against the backs of stores on Main Street. They were wrong. The watchman had to check on supplies in the backyard, so daytime he mostly left a back door unlocked. I reached that door and swung it open.

Standing in the doorway, I took a good look at that pair coming down the path. They were still grinning and in no hurry. In another minute, they would reach the back door and have me blocked from getting out of the building. They apparently didn't realize I could go out a front door I could unlock from inside. I'd be on Main Street with lots of people and maybe a cop.

I didn't have time to diddle around. I ran for my life through a maze of unfinished rooms—one room to go before I'd reach a big gallery and the front entrance.

I always figured I was good at thinking ahead, but not this time. Cooper's big thug grabbed me by the arm as soon as I entered the room. I wrenched free, but this monster backed me away from the door. Now it became obvious: Cooper and his smaller thug had virtually herded me down here. I knew in a few minutes they'd join us—to have their fun in a big unoccupied building.

Meanwhile, the bigger kid decided he'd start the fun. I guess he was still sore I stepped around him so easily when Lawrence was trying to shake me down for lunch money.

"I'm gonna kick the shit out of you."

"Shouldn't you wait to see if that's okay with Cooper?"

He just grinned, sopping up my fear.

Frantic, I looked for a weapon. We were in a room where carpenters still had work to do, but I didn't see any saws or chisels. I did see two-by-fours, but the shortest piece of lumber looked to be ten or twelve feet long.

Ray's fist came at me. He wasn't that fast, but he wasn't going to miss. I half turned and took the impact on my raised shoulder. It knocked me to the floor. I rolled, expecting a kick, but none came. He smiled down at me, practically drooling with anticipation, waiting for me to stand up.

Fate smiled on me, in the form of a manageable length of two by two within reach. I made like I was groggy while I planned. The instant my feet felt fully under me I swung the length of wood with all the force I could muster. He raised his left arm to protect his face and head, but I'd aimed for a spot between his ribs and his hip. I missed that spot, and broke the piece of wood on his rib cage.

He staggered a bit and looked surprised, but all I really accomplished was to make him more pissed off. I still clutched one end of the broken two by two, nearly three feet long with a jagged point. I kept the point aimed at him while he moved from side to side in front of me. I doubted if my make-shift spear would hold up for a solid thrust into his body. He probably doubted it too, but he had a lot to lose if he was wrong.

"Oh, for Christ sake, Ray, what you think you're doing?" Cooper's voice cut through our tense standoff. For a few seconds I felt relieved. Then I realized it was now three to one.

"He broke that stick on me." Roy whined.

"Why did you let him get that close to you?"

Ray shrugged. "I had to get close to slug him."

"Well, Ken, there are now three of us, so your piece of wood is just going to be a little inconvenient—no real problem, for us." Cooper sounded friendly and reasonable.

He was right. I had no chance in an all-out fight. Maybe if I played his game I'd survive. I tossed down the stick.

"Now, see, Ray, he doesn't have his stick. So, what are you going to do?"

Ray knew what he was going to do, but it took him a minute to figure out the most enjoyable way to do it. Then he started for me.

"Hold it right there." The command came, in a loud, adult voice.

It was my friend the watchman. He'd entered the gallery from a hall. No one noticed him until that moment.

"We're just playing a game. Right, guys." It was Cooper at his oily best. "Now we'd like to finish the game, old man." I don't know how that bully could sound so friendly and still be so threatening. "We won't do any damage in here. And we won't steal anything. Honest."

"I want you out. Now."

"You shouldn't be in such a hurry." He and his two thugs began to close in on the old guy. I was worried. He was my friend.

The watchman reached into his jacket and hauled out a .45 revolver. "Out."

Lawrence didn't give up easily. Maybe he was afraid of losing face. "Now, gramps, you're not going to use that gun on anybody."

Cocking the hammer sounded loud in the room. "You're first, smart ass." He held the gun steady, aimed at Cooper's chest.

No one said anything for several seconds.

My friend moved the gun to each of the two thugs. "Or does one of you want to go first?" Then the gun was back on Cooper.

I suspected we were all thinking about the same thing. Would a watchman protecting property be in trouble if he shot some kids? Maybe in self-defense? He'd have me for a witness. This was Durango. People got shot.

Cooper held up his hands in a placating gesture. "Let's not get antsy. We're going. Come on, Ken."

"I'm staying here."

Lawrence started to argue. He glanced at the watchman, who studied the bully like he was curious about this kid who was about to get himself killed.

Cooper and his two sidekicks left the room. The watchman and I followed and watched them start up the path to the alley.

Before leaving, I thanked the watchman. He leaned in the open rear door of the new building until I reached the alley. But he couldn't stick with me forever. I knew this thing with Cooper wasn't over.

The next morning, I woke up worried. By the time I ate breakfast, I was in a clammy sweat. Mom asked me if I was okay. No point trying to explain to her, nor pleading sickness to postpone what was going to come. I dressed, swallowed as much cereal as I could get down without puking, and started for school. Nothing happened on my way, but I didn't feel any relief. I figured they'd wait.

In the cafeteria, I was hungry enough to eat. I was on the canned peaches, desert, when Cooper slid into the bench beside me. "Hi, Ken, how's the hash?"

My body stiffened. "Fine." I tried to breathe normally. The rest of his gang was nowhere in sight.

"Ray's got sore ribs." Cooper chuckled.

Where was he going with this. No place good, I was sure.

He continued, "Ray will hold a grudge. Italians are like that, you know." He paused. "Would you really have rammed that broken piece of lumber into him?"

I put my spoon on the tray and looked at Cooper straight on. "Yeah, I would have." This may not have been a fully truthful answer, but I figured any plausible threat I could level at these bullies was to the good.

"I thought so." He nodded. "You know, Ken, that friend of yours with the big gun can't be around everywhere, here at school, on your way home, downtown." He smiled. "And you can't carry a spear with you all the time, can you?"

"What's your point, Lawrence?"

"You'd be a lot safer in a gang, Ken, my gang. Consider this an offer."

I didn't see this coming. I stalled.

"Why the offer?"

"You're smart and you got guts. I like you. "

I did not like Lawrence. "Maybe I don't want to join a gang."

"Then you should change your mind." He wanted it his way. He reminded me of the fat guy who sold me on the newspaper business, except Lawrence was more convincing. "Look at it this way. In the gang, you don't have to be afraid of anybody at school, and you'll make some real money." He shrugged and sighed with labored regret. "If you're not with us, every day for the rest of the year, Roy and Vick will be on your back. Every day."

"How does the gang make money? You can't be shaking down that many kids here at school."

"True." He chuckled. "But it's steady income." Abruptly, he turned grimly serious. "What I'm going to tell you now, you don't ever tell anyone. You understand?"

I nodded.

"I got some friends, older guys, who operate flea markets, used merchandise shops, that sort of thing."

I waited. I couldn't imagine an eleven-year-old kid operating a stall at a flea market. "So what's your connection?"

"I'm a supplier." He said it with a certain amount of pride. "Hub caps. Fishing tackle. Other stuff from sticky-finger purchases. If we see a car with nobody in it, but with some goodies like radios, new clothes, wrapped packages, we take the stuff."

"If the car is locked?"

He looked at me as if I'm really slow. "We smash a window, or move on. You'd be surprised how many people don't bother to lock their car." He shifts from explanation to business. "So, you in or out?"

"I'll have to think it over." Working for the fat guy had given me enough taste of the shady business world in Durango.

Cooper shook his head. "No, you don't think it over. Decide now."

His direct order didn't invite argument, but I could try. I smiled and tried to keep an agreeable tone. "What if I'm no good at shoplifting or that other stuff?"

"You can learn, starting today. When school is out, I'll meet you at the corner on Oak Street." He got up, started toward the cafeteria door, stopped and looked back. "Ken, you want to be there." He said it as if solicitous of my welfare, but I got the message.

So began my career in crime. At first, under his direction, I practiced with candy and gum in grocery stores. In two weeks I graduated to lifting office supplies and small tools and sports equipment. Cooper said I was really good, a natural.

Fear of being caught plagued me. Finally, I mentioned this to Cooper.

"That's good. That keeps you on your toes. Anyway, Ken, what are they going to do to you? You're just a kid."

Mom worked hard. A good reputation and living by the rules were important to her. I imagined her hearing cops tell her I was in jail. She'd be mortified, and she'd take it out on me.

My problem came to a head one Saturday morning five or six weeks into my life of crime. I was in the Gun and Sports Store planning on picking up a few fishing flies.

They came in long, narrow boxes, the expensive ones in a glass-topped case on the counter. All I needed was half a minute to lift the glass lid, grab a handful of boxes and stuff them inside my jacket. I looked around, reached for the edge of the glass top, and took a last glance around.

An older clerk, hawk-eyed, watched me from thirty feet away, just waiting. For sure, he might as well have been reading my mind. I let the case close and walked out of the store. Three doors down I stopped in front of the J.C. Penny store and looked back. He was not behind me.

That was too close. I had to do something. I didn't know any city cops, but I did sort of know the man who ran the county jail. Dad and Mom knew him; I'd met him two or three years ago. I wished Dad was around to help me contact him, but he wasn't. I didn't want to burden Mom with my problem.

A couple of days later, I walked into the granite building that housed county offices, and found the jail. I walked to the jailor's office. While I waited outside his office, I stared down a corridor with cells along one side. Vertical bars defining cells looked thick and heavy, reinforced by horizontal bars about a foot apart. Our gang, including me, could end up behind those steel bars. Clammy fear almost overcame me. I gripped the armrests of the heavy wooden chair I was in and held tough. I figured if my nerve deserted me now, I'd not be likely again to work up enough courage to come here. I'd be a slave to that bastard Cooper as long as we stayed in Durango.

I told the jailor how I was forced to join the gang, what we did, and their names. He took notes. After twenty minutes, he nodded, thanked me, and told me to go home.

Four days later, I walked along Main Street. A city police car, with two cops instead of the usual one, pulled near the curb and stopped. The cop not driving got out and walked across the sidewalk toward me. A big queasy hollow replaced my stomach. I just waited. He asked me if I was Ken Bailey. I said I was. He told me to get in the back seat. Lawrence Cooper and Roy were already there. Cooper wasn't smiling at all.

They took us to the jail office and photographed and fingerprinted us. Then, one at a time, we were interviewed by a big, beefy, mean-looking cop. At the end of my time with him, he didn't ask for a confession or even a statement; he just sent me home. A few days later, I found out that roughly the same thing happened to Lawrence, Roy and Vick, except the cops did take signed statements from them.

I don't think many ten-year-old kids were arrested as part of a gang—at least not in those days. It bothered me some that I was a snitch, but I figured I acted in self-defense. So far as I know, Cooper never found out how they got turned in, thank God.

So ended my career in crime. My troubles in Durango did not, however, end.

CHAPTER THREE

I had few friends at school. At times, the loneliness bothered me enough to make me want to join in whatever more popular kids were doing. In mid-spring, they were fighting a battle of tacks. The rules were simple. If you could plant a thumbtack so someone else scratched himself or herself on it, you scored. I'm not sure what you scored, but at least you were in the game. The highest achievement was to plant one so someone sat on it.

Mom being a teacher, we had thumbtacks. I took a half dozen to school and, at recess, put one on the seat of a scrawny, not very popular kid. It was kind of cowardly to go for a safe target. After recess, he spotted the tack and decided, I suspect for pretty much the same reasons I did, to use it. He went for broke. He got back from recess a little early, and, with a few other early returnees watching fascinated, he planted the tack on the teacher's chair behind her desk.

Our homeroom teacher, a heavyset, stern woman, with no sense of humor whatsoever, called the class to order and started for her seat behind the desk. By now, half the class knew what was going on, and they waited with breathless anticipation. She sensed something was up, I guess. She paused, looked around warily, and, with her eyes covering the whole class, went to her chair and sat down.

Her response was better controlled than we hoped. After a passing moment of surprise, she appeared to reach under her butt. She stood up, holding the offending tack in front of her chest. There was no mistaking the barely contained rage while she looked around the room.

"Who put this in my chair?"

No one spoke. I glanced at the scrawny kid. He looked sweetly innocent.

"Someone knows who did this." She waited.

By now, almost everyone in the room knew who the villain was. No one spoke.

"One of you brought thumbtacks to school. Who has them?"

I felt uneasy. I had a half dozen in my pocket. I wasn't sure anyone else had any that day.

"If you won't confess, I'll search every one of you until I find them."

Thinking back three years later, I'm not sure how she'd work that. But then she spoke with the threatening confidence of a Nazi prison guard. I didn't doubt her, and I'm sitting with a pocketful of the offending contraband.

"I have some tacks." I held up my hand, trying to keep it steady. "But I didn't put any tack in your chair."

Every kid turned to look at me, a few with sympathy, most curious.

"Then you're responsible." Clearly, she had found a target for her outrage, and she wasn't interested in fine points of justice. "Come with me."

She strode along the side of the classroom to the door, picking up a yardstick on the way. The yardstick was not a flimsy giveaway from a lumber store. It was seasoned hardwood, a third of an inch thick. Even so, I counted myself lucky that she decided to handle this herself, rather than involve the principal. Mom would be seriously annoyed if I got ejected from another school.

We departed from an absolutely silent class, and entered an empty room a couple of doors down. She did nothing fancy like have me bend over a desk or drop my pants. With her left hand she grasped my left arm below the shoulder, and with her right arm administered justice—quite a bit of justice. I didn't yell, but tears streamed down my face and I sort of gagged.

"Have you learned your lesson?"

"Yes, I have."

She studied me for several seconds. "Do you want to go home for the rest of the day?" She said this almost kindly. I was amazed.

I shook my head.

"I'm sorry I brought tacks to school," I said. "But I wasn't the one who put that tack in your chair."

"And you're not going to tell me who did, are you?"

I shook my head again.

"Go blow your nose and rinse off your face before you come back to class." She turned and went out the door.

When I entered the classroom quietly from the back a few minutes later, word seemed to sweep up to the front. Some students looked at me with maybe a little respect.

I still had to fill long late afternoons. Downtown wasn't so attractive, because Roy and Vick were still running free and not friendly. To pass some time in our apartment, I assembled temporary models of machines or buildings from a kit with dowels of various lengths and spools with holes the dowels fit into.

One afternoon I got a dowel stuck in one of the spools. Some sort of tool was needed to push the dowel out from the other side of the spool. The first thing that came to hand was a two-pronged carving fork. Not the best choice, but I was in a hurry to get on with whatever I was building.

With one prong of the fork, I pushed on the dowel as hard as I could. The fork slipped and the other prong went through my left index finger near the first joint. It went through cleanly, so deep it must have come close to scraping bone.

I dropped the dowel and spool. Now I held a carving fork in my right hand, one prong of which was sticking through a finger on my left hand. I had to hold fork and finger in the same relation to each other, or have a carving fork suspended from the flesh of one finger. That didn't seem like a good idea. There wasn't much blood, and if there was pain, I didn't feel it, yet.

But I was anxious. Not until later did I understand shock, but I knew something was going to hit me as soon as the surprise wore off. Mom wouldn't be home for another hour, maybe two. I wasn't sure I could go around holding a carving fork that long. I knocked on the landlady's door. No response. Lamar's Florist Shop was probably closed by now. Anyway, I wasn't sure I could walk that far carrying this mess with both hands. Desperation seeped through my thinking. Somewhere, I'd read that you could fight off lightheadedness by moving around; it was what boxers did after taking a solid blow. So I rapidly paced up and down the length of our small apartment about fifty times. That seemed to work because the panic passed.

In the small kitchen, near a window, I sat and stared at my finger and the attached fork. If I'd thought very much about my next move, I'd have been paralyzed. But I didn't think. I pulled the fork out of my finger. While I had some momentum, I opened our medicine cabinet to get alcohol and pour it over both the entrance and exit wounds. It hurt like hell, so I figured it must be doing some good. I gave the finger a second dose.

Then, kind of numb, I sat on our well-worn couch and waited an hour or so until Mom came home.

I showed her the injury and told her what happened.

"We'll have to put iodine on it."

"I already put alcohol on it." Iodine would burn as bad as alcohol, and this was a deep wound.

She studied the exit point, turned my finger over and looked at the entry hole. "Did it bleed much?"

"A little, not much."

She went to the bathroom, turned in the doorway and looked back. "I'm proud of you for pulling the fork out by yourself."

"Would Dad have been able to do that?" I have no idea why I asked that.

She smiled. "Yes." She put down the small brown bottle with the skull and cross bones. She looked over the fork carefully. "I don't think you'll need shots." That was a blessing! She dabbed on the iodine and covered both holes with band-aids, the closest we had to bandages. She went into the small kitchen to get dinner.

Over our plates Mom raised the option of me finishing up the last weeks of fifth grade at the school where she taught. "I'll be nearby if you have another accident. It will take some paperwork, but I'm sure I can get permission."

I shook my head. I appreciated her concern, but Durango had cost me a lot of adjusting and I didn't want to start over. Rural schools could be even tougher than Durango. "It would cause you too much trouble for just a few weeks."

She shrugged. "How's the finger doing?"

"Fine." It throbbed a little. With Mom here I didn't feel so alone.

One Sunday morning a few days before the end of the term, Mom announced, "I've got to go to teacher's college in Millersburg this summer, to get certified." Millersburg was sixty miles from Durango. "I can't take you with me. I'll be there all summer."

"Why can't I go with you?" I figured she wouldn't just abandon me by the side of the road, but a summer seemed like a long time.

"I have to concentrate on getting these course credits. Do you remember the Ambersons, the family I stayed with when you were five?"

"Yeah." I also remembered the trombone player she'd planted me with because Ambersons didn't want to be bothered with me.

"You'll stay with Ambersons."

"How come I couldn't live with them five years ago and now I can?"

"They're going to have you work for your keep."

"Doing what?"

She shrugged. "Whatever jobs they have. Hoeing weeds in corn fields maybe, things like that."

A few days later, she'd packed up for a long stay in Millersburg and I was deposited with the Ambersons. Their house was large, and I was put by myself upstairs in a bedroom I shared with a pile of hundred-pound sacks of flour ground from wheat grown on the farm. My hosts put me to chopping weeds out from around emerging corn plants. I had to pay a little attention to avoid taking out the corn plants. It was tedious work, and boring.

The Ambersons were Seventh Day Adventists. No pork and no duck. And no reading fiction, but I figured a way to beat that. I borrowed books from a friend who lived about a mile away. Characters in the books were animals with some human traits. I claimed the books were instructional: I learned about the animals. That was stretching a point, but I was only there for three months, so the Adventists didn't push it.

A very pretty girl was a major attraction, for me, in Sunday school.

I wanted to go to a one-week summer church camp. Mr. Amberson wrote to ask Mom to okay it. She didn't get around to answering until it was too late, so I spent the week with some Ambersons who stayed on the farm. I didn't understand why Mom couldn't take ten minutes to send a note saying it was okay to send me to church camp.

During haying season, another kid about my age and I set slings on the wagons and sleds that brought the hay to a stack. One sled was pulled by a pair of magnificent black horses. The slings were laid out so that when a load of hay came in, a crane lifted the load and swung it over the haystack. Then a jerk line on the bottom of the sling would cause it to separate in two halves and dump the load on the stack where a worker would spread it out. Setting the slings and jerk lines wasn't complicated, but God help us if we got it wrong and a jerk line wouldn't release or a load would dump on a wagon as soon as the crane started to raise it.

The summer went pleasantly enough, but for one incident. The boy who loaned me books and I went fishing at a big reservoir. Permission was given on condition we get back well before dark. The fishing trip was adventuresome but produced no fish, until finally near dark we gave up and started back. We decided to take one more try at a small outlet pond just below the reservoir.

We hit the jackpot. Small but legal perch abounded. This was fun! We hauled out several apiece before we noticed it was night and for both of us home was more than a mile away.

We walked together to a main road where we split in our separate directions. I'd started up the lane past a couple of fields to the Amberson farmhouse when I saw a pair of headlights coming toward me. The car stopped and one of the Amberson boys told me to get in. We drove to the house in silence. I got no dinner that night, and my haul of fish was ignored. The two sons, eighteen and twenty, said nothing. I guess Mr. and Mrs. Amberson felt acutely responsible to my mother, and our fishing destination had sufficient danger for inexperienced ten-year-olds. Mrs. Amberson pointed out to me that I'd not kept my promise to get back before dark. I'd caused a lot of worry, and I'd lied.

The next day, mid-morning under a hot sun, she ordered her younger son, Earl, and me into the car. He drove down the farm lane until we stopped at a patch of willows near the road. We all stood near the car, waiting. Mrs. Amberson told Earl to cut two sturdy willows. He took out his jack-knife and did so. I didn't have to be a genius to figure out where this was going. Earl was about six-foot tall and solid, and if he really laid into me it would hurt like hell. My eyes watered a little looking forward to that. It didn't help at all to know I deserved what was coming.

Mrs. Amberson told Earl to give me a whipping.

Earl didn't say anything for half a minute. Then he shook his head. "I can't do that, Ma."

"Why not? What's the matter with you?"

"He's just a kid."

She studied Earl for several seconds before she sighed. "Then give me that willow."

He handed it over and glanced at me with sympathy.

So Mrs. Amberson gave me a whipping, such as it was. She was pretty frail, at least compared with Earl. I wouldn't stand still, Earl refused to hold me, and she didn't have much strength to hold me with one hand and lay on with the other. While I circled her a couple of times, she'd got in maybe a half dozen fairly solid hits on my backside.

"That's probably enough, Ma," Earl said. "I think he's got the idea. Right, Ken?" I did get another whipping, but it hardly counted. I stayed overnight with Glen Brown and his family, fellow Adventists. I guess we'd teased Glen's sister pretty hard. Mr. Brown took a razor strap to Glen and me. He used the cloth side on me, so it didn't hurt much. Glen got the leather side, but he didn't cry out.

CHAPTER FOUR

Near the end of the summer, Earl Amberson drove me into Durango and stopped in front of the Strater Hotel. "You're supposed to wait for your dad in the hotel lobby." He paused. I think maybe he even swallowed before he went on. "So long, Ken, you're a good kid. We were glad to have you stay with us. Good luck." He said "Good Luck" like he wished for something he wasn't sure was going to happen. He put my suitcase on the curb.

In the lobby I sat in an over-stuffed leather chair in one corner where I could keep an eye on the entrance. The lobby looked like a place for rich people. Even in clean jeans and shirt, I felt vaguely uncomfortable. Mom was not in sight, nor did I expect her to be there.

When Dad came in, he immediately spotted my location and came toward me. I stood up beside the big chair. He smiled like he belonged there—and I guess he did. We hadn't seen each other for over a year, but we didn't hug or any of that nonsense. I didn't feel any great rush of joy, but I was relieved to see him.

In the elevator, we went to the fourth floor and down a hallway. He opened the door to the biggest hotel room I could imagine, actually two or three rooms. It was in a corner of the floor, and windows looked out on both Main Street and a side street.

"Set your stuff in that smaller room, and we'll get some lunch. Your mother is finishing up her course work. Later today, I'll drive over to Millersburg and pick her up." I was glad to hear that Mom would soon join us.

Now on the train to Oregon three years later, I'm not sure I should have been happy about that. The outcome of Mom and Dad getting together wasn't that great for me.

That evening we had dinner in the hotel dining room. I did not order sauerkraut and hot dogs. I have no idea what I did order. Even with me barely over ten, there was no ignoring a tense atmosphere between my parents.

He had come to take Mom and me back to the ranch. "Why did you give up a good newspaper job in Alamosa to come back to the ranch?" she asked.

"I missed you a lot, you and Ken."

"Bull shit." Mom swore only when she was really mad. "You could have taken us to Alamosa."

I wished when he said he'd missed me, she hadn't decided he lied.

Dad sighed with frustration. She was backing him into a corner. "I didn't think you'd want to leave Ridgeway. Your friends and all that." It was a poor argument: Mom and I had been living in Durango for the past six or eight months, sixty miles from Ridgeway and familiar friends.

"You decided that, did you?" She turned to me. "Your father is a liar." She turned back and stared at him, until I could see him decide to tell the truth.

"Mother said the ranch was about to go under. The sisters seconded that. I had to come back to take over, or we'd lose it."

"You gave up a good job in Alamosa, to come back to that ranch? Why doesn't one of your brothers take it over?"

From a few family stories, even I knew the answer to that. Dad's younger brother had left the ranch when he was sixteen. He'd announced he had no intention of ever going back. Dad's older brother was a mess mentally, brilliant but incapable of managing anything. It seemed playing dirty for Mom to lay that on Dad when she already knew why he didn't go to his brothers.

"We'll talk about it later," he said. And they did, for a week or so, while we lived in perhaps the finest hotel suite in Durango. I was sent elsewhere most evenings, sometimes to keep me from hearing them fight about the issue of whether to go back to the ranch, sometimes because they just wanted privacy. The hotel had three lobbies, and I hung around in them for a while. I discovered, tucked in one corner of the building, a drug store with a soda fountain. It had a large display of comic books, and I could nurse a coke through a couple of hours while I read them. Sometimes it would take two cokes. The guy who ran it was very tolerant of me being more or less a deadbeat. Maybe he had some idea why I was down there and felt sympathy.

The battle was, as usual, Mom versus Dad's family. She seemed able to tolerate his abrupt departures from jobs and his womanizing, but she hated his willingness to abandon his career whenever his mother and sisters called him back to the ranch.

As I looked over at her sitting upright and asleep on the train, I realized why we're on our way to Oregon. This time he didn't rush back when his relatives called. Instead, he stayed on his newspaper job in Albany and asked Mom to come to him.

But three years earlier in the Strater Hotel Mom had less reason to trust him. He'd blown off the job in Alamosa and done what his mother and sisters wanted and returned to the ranch.

What could Mom do now? She didn't have a job lined up, and we were near the start of the school year. She could maybe get a job at a rural school somewhere. I hoped she'd want to avoid me going through another year like the past year in Durango, but I'm not sure that even entered into her decision. In any case, she decided to go back to the ranch with Dad. She'd resume life in that primitive house, and I'd go by school bus to Ridgway public school. Maybe we would be a family again. I hoped for that.

After a week in the Strater Hotel, we all got in the big Buick and headed for the ranch eighty miles away.

Dad went back to working our farm and taking a few piecemeal jobs, but it was clear he didn't want to work the same killer schedule he did earlier. Maybe he couldn't. Mom took the car into Ridgeway and stocked up on groceries. While she was there, she signed me up for sixth grade.

I may have been only ten, but I recognized my teacher was a good-looking woman, and unmarried. But for us grade school kids, fantasy is as far as it went. Rumor had it, however, that she was having a torrid affair with a high school student.

We settled down to a routine. Every weekday morning I'd walk down the road, cross the railroad tracks, and go up a slight hill to the highway between Montrose and Ridgway. A school bus picked me up. The order reversed every afternoon. Two school buses brought enough students in from the countryside to keep the school legally open and, more to the point, enough male students to field athletic teams. Ridgway played Ouray ten miles further up in the mountains and schools down-valley as far as Delta forty miles away. Even then getting a necessary minimum number of athletes was sometimes a close call. A couple of weeks into the fall Johnny Forseyth had to play football, both offense and defense, with three cracked ribs.

A month into the fall term money was really tight. Dad showed the strain of holding it together. One late afternoon he came back from a business trip to Montrose with a young couple, Bethel and Bruce McAllister. He explained to Mom he'd picked them up hitchhiking along the highway, and he told her they'd be joining us for dinner. He didn't add they'd be with us a lot longer than dinner.

Bethel and Bruce were complete strangers to Mom and me, and I think to Dad. Their possessions were limited to the two suitcases they had when Dad picked them up and the clothes on their backs. They had gone through high school at most. She had fine features, with shoulder-length dark hair. He had a few days growth of dark beard, and he could use a haircut. They smiled and asked what they could do to help. Mom put Bethel to peeling apples.

Mom and Dad went out past the back porch. I tagged along.

As soon as they were out of earshot of the house, Mom turned on Dad. "Who are those people, and why did you bring them here?" She was more than curious. Maybe because Bethel was pretty, she was suspicious and a little hostile.

"I'm going to have to raise some money, Marie."

I didn't see any connection with the young couple, but Mom did. She waited.

"Bruce says he knows how to handle a tractor and other equipment, and he can manage a ranch."

"Where are they going to live?" Mom asked. It was a good question. Ridgway, the town, was a couple of miles away.

"Here."

"Here!" Mom didn't scream at him. The cold anger in her voice and look were scarier.

"Yeah, I figure we can put them in Ken's room. He can sleep on the couch in the living room. It'll work out just fine. She can help you in the kitchen and garden, and he can handle the ranch."

"And what will you be doing?" Her voice seemed to dare him to answer.

"In Montrose I got a strong lead, an offer actually, to take over advertising for a paper in Olathe. Just through the Christmas season, until a man on medical leave gets back. They'll pay me a salary plus commission."

"So you'll be doing just what you've always wanted to do?" she pointed out.

"Yes. I can keep the ranch afloat at the same time. It's providence."

"And how do Ken and I fit into this providential plan?" Her tone said she was still on the attack, but she couldn't quite figure out how to get at Dad.

"Well, you'll stay on the ranch, keep an eye on things, and Ken will continue school in town."

"You don't know whether this McAllister guy knows how to drive a tractor, do you?"

"He says he does, and I believe him."

"And Ken and I will be here without a car?"

"No, no, not at all. The newspaper will provide me a car. The Buick stays here with you."

Dad left for Olathe by bus two days later. Bruce made a reasonable pass at plowing under stubble in a field above the ranch house. Mom managed the meals and housekeeping. I'm not sure what Bethel did. By a couple of months before Christmas, things had settled down. We still had no running water or electricity, so life wasn't easy. Bruce reminded the Bentons to keep up the coal supply, and whether because Bruce looked tough or they remembered Mom from a year earlier, we never ran short of fuel.

A telephone line had been extended as far as our ranch. I overheard Mom talking to a friend in Ridgway about how if Dad had the guts to stand up to his family, we could be living in a civilized home in Alamosa or Olathe. She sounded bitter, not likely to trust Dad again.

Mom and I shared the small ranch house with the McAllisters. Being back there at all was hard enough on her, and Bethel was a freeloading slob. That just about sent Mom over the edge, as I'd discover in a few months. Bethel and Bruce seemed to figure Dad was the only one they were responsible to. I got along with Bruce okay and numbed out on the rest of it most of the time.

I think the oldest Benton boy soon got a thing going with Bethel. A few weeks after the McAllisters moved in, he showed up on horseback at the house, told me he had a message for Bruce. He told me to take his horse up to a field where Bruce was running a cultivator and deliver the message. I'd never been fond of horseback riding and I said so. The Benton boy insisted. He told me the horse was tame as a lamb. I knew that was crap, but I got kind of bullied into going. Outside, I swung into the saddle, and set off up a trail to the top of the mesa overlooking our house.

At the top of the trail, two things happened. The horse reared. I grabbed the saddle horn with one hand and held on. I guess the horse figured he'd given it a try, and he stood still. The other thing that happened was I realized why I'd been sent on this errand. Bethel and the Benton kid wanted some time alone—though I'm not sure what they could do in the time it'd take me to deliver the message, maybe some smooching.

I sat on the horse deciding whether to keep going or turn back and tell Benton to deliver his own damn message. I realized I could be sprawled out on the rocky trail, maybe smashed up pretty good. That should have scared me into going back, but it just made me madder. So I delivered the message and reported on Benton who was still back at the house.

Bruce listened to my report, read the short note and growled, "Son of a bitch." He wadded up the note, stuffed it into his pocket, and shifted the tractor into gear. I rode back to the house, thankful I wasn't the Benton kid. But nothing ever came of it.

A few weeks later, the McAllisters wanted to go into Montrose with a couple of friends. Mom had to go to Ridgway on some business, so I ended up going to Montrose with that foursome. Basically, what we did was barhop. About every bar had a jukebox. We heard a lot of "I Got Spurs that Jingle Jangle" and "Give Her One Dozen Roses"—really stupid songs I can't get out of my head three years later.

We varied the bars with other adventures. Bethel would go into a department store to try on dresses. Clerks sometimes seem to have a sixth sense about people like Bethel. She was smart enough not to steal any clothing, but some dresses and other women's garments had little decorative pins. She'd remove the pins, sometimes without even going into a dressing room, and slip them to me. We were pretty slick as a team. I didn't feel guilty. These were grownups, and this was more like a game than stealing. I didn't tell Mom much about the afternoon, and she didn't ask.

Mom put her name in for a teaching job in Ridgway. For her to get hired in the middle of a school year a teacher would have to quit or be fired. In late winter, the 7th-8th grade teacher threw in the towel. Mom got the call. A friend on the school board offered to put up the two of us for the rest of the school year. Mom had a car, but driving from the house up to the highway was sometimes tricky in bad weather. She could manage it, but why take a risk "just so she could keep an eye on that bastard's ranch" is the way she put it. We moved into town, into the Hoovers' home, which seemed luxurious and roomy to me.

It's a tossup as to which of my parents deserted whom this time.

In late April, Dad came to Ridgway for a few days. Actually, he stayed in a hotel in Ouray and drove down to check the irrigation system and equipment at the ranch. Sometimes he'd just show up in the evening and invite Mom and me to dinner at the one café in Ridgway, or we'd drive up to Ouray. Mom didn't talk to him much, but I did. I think he missed her a lot. He said he had a job with the Army and would be gone to Alaska for a couple of years. This was going to be a long-duration split for them. Mom didn't seem to care much. She figured he'd double-crossed her on the last move to the ranch. She swore it would never happen again, and she meant it.

Apparently, though, Mom and me being on the ranch had kept Bruce McAllister trying to look like he was doing his job. Things had really gone to hell after we moved into town. Maybe that's when Bruce found out his wife was up to something with the Benton kid.

I was with Dad when he drove out to the ranch to settle with McAllister. He stopped the car and got out. Bruce invited him in for a cup of coffee. Dad ignored the offer. The two men stood in a cold, clear mid-morning on the packed-earth parking area outside the back porch.

Dad explained in about two minutes the neglect he saw on the ranch. "I want you off this property. I'll be back at three this afternoon to take you into Ridgway."

Bruce protested, "Look, Al, we've got sort of a contract, at least for the rest of the year."

"I don't have any contract with you, and I never said you could stay here. You're too damn hard on my equipment."

"You can't just throw us out." Bruce got a little whiney. "I got rights."

"Three o'clock. I'll have a gun," Dad said.

On the way into town, I reminded Dad, "There's guns, at least one hunting rifle, in the ranch house." I was worried.

"Yes, of course. My 250 Savage." He looked across the seat at me. "Don't worry about it."

As we drove back to the ranch, on the seat between us, holster and all, was Dad's favorite gun, his .44 Special. At three, when we drove into the parking area, the two McAllister's waited with doleful expressions and packed suitcases. Dad slipped the revolver under the seat.

I told Mom that Dad had kicked the McAllisters off the ranch. She just nodded with a sort of "Who cares?" expression.

"He said he's going to Alaska for two years," I reported.

"He never told me that." Her interest perked up. "Who's going to take care of the ranch?" That was about the last thing I'd expect her to be concerned about. Maybe she said that to cover up what really bothered her, that he was cutting out on her for years and hadn't bothered to explain or even say goodbye.

I told her as much as I knew. "Come summer, Bentons will cut and bale the hay that's fenced in. He's renting the rest of the place to a sheepherder."

"For two years? That's going to be hard on the land."

"Yeah, I suppose so." That depressed me a little, like Dad had given up on the ranch—and on us ever being a family.

Mom looked across the breakfast table and said, "I guess you won't see him for quite a while, maybe never. I'm sorry about that." She didn't sound very sorry.

But here we are three years later clacking along on a train to join Dad in Oregon.

I reminded her she'd said, "Never again."

"This isn't the same," she replied. "He's got a solid job in Oregon. We're not going back to that god-awful ranch. And I've got my teaching certificate if I need it." Mom usually tried to have a backup plan. As near as I could figure, she didn't trust anyone. I'm learning that from her.

The last half of sixth grade, in Ridgway, went okay for me. Mom coached the junior high basketball team. Next year, she'd be coaching me. Weird, when I think of it. I'd get no special favors from her as a teacher or a coach, and no one ever said I did.

When the team had an away game, we'd travel on the school bus with the varsity. If the varsity wasn't playing, she'd get a parent to take part of the team, and she'd load the rest, five or six kids, into the Buick. I remember one time when she took the team out of town. I stayed home alone with a headache.

I could see one of these headaches coming when muscles in my shoulders and neck would get tighter and tighter. There was nothing I could do to block the growing pain. Aspirin was useless. I'd stick it out as the torture got worse. I felt if someone could drill a hole just above my eye socket, it would relieve the pressure in my skull. I lacked the guts to take a hammer and nail and do it myself. Sometimes it helped to pace rapidly around the room. I didn't like being alone, but this time Mom had an away game, so it couldn't be helped. I paced and counted minutes until she'd get back—a lot of minutes.

The year I was in the seventh grade, we stayed in Ridgway. We'd used up the Hoover's hospitality, and Mom wanted to move closer to the school. She rented a log cabin in a local family's backyard, about a quarter mile from school. Log cabin might sound rustic and charming. It wasn't. The cabin consisted of three tiny rooms. I slept on a couch in the living room. At least, my bed was near the stove. We had electricity, but the water supply was a faucet in the backyard about twenty feet away, and the privy was about fifty feet in the opposite direction. Except for the small size, this cabin was an improvement over the ranch house—more convenient and much less isolated—but I was back to primitive plumbing.

That year in school, Mom worked hard teaching two grades without a heck of a lot of resources beyond a blackboard. Coaching the junior high basketball team was mainly a matter of scheduling practices, getting the team to games, and managing the roster during games. I was just another student and second-string player on the basketball team.

She did a good job as teacher, and she took her job coaching very seriously. In one game, the team from Delta announced its arrival, with the junior high team, which our high school coach had neglected to tell Mom would be coming. Mom was furious, but she'd be damned if she'd forfeit. With phone calls and dashing around the countryside to gather a car full of players, she fielded a team. When the game was underway, she strode the length of the spectators' viewing gallery to make some remarks to the high school coach. By then, most spectators knew the varsity coach had left Mom out on a limb by not telling her the junior high team would be coming. As she marched the length of the narrow gallery, her face set in stony anger, people backed out of her way in respectful silence. After their chat, the varsity coach was conscientious about sharing information with Mom.

Mom was a fairly strict disciplinarian. She was usually a step ahead of troublesome students, so she didn't have to exercise discipline often. Once, however, she kept the whole room in during recess. When she had to leave the room for playground duty, the kiddies got restive and were on the verge of trashing the room. I gave a short speech on how we deserved the punishment and would gain nothing by behaving like children. The students decided not to rebel. I was proud of myself for helping Mom avoid trouble.

We did hear from Dad a few times that year. For Christmas he sent me from Alaska some sled gloves made by natives. I guess if you had to keep using your hands in sub-zero weather, it was important to keep them warm. These mittens would cut the wind with walrus hide on the outside and rabbit fur for warmth on the inside. They were attached to a shoulder harness which went over the sled driver's head, to prevent them from being lost in a blizzard. The set of mittens gave me a sense of how it would be to manage a sled and team of dogs in deep winter. It seemed that Dad must have been really thinking of me to send them to me. He also sent a couple of other presents on no particular occasions: a pair of moccasins with Indian beadwork and a box of marbles with two agates. Kids in Ridgway measured wealth in the round pieces of glass and in the prized agates. I think Dad knew this and sent me something I'd really value. Maybe he even enjoyed picking them out—at least, I'd like to think so.

I kept the marbles close at hand, since during warm weather we played several times a week on packed earth in a vacated service station parking area. A player put marbles at risk. I was good enough to pretty much break even over time. I never risked losing the agates.

CHAPTER FIVE

The summer I turned twelve, Mom decided we'd go live with her sister's family in Malta, Montana, in the eastern part of the state up near Canada. It was fairly flat country, at least compared with Colorado and Western Montana, and in winter it could get bitter cold, dangerously so when a hard wind blew. She signed into the public school system to teach second grade. I started eighth grade in a junior high attached to the high school.

I didn't know why Mom left Ridgway for Montana. Maybe she wanted to get faraway from Dad's mother and sisters and be with her own relatives for a change. Maybe she wanted to teach in a larger and somewhat more civilized school system. Maybe she didn't think it would be a good idea to teach me two years in a row. Maybe she just wanted indoor plumbing.

We moved in with Mom's sister, Etta, her husband, Newton Cummings, and their three kids. The youngest, Ruth, was my grade, and we were sort of in competition from then on. Doris, a couple of years older and the object of my fantasies, scarcely knew I existed. The oldest, Everett, was a senior. I'd like to say we all became a close group, but we didn't. There wasn't much friction, however, considering that Mom and I moved in to share a small house with them.

A generation earlier, Newton and his new wife Etta took advantage of a veterans' deal to get a quarter section, 160 acres, free if they could homestead it for one year. Newton took his only option that first year: he raised winter wheat, and he broke even. He and Etta lived in a house, dug out of the earth, and roofed with squares of sod. The first few years he worked like a dog to keep his homestead.

Other homesteaders didn't make it past the first year or two. Newton acquired as much of their land as he could. When Mom and I moved in with them, he owned 2,500 acres outright and had a long-term lease on another 3,000 acres of government land. He ran purebred beef cattle on this ranch. In addition to their house in Malta, they owned a modest house near his acreage. Out of pure tenaciousness and toughness he'd survived when most didn't. Now he had a big payoff, but he didn't build a mansion, and he didn't stop working. There were other millionaires living in four or five room, wood-frame houses in Malta; they liked it there, mosquitoes, blizzards, and all.

In Malta, I made friends with other eighth graders, got on the basketball team, and took piano lessons for a while. At a little recital, I messed up, like most students. But some parents praised me for the "feeling" in my music. I figured if they were that hard up for something good to say I must have been terrible. I never took another piano lesson in Malta.

I was in choir until I got kicked out for being disruptive. It was a bum rap: another kid and I were horsing around, he started it, but I was in the field of vision when the choir director got fed up with us. She was a fair and reasonable person, but managing junior high kiddies in Malta kept even conscientious, new teachers constantly alert and aggressively defensive. The experienced teachers were more comfortable, less threatened. They'd come to terms with us. A couple of the male teachers had quietly established a reign of mild terror. One younger, well-built woman would sit on the front of her desk and cross her legs; no eighth-grade boy wanted to make her unhappy. She was actually an effective, no-nonsense teacher.

One time four of us boys went into the low hills near Malta on a camping trip. We didn't plan for cold nights, nor did we take enough food and water, so it was a memorably miserable night. At least I had friends.

The bullies that had so dogged me in Durango didn't get to me in Malta, with one exception, and I kind of drew that one on myself. One warm fall evening, some neighboring kids and I were playing kick-the-can in the front yard. Buddy McNeese, big and something of a loner, in the eighth grade like us, showed up and tried to horn in on the game. I'm not sure McNeese liked being a loner.

He was off a farm, where he did a man's work, driving a tractor and stacking hay bales among other things. He was tough and seemed to have a chip on his shoulder. Even seniors avoided provoking him.

I unwisely decided that since it was my yard, I was responsible to tell Buddy to get lost. I guess this hurt his feelings. He didn't like having his feelings hurt, and in hindsight, I was being kind of pissy-assed. Words led to more words and then to some shoving. While the rest watched, Buddy and I squared off for a full-fledged fistfight.

I'd like to say I won, but the fight wasn't even close. He beat the crap out of me. We punched at each other for a few minutes, mainly because I wouldn't back down. Mom came out on the porch and watched for half a minute, then went back into the house. Later she'd explained that if she stopped the fight, it would be worse for me down the line. She'd come out to make sure I wasn't getting seriously maimed. I agreed with her decision. In that time and place no one would fault her for not interfering.

Eventually, the fight ended, I guess because McNeese got tired of hitting me. I didn't go down, but my face got messed up pretty bad.

The next day, I went to school with a beautifully black eye, scrapes and bruises on my face, and a fat lip. At least, I hadn't lost teeth or got a broken nose. It took some courage to show up at school, the obvious loser in a fight. To my surprise, no one teased me. A few showed considerable respect. Word of the fight spread fast, of course. What I didn't know until later was that Buddy McNeese gave out word that I hadn't backed down, and that he'd take a dim view of anyone who teased me. He and I became good friends.

That summer after the eighth grade, the good life, with friends and things to do, continued. We all moved for a month or so out to the house on the rangeland. Uncle Newton put me and his two daughters to picking rock—literally—for several days. We went over raw pastureland, picked up more or less fist-sized rocks and put them in a bucket. When the bucket got full, we'd dump it in a central pile. We were clearing the land for cultivation. I was a skinny twelve-year-old, and this work was backbreaking. At the end of our two-week stint, Newton paid each of us a silver dollar for every day's work. Fair enough, but I wouldn't want to make a living doing that. I was proud of lasting through it, and I had a fistful of silver dollars.

School started in the fall, and I was a fairly happy guy. About two weeks into the ninth grade, Mom got this letter from Dad in Albany, Oregon. She decided to respond. I don't think I'll ever understand this hold they had on each other.

That's how I found myself on a train crawling across Montana, through the mountains, and on to Oregon to live with a father who'd been barely on the fringe of my life for three or four years. It seemed unfair to pull me out of ninth grade for a very "iffy" future.

CHAPTER SIX

I watched factories and warehouses and then neighborhoods of small, run-down houses come into view and pass. I could match poorness with any of them, but I hoped for better things. Outside Portland a few miles of another track ran parallel to the one we were on, and as the jumble of houses, warehouses, and factories got closer together, we joined four or five tracks into the Portland station. The size of this city made me feel kind of helpless. Mom looked like she'd handled herself in cities and train stations like this dozens of times. Probably she had, before I was born. She'd been in Chicago and Denver that I knew of.

The train came to a stop beside a long concrete platform. Along with a crowd of other people exiting from the train, we emerged directly from our car onto the platform. A porter set our five suitcases a few feet from the train.

We scanned up and down the platform. Dad had told Mom he'd meet us at the train, but he was not in sight. Mom shrugged and waited a few minutes. When the crowd thinned out, she gave me some quarters and pointed to a stand for carts sixty yards or so up the platform. "Go rent us a cart. I'll stay here with the luggage. Keep your eyes open for one that's been abandoned, so you can save us a dollar."

I felt carts weren't the only things abandoned on that platform.

The question just came out. "What happens to us if Dad doesn't show up?"

"We take a bus to Albany and find the newspaper office and your dad. And then, by God, after that letter, he takes care of us." I wasn't all that positive, but I figured she ought to know. I sure as hell didn't have a plan.

The automated rent-a-cart machine was unfamiliar. I was afraid of screwing up and wasting a dollar, so I studied it carefully. As I was about to put coins in the slot, twenty yards or so further up the platform, a couple pulled their suitcases off a cart, and went on to board early. I grabbed the cart just before a woman with a couple of little kids in tow got to it. I felt bad about that, but this was the big city and Dad was missing. I figured I needed every advantage that came my way. I looked away from the woman and started managing the cart at a brisk pace back toward Mom.

"Ken." I recognized the voice, with a flood of relief. "What's your hurry?"

"Mom sent me for this cart." That sounded dumb, I knew, but it was all I could think of.

Dad fell into step with me. I was really curious about how Mom and Dad were going to greet each other after nearly three years apart. Would they fall into each other's arms, like in the movies? Not likely, I figured.

And I was right. He was considerate and cheerful. Mom was wary. At least, they were talking, focused on getting our stuff loaded in the roomy trunk of his car— naturally, a big Buick.

We drove nearly two hours down the Willamette Valley to reach Albany. Mom asked how Dad's job was going. He told her he was one of the key people at the newspaper, and the others were nice people to work with, though he'd been there only a month or so. He had planned to go to Colorado, but coming back from Alaska, in a bar in Portland, he'd run into this man who told him about this job in Oregon. To Dad, it sounded interesting.

"So you decided you didn't need to go back to the ranch?" Mom asked, sounding casual.

"I knew you'd never join me there again," Dad said. "This seemed like a better deal for the two of us, but I needed to make sure it was a job I wanted."

"And is it?"

"It's dead on target for me. They need someone to build up advertising revenue, and they'll pay a modest commission over my base pay."

Mom seemed to relax a little.

So did I. This looked like it might really work for us. But, like Mom, I was still wary—and, as it turned out, with good reason.

Albany was twenty or twenty-five thousand people in the middle of lush farmland, a lot of truck gardens and orchards. Early October, harvests were about over, but the land was still green. We drove through suburbs that seemed to go on forever. The town was up against the river on one side, and tended to spread out from there. The size of the town intimidated me. I didn't know what to expect. I hoped it wouldn't be a bigger version of Durango, with gangs and bullies.

The center of town was a large grassy square with a four-story courthouse. About three blocks from the town square, Dad pulled into a driveway beside a large, attractive, two-story brick house. "This is it. We have the second floor. I think you'll find it roomy enough."

I capped the urge to say something like, "Gee, I don't know, Dad, we're used to our own log cabin." He seemed satisfied that, of course, this would make up for all the time Mom and I had lived in quarters that were either crowded or primitive or both. I didn't want to rock the boat. I also sensed, however vaguely, I'd picked up some of Mom's hostility—even though she wasn't showing it now.

The three of us carried Mom's and my total belongings up one flight of stairs. The apartment did not disappoint. Even Mom nodded approval. Compared with where we'd lived before, it was roomy and plush, with a fireplace in the living room. It was comparable to my grandparents' house in Montrose, and I knew this one had, for my mother, one great feature over that one—no mother-in-law on the premises. I had my own room. A big living room separated the bedrooms from a kitchen and breakfast nook. Lots of windows looked out on a large, manicured backyard. This home is where we were to resume family life.

So far, so good, but I didn't trust it to stay that way. I was starting ninth grade, in junior high, where ninth graders ruled. School seemed to be a closed society, and I knew no one. This was not new for me, but it seemed a more acute problem than ever before. There were no neighbor kids, except for a girl in a first-floor apartment, who made clear from the get-go she wanted to have nothing to do with me.

In my second week there, crossing the schoolyard long after classes were over for the day, I was stopped by a couple of boys.

"New kid, huh?"

"Yeah, that's right." I started around them.

One of them stepped in front of me. "Too stuck up to talk to us, is that it?"

I marked them immediately as bullies, mean ones, and big enough to inflict real damage.

"No, I'm not stuck up. I just got things on my mind."

"Hear that, George, he got things on his mind."

I could predict George's response. "What things you got on your mind, huh?"

"I'm trying to figure out how I can explain my recent move to my probation officer," I said. This was going out on thin ice, but I didn't have much to lose.

This stopped George and his friend for a few seconds, but they seemed to suspect a bluff. "What you on probation for?"

"I cut a guy up some. He had it coming. He was an asshole, like you guys." I could see these two were trying to decide how to deal with this frontal assault.

I 'd carried a switchblade knife for a couple of years. It was handy for cutting string or whatnot, and it gave me, probably misplaced, a sense of confidence. At the moment, I hoped it would make my bluff more believable. Would I have tried to use the knife, if it came to that? Yeah, I think so. Why not? If these thugs did bad things to me, I could see them in jail, but I could be really messed up.

I brought the knife out, and held it at my side. I made sure the bullies saw what it was, but I didn't flip it open.

"I've answered your questions." I thought that would make me seem a little more agreeable. "Now, I got things to do."

I walked past them before they could react. Fifty yards away, I turned and looked at them, as if wondering if they'd come after me. I really was curious about that. They didn't.

At home after dinner I told Dad about my schoolyard adventure. He would, I thought, at least comment on my courage and say well done or give me advice on how to handle such situations later. We could talk about it, like father to son.

He nodded and said, "You should be careful flashing a knife, unless you intend to use it."

"I did intend to use it if those boys came at me." I'm not sure that was true, but it might have been.

Without further comment, he started talking to Mom about some household bills.

I wanted to say, for Christ sake, I could have killed someone or got the hell beat out of me, and that's all you have to say. But this is just the way he was. I kept silent.

I don't want to make it seem that he wasn't interested in me. Twice that year he brought home stamps for a collection I had started. Nice stamps: one a special issue sheet with reproductions of the first U.S. stamps and the other a plate number block of five cent stamps in the national park series. His interest in me seemed to run hot and cold. I wasn't sure the stamps were totally for my benefit: the owner of the stamp and coin shop often employed his daughter, who'd been Miss Albany a year or two earlier.

Dad made friends with people at the newspaper and a couple of local politicians. We'd have picnics and dinners with some of them. These were relaxing and fun, unless it was a state legislator. Then Mom would get anxious about the quality of our furniture and plates and the rest. Such things never bothered Dad at all.

I was a loner, so lack of friends at school didn't bother me much. Except for the one run-in, I had no trouble with bullies. Studies came easily. Occasionally, I'd meet Dad at the newspaper and hang out there for a couple of hours after school and watch him work. These were special times.

Once when I was at the paper, sitting at a desk in his crowded office, keeping my mouth shut, the chief editor came thundering in. "Al, dammit, Ed Jason called. He's mad as hell, says you changed the copy on his half-page ad that came out yesterday without consulting him. That true?"

Dad was totally calm. "Yes, that's true." Then he waited.

The editor quieted down just a little. "Why did you do that? You know his account is a big one, and he's touchy as an old maid with hives."

"His ad was garbage. He was making claims for his used cars that he can't back up, and it doesn't take a genius to know that. I shifted the focus to services he can provide."

"Well, Al, suppose you call him up and try to explain that. You can start with an apology."

I'd never seen Dad apologize to anyone for anything, except maybe to Mom.

Dad picked up the phone and got Jason's car dealership on the line, gave his name, and asked to talk to Mr. Jason.

"Hello, Ed. This is Albert Bailey over at the newspaper. . . . Yes, I changed the ad, and I didn't have time to get back to you before the paper went to press. . . . Ed, I'm responsible for doing my best for our clients. I know you understand that kind of responsibility."

Dad listened for a couple of minutes. Apparently, Ed Jason had a good deal to say about responsibility to clients, and I doubt if much of it was praise for my father.

After Jason vented, Dad asked, "What do you think are Jason Automotive's strongest appeals in the community. Are you reliable? Are you convenient?"

Apparently, Jason agreed those virtues fit his business.

"So, Ed, that's what I think too, so that's what got emphasis in the ad. Tell you what: Give it a try. If it's a complete bust, I'll personally pay for running your original ad. It will cost me a day's wages, but our editor will want it that way. He insists on doing the right thing for our clients, and so do I."

They chatted for a few minutes about how Jason's business was going. Dad concluded by saying, "When you do your next big ad, I'll be glad to take a look at it, if you want." He chuckled. "Yes, well before press time."

He went in to assure the editor that Ed Jason was still a client, and, in fact, intended to run his next big ad past Dad.

The editor said, "Fine." Then he turned to me. "Your father could charm the bark off a tree."

Yeah, I thought, but he may have met his match with Mom.

At that moment I had warm, proud feelings for both my parents.

★ 81 ★

CHAPTER SEVEN

One late afternoon two weeks after school was out for the summer, Mom got the call. It changed everything.

Dad had a heart attack. He was rushed to the Albany hospital, where he was now critical. He'd asked for her.

Mom brought the back of her hand to cover her mouth as she put the phone back. She stared into space for several seconds. I think it was the only time I ever saw her eyes water. I wanted to say something comforting, but I had no idea what. So I kept silent and watched.

After a couple of minutes, she stood. "I have to go to the hospital." She picked up the phone and in a firm voice called for a taxi. "You stay here."

"Why?"

"Because I say so." Her tone did not invite argument. I'd never liked hospitals anyway. An hour or so after she left I realized she didn't want me to see my father helpless or dying. I didn't want to see him that way either.

I began to read a history book, then switched to a novel. After a few minutes I got up and paced, then sat on a couch, then paced the length of the apartment and looked repeatedly out the bedroom window at the street. Late afternoon turned to twilight and then to night. A streetlight on the corner came on.

I stood in my parents' bedroom and stared out into the night. We had come so close, it was not fair for Dad to die now. My eyes watered. A few tears spotted my shirt. But I'd not cried before, and I was not about to start now.

I tried to think back: Was that really true I'd never cried? Probably not. According to Mom, when I was two or three years old, I'd sometimes get frustrated and throw myself on the floor or ground in a temper tantrum. Her solution, at least when she could, was to throw a bucket of water on me. She admitted to a lack of parenting skills.

Standing in that dark bedroom, I felt very much alone.

A car stopped in front of the house. A door slammed shut. In the silence of the night, I heard the front door open and close. I moved to sit in the living room and watch the entrance to our apartment.

Mom came in and sat in a chair across the room from me. She didn't seem to know that I was there, until I turned on a lamp by my chair. Even in that dim light, she looked drained. I was sorry I'd turned the lamp on. I couldn't go back to the comfort of darkness now.

Finally, she glanced at me. "The doctors think he's past the crisis. As near as they can tell, his mind is still okay."

"When does he come home?"

She shrugged, then seemed to decide that wasn't enough of an answer. "They'll keep him in intensive care two or three more days, then probably another week in the hospital." She seemed to squint into her own mind. "The doctors just don't know. I've got to let the newspaper know what's going on. And, damn, I'll have to call his sisters." She smiled bitterly. "They'd never forget it if he died, and I hadn't told them about his heart attack."

The next morning, she took a taxi to the newspaper office. An hour or so later, she returned in Dad's car. I asked, "How did it go at the newspaper?"

"Fine. The publisher volunteered to hold your dad's job open until he's recovered and can come back to work. That's great news."

That afternoon, she drove to the hospital. I didn't go with her. She said, "Give it a day or two before you see him. I may be there the rest of today. You can find yourself something to eat in the fridge or at the grocery store." She laid out some bills and left me.

Until Mom got back in the late afternoon, I stayed around the apartment, trying to reassure myself that Dad would get well and it'd be like before. It was no go; I'd learned that bad news can, and often does, lead to worse news. He'd worked hard at times in the past. He was strong, I told myself. Dad wouldn't die or be crippled.

Why was I so concerned? I tried to sort that out. For one thing, he was my father, and that should count for something. I felt guilty that it didn't count for more, but the tie between us was not strong to begin with, and Mom had gnawed it even weaker. If he died, Mom and I could make it on our own. We had in the past.

More puzzling, why was Mom so shaken up? That didn't fit. The summer I was eight, he had a job in Pueblo and we were living with him. He got really sick for a couple of weeks and had to be taken care of in our apartment. Two of his girlfriends shared the job with Mom. She'd never talked about it, but I remember them clearly. One was really pretty, and the other one was at least average. I guess they got along okay. Even young as I was, that arrangement seemed odd to me.

Mom came in the door carrying a sack of groceries she'd stopped to buy on the way home from the hospital. I guess letting me know how my father was doing was lower priority than having fresh milk and cereal in the house.

I put the food away while she sat in a kitchen chair and stared into space. I think I knew what bothered her. She had a call to make.

"How's he doing?" I asked.

"He's coming along okay." She paused. "Go to your room while I'm on the phone. And close the door."

All that came through the door was an indistinct mumble. The only words I heard were when my mother raised her voice, "It's not necessary. I'll keep you informed."

A few minutes later, she came into my room and sat heavily in a chair. I knew she'd lost the argument. She said, "Your aunt Frances is coming out to stay with us for a while. She'll have your room. You will sleep on the couch in the living room. I hope it will be a short visit."

I knew letting any of his relatives back into his life made Mom anxious —in fact, it made her furious—and I didn't blame her at all. They'd not been hostile toward me, but contact with his mother or sisters often meant trouble for us as a family.

"How long will she be here?" I asked.

"How can I know that? Maybe just until it's clear he's getting better. A week or two."

"Why is she coming?"

Mom smiled cynically. "She doesn't trust me to take care of her precious little brother."

That made me wonder, would Mom would take good care of him? I remembered when she'd treated his boil on the ranch. Yeah, she'd take care of him, probably better care than she'd take of me. The two women in Pueblo were extraneous; he just seemed to need to have girlfriends around. Maybe they made him feel better about himself.

I moved some clothes and other stuff from my room into a hall closet. The next morning, we left for Portland to meet the afternoon train. Neither Mom nor I felt cheerful. I still hadn't seen Dad in the hospital, and that worried me.

Frances moved two suitcases into my room—bad sign—and immediately went to the hospital in our car. Mom fixed dinner for the three of us, and we waited until Frances got back about eight o'clock at night.

"How is he?" Mom asked.

"You mean you haven't seen him at all today?"

"There wasn't time after visiting hours opened before I had to leave for Portland to pick you up."

Frances gazed at a forkful of mashed potatoes. "I see." That got across the strong disapproval that she was afraid to say directly to Mom. I was proud of Mom. Aunt Frances wasn't afraid of much.

This tense truce, with Mom providing meals and going with Frances to the hospital went on a week.

After the first day, Frances agitated for me to go with them. Mom resisted. On this issue I hoped Frances would win, and two or three days later she did, mainly, I think, because Dad asked to see me. Apparently, a lot of time at the hospital was spent by Mom and aunt Frances arguing about what should happen when he got out, with Dad sort of refereeing. He was getting tired of it. I guess he thought I'd cause a change in the topic of conversation.

Dad looked pretty good. He was out of intensive care, though he still had a couple of monitors hooked up. He smiled and asked, "Are you doing okay, Ken?" His question made me feel wanted, or at least relevant.

"Yes, I'm doing fine. How about you?"

"I'm good. The damn doctors won't let me out quite yet. I want out of this place. People die in hospitals, you know." Then he grinned. "But the nurses are okay. A couple of them are pretty cute. So I guess I can stay a while longer."

I glanced at Mom and Frances. Neither of them showed any reaction to his crack about the nurses. They both cut him a lot of slack on that sort of thing, so I guess I would too.

After a week, the doctors decided he still needed rest, but he could get it at home. Mom did her share of taking care of him as well as managing the household. She and Frances didn't get in each other's way. After another few days, he was moving around the apartment.

He called his editor. "I'm coming along fine. In fact, I'm well, as the doctors will admit shortly. . . . Marie said you were holding my job. . . . I appreciate that. . . . Yeah, you might keep him around until I'm up to full steam. I'll drop in day after tomorrow, see how things are going, get back into the swing of things."

He'd talked on the phone in the living room, and both Frances and Mom followed his end of the conversation. I realized they were both girding for battle as they listened.

Mom asked, "I suppose he wants you back as soon as you can make it?"

"Yes. But he's really not putting any pressure on me. My salary continues, but no commissions until I start earning them."

"I don't think you should rush this," Frances said.

Both Mom and Dad looked at her in surprise. I could already see an argument shaping up. I just never expected it to get as bad as it did.

Dad said, "I won't be bringing in serious money until I go to work. I've a lot of loyal clients, but they won't stay loyal forever."

I glanced at Mom. She stood pat, as they say in poker. She looked victorious, but there was a tentative twinge in her expression.

Frances said, "This isn't your first trouble. You've had a delicate heart condition since you were a child on the ranch. You must find an easier job, or at least wait longer to plunge back into work."

"I'm supporting a family, Frances."

"You can't ruin your health just to make this family comfortable."

I figured that drew the issue clearly. I hoped Mom would ask my aunt, "Where the hell were you when he worked his tail off to save that damn ranch?" But she said nothing, just watched Dad, waiting for him to take a stand.

He said, "We'll discuss this tomorrow," and went into the bedroom.

Mom said, "What makes you think this is any of your affair, Frances, because it isn't."

"He's my brother, and I'm not going to see you work him to an early death."

I thought that was a laugh after how hard he'd worked on the ranch. I was sort of like Mom, waiting for Dad to tell his sister to mind her own business.

But he didn't. Four days later, he got clearance from his doctor, resigned his job at the paper, and was with Frances on his way to Chicago.

Mom didn't say anything about that. But her grim expression told me that my last chance to have a real family with a real father had just gone south. Depressing, but I was fourteen and could handle this—I knew how to numb out.

The first order of business was to find a cheaper apartment—a much cheaper one. Mom always traveled light, so it didn't take long to move.

We climbed one flight of stairs to a moderate-sized room with a kitchen at one end and an alcove as a bedroom. The only windows were in the far end of the alcove and over the small kitchen area—not too sunny! We shared a bathroom, in the hall, with at least one other family. But that beat an outdoor privy, and I didn't take many baths anyway.

I slept two floors down in what once must have been a basement storeroom, just big enough to hold a rollaway cot as its only furniture. It could have been a jail cell, but I only slept there, so I didn't think much about it.

Mom wangled a teaching job, starting in the fall. Until then, we were barely solvent. I raised money working in the fields. Picking pole beans was a standard summer job. They raise a lot of green beans in Oregon. Cherries were okay, if you were careful not to fall out of a tree, but there was a lot of competition from older, more experienced pickers. Strawberries were harder than picking rock had been in Montana, because it took a lot of scooting along and checking each plant to get enough berries to make very much money. I went for beans.

Each morning, not long after sunup we'd catch a bus or, more commonly, a flatbed truck with side rails and benches. We were quite an assortment: a few middle-aged women and men. Even Mom went out occasionally, until she got a part-time job selling in a department store, a job she'd hold for several years. We rarely saw winos, as the drivers were told not to pick them up. Most of the crew were more or less regulars. A lot of us were kids, around twelve and up. At eighteen we'd be old enough to get jobs in the canneries. Both girls and guys worked in the fields, so there was a certain amount of making out—probably a tiny fraction of what was rumored—and relaxed flirting.

We'd be taken to a field and let out. Usually in pairs, we'd take the next row up and put the beans in our buckets. When my bucket got full, I'd dump it into my sack. When the sack was full, I'd take it in and get it weighed. A foreman would punch the weight on a card he'd hand me. I'd accumulate cards for a few days before cashing in, sort of like money in a bank. If I got paired with an Okie kid, I'd have to really work to keep up. These kids were fast, and when they got ahead they would grab clumps of beans on my side of the vines. It was cheating, but often they'd be part of a big family working the field, so I couldn't do anything about it. Some of them were fair enough, I guess. Man, they could work.

That summer I met this girl, Marian Mason. We both picked beans, though she wasn't as regular as I was, and we rode the same truck back and forth to town. I don't remember how it started, or even who started it. "It" wasn't a romance, exactly. Somehow, we began to sort of role-play as brother and sister. We weren't trying to fool anyone. A sibling relationship seemed easier to manage than a "romance," which in my limited experience meant sex, consensual from the get-go, or at least pursued. Did we feel close to each other? I think so. We didn't occupy a big chunk of each other's life, at least not at first. We did, however, have a special kind of bond. What we felt toward each other wasn't quite like between brother and sister, but our playing those roles enabled us to avoid dealing with anything deeper.

She had short dark hair. I guess it was naturally curly because I can't imagine her spending time with a curling iron. She had an easy smile. I thought she was beyond beautiful. Maybe she was. We both came from less than routine, ideal families. She was pretty much on her own, with an older sister to help her financially and keep an eye on her. A few years earlier some guy murdered her mother, and she witnessed it. That topped any train wrecks in my own life. I guess we were each glad to have a fake sibling.

This relationship between Marian Mason and me may not appear significant in the splotchy scheme of my growing up. Eventually, it went nowhere. Next to my wife, however, this was the most important relationship with a woman I ever had. With my father as my model I botched it badly.

The special thing between us that started in the bean fields didn't carry over into school, at least not consistently. We had some dates, and some fights. The fights usually were carried out by disengagement from each other—sort of a siege until one or the other, usually me, gave in. Her part-time job during the school year was in a movie theater, selling tickets or running the concession stand. Mine was in an office supply store. I don't recall her ever coming to see me there.

One sunny afternoon, I found myself standing in front of a counter over a bin full of popcorn and trays of Milk Duds and chocolate bars. "Look, Marian, I didn't mean what I said." I wasn't clear on what I 'd said three days ago that so ticked her off. It had something to do with me saying a particular girl in class looked interesting. Marian had exploded at my lack of taste. I couldn't see anything wrong with noticing good-looking women, and I don't think Dad ever backed down or apologized if he was called on it. What I didn't take into account was that Marian had not had the most secure life. Beneath a tough shell she was easily threatened.

"Then why did you say it?" Marian asked.

"It was just to say something, like I might notice a new Cadillac."

"So, to you, girls and cars are the same?" She was pummeling me. What would Dad do?

"Yeah, except for you. There's no car to compare to you."

She smiled a little.

"You want to take a short hike down by the river when your shift is over?" Actually, by short hike, I did mean a walk. All through our relationship, despite some heavy necking, she remained celibate. Staying chaste wasn't true of other girls I had dated. I didn't think of sexual aggression as immoral or not.

"No" she said, "I've other things to do."

"What things?"

"You know, Ken, it isn't really any of your business, is it?"

At times, I knew enough to quit when I was losing. "No, I guess not." Like hell it wasn't my business. She was doing a job on me, and I was taking it. "So, Sis, are you still willing to go out with me sometime?" I couldn't believe what I'd said. I was practically begging.

"Yes, little brother, I'll still go out with you." The "little brother" wasn't necessarily intended as an insult. She was nearly two years older than me. I'd skipped a grade, and she'd spent the better part of a year in a hospital, she never told me for what.

When stocking shelves at D&P, the stationary store in Salem, I had to put price tags or stickers on staplers, packages of paper, pencil sharpeners, file folders, and a host of other items. I took the costs from invoices and used whatever formula applied to get the retail cost. It was hardly advanced mathematics. I was so anxious to avoid mistakes in the math or where I put the stickers or tags that I'd repeatedly go back and check what I'd done. It slowed me down terribly. I knew I was way too anxious about not making mistakes, but I couldn't seem to help myself. I lacked the self-confidence that would free me up to work briskly. The store owners seemed remarkably tolerant of my snail-like pace.

Another way I wasted D&P's time was occasionally I'd get in an argument with a classmate that would carry over on a street corner after school. The arguments were about impersonal issues: higher tax rates, access to medical facilities, rights of police versus the public, and so forth. Sometimes they'd go on for an hour or more. I'd get to work late, but no one ever docked my pay or even complained.

This tolerance for my wasteful tendencies puzzled me. I finally decided they regarded having me on the payroll as a sort of charity. But Mom and I weren't in poverty, so why did I deserve this generosity? I never figured it out. This pattern of my faults being tolerated and me getting undeserved breaks continued long after I left D&P.

Sometimes, it worked the other way. By some fluke I got the highest grade point average in my class of about seventy seniors. I'm afraid the bar was pretty low. The principal called two of us down to his office shortly before the end of our senior school year. He explained I would be valedictorian. The other fellow, Samuel Leifkowitz would be salutatorian. We'd both give speeches at the high school graduation ceremony. There was a routine selection process: the list would be sent around for approval by the school faculty, strictly *pro forma*—usually. A few days later, the principal called me into his office and told me the order was changed. Leifkowitz would be valedictorian. Three teachers had blackballed me for the top honor.

It made no difference to me. I'd still give a speech at graduation. I was kind of curious who the three teachers were, but the principal refused to divulge that—and properly so. I still speculated. One, I was sure, was the typing teacher. Fair enough: I dropped her class because I was probably getting a poor grade and could see a little point in most of what she taught. She also was an advisor for the Honor Society, the meetings of which I didn't take seriously. Someone would usually be dispatched from the meeting to the gym to get me out of a pickup basketball game.   Another, I think, was a math teacher who'd remarked that I would go far in life . . . at the end of someone's foot. There were other candidates.

I was not a hooligan or a bully or in a gang. In fact, in the week or so before graduation, when everyone else was partying, I worked on a letter of complaint for some kid the cops had given a ticket and banished from a city park for reasons that seemed arrogantly frivolous. I took time away from preparing my graduation speech, and that was important to me, but this kid got a raw deal. The cops cancelled the ticket, so I guess I was right. My graduation speech went fine.

I didn't begrudge Leifkowitz's top honor. He was kind of frail, and his mother walked him to school. He was hopeless at sports, so P.E. grades killed his average. He also was a very conscientious and hardworking student. I wasn't. It wasn't that I was a rebel. Rules just weren't important. An assigned five-page paper would come in at ten pages and a week late, but it would be a good paper.

CHAPTER EIGHT

I said that while I was in the ninth grade our chance to be a family went into the junk heap when Dad went back with aunt Frances to Chicago. That's true, but not technically accurate.

Near the end of my sophomore year in high school, several months after he'd cut out on us, Dad showed up again in Albany. He moved into our tiny apartment. That made it really cramped.

"Are you and Dad going to get back together?" The setting sun shed diffused light into the apartment. Mom and I hadn't turned on any lights, so a deepening gloom prevailed. Dad was somewhere else, and we had no idea at what hour he'd return home or in what condition.

Mom seemed to study me for a minute, as if calculating how I'd fit into an equation. She took several seconds more before she answered, "No, we're not. I'm sorry, Ken. I just don't want to go through any more of his irresponsibility. You got this far without your Dad most of the time; you can make it from here."

She was right, of course. But for a moment I felt icy pain in my chest. In those times that we three had been a family, I'd gotten an idea of how a family could be. Realizing it wasn't going to be that way ever again depressed me. I tried to stop thinking about Dad.

In a vague way, I knew he went out to bars just about every night. Maybe he was escaping our dreary little apartment or Mom's coldness. He was probably making a desperate attempt to get back on track. He'd come to Mom hoping she'd help him, as I guess she had several times in the past. This time she barely tolerated him.

He'd tried to get back on at the newspaper. They turned him down. That must have been hard to take. His life had gone to hell. Within two weeks, he returned to his sisters in Chicago. On his way to the train station, he left a package for me at D&P Office Supplies. It was the size of a large and heavy book. In support of Mom's determination to cut all ties with him, I didn't open the package. But I kept it.

Mom was clearly relieved. I guess I was too, though I barely noticed he'd gone, except that the apartment was less crowded. He and I hadn't talked much. We didn't seem to have much to say to each other.

Mom's view of life seemed pretty grim. I didn't appreciate until later how she'd fought for almost everything she got for herself and me. If we were going to have a comfortable home, even in an apartment or trailer park, she would earn it herself, and that meant finishing her teaching degree. For years she'd taken the least desirable teaching jobs, often facing tough kids and handling several grades at once, and kept one step ahead of minimum requirements for provisional teacher certification. Her standards for success were modest, but, in her circumstances, they were not easily achieved.

Dad, on the other hand, had always seemed confident of getting what he wanted— jobs, money, influential friends, women—though not always effortlessly. His apparent right to success was part of his charm. Now, suddenly, it seemed, on his last visit to us in Albany, the rules for him had changed. Exercising his charm in second-string bars downtown was a hollow façade he maintained in his effort to feel better about himself. Much later, I'd begin to understand how desperately depressing this must have been for him. I wished we'd been able to talk, not just to help him survive the constant pain of failure, but because I might have learned from the confident, open approach that had governed most of his life. But we didn't talk, and thoughts about Dad and the future sank into the swamp beneath the surface of my mind.

During the high school years in Albany, I tried to live a pattern that didn't really fit me. A conflict between what I was and what I was expected to be produced fairly extreme depression at times. Mom defined success as financial security and social acceptance, and I should follow a prescribed path to get there. I suppose her ideal goal for me would be to become department head in a university, and then move on to dean.

That I couldn't commit to Mom's pattern for success should have been obvious even while I was in high school, but it wasn't. I needed my father to make explicit alternative views of getting on in life. He was pretty much out of the picture. If I thought of him at all, I saw him as impotent. So, I had one model, Mom's, and I failed to measure up. I assumed that to deliberately reject her goals would probably be mere rationalization.

Failure is what it is. Living with a deep sense of failing erodes the soul, and it plays hell with confidence. It's also painful.

Mom couldn't figure out what was keeping me from getting with the program (nor, for that matter, could I). Obviously, lack of focused ambition was a symptom, but she couldn't find anyone to deal with that.

The final three years of high school, after Dad moved east, were not dismal. I made some friends, and I had Marian Mason and a few other girls.

The girls, at least those who went out with me more than once, had to tolerate behavior that was sometimes less than rational. Vicki was one girl with low tolerance for mild insanity.

One evening, parked outside my apartment building in her parents' car, I tried to persuade Vicki to break a date a couple of days later so she could go to a party with me.

"Don't you want to go out with me again, Vicki?" She was behind the steering wheel. I took her hand, and looked soulfully into her eyes.

"Of course I do, Ken, but I can't just tell this fellow I've changed my mind about Friday evening. How would you feel?"

"If you'd rather be with another guy, I'd want you to say so and break our date," I said. That was bullshit, but these situations seemed too trivial for it to count as a lie.

She seemed to think about it. My hope surged.

Then she spoke. "I can't break the date. He's an old friend, and we've been going together two months."

"Are you engaged or something?"

"No." Vicki was a beautiful girl, long, blond hair, and the rest. We'd been necking a little, and she was good. I really wanted to show her off at this party, as well as enjoy her company.

"So?" I paused and lit a cigarette. Practically everyone past mid-teens smoked. "What is your problem?" She looked at me with just a shade of irritation, so I shifted my line of attack. "I really want you to go with me to this party. Really. I'm stuck on you, probably more than this other guy is."

She smiled. "I'm sure you can get someone else." She added casually, "And you'll recover." She was still smiling.

I just looked at her. "You think I'm just kidding don't you?" I jammed the lighted end of the cigarette into my arm. Was there a faint sizzling or smell of burning flesh? I didn't notice. "I'm not kidding."

For a half a minute, she stared at my arm, surprised, and a little shocked. She removed her hand from mine. I don't think she was worried about getting burned. I'd been careful to aim for the middle of my forearm.

"Do you have something to put on that?" she asked. She sounded mildly concerned.

"Yeah, I've got something upstairs in my apartment, I think." I wasn't sure what medicine that would be.

"Then you better go take care of that wound. It's ugly." She didn't order me out of the car, but her intent was pretty clear.

I opened the car door. Before I closed it, I leaned in and said. "How about a date for a week from Friday, a movie maybe?"

The night had closed in; I couldn't see her clearly across the front seat. She said, firmly but without rancor, "No," and started her engine. I saw her at school a few times. We were polite, but we never dated again.

On a date with another girl, Kate, sitting in a dark car on a side street, I ran out of things to talk about. So I told her about the rare blood disease that would kill me within a very few years. She seemed to buy my story, at least she was curious.

"When did you find out you were sick?"

"Oh, a year or so ago."

"What are your symptoms?" Kate asked.

"Trouble concentrating sometimes. Eventually, the mind sort of detaches."

"Is it contagious?"

"Not at all, no possibility of that." I needed to reassure her on that point if I wanted this date to work. "You're born with it."

"Does it depress you, knowing you're going to die?"

"No point in being depressed," I said bravely, and leaned in for a long kiss. How could she resist a dying boy, though eventually she decided she'd gone far enough for one evening.

To me this was an exercise in what you might call creative conversation, and I did it frequently over several years—abandoned by a vicious father, nearly starving, and so forth. Sometimes it would be awkward at the end of a date to explain that I'd been making this up. So, I'd leave the other person to figure that out. Sometimes they never did. When I dated a mutual friend, Kate had told her, I learned later, "Did you know Ken is dying of an incurable disease?" That took some careful explaining to the new girl.

I don't think these stories were motivated by anything as dramatic as a death wish, but they might indicate I wasn't entirely happy in my own skin, nor was I any Rock of Gibraltar in mental stability.

A more significant mental twist was my tendency to be self-defeating. One relatively normal way this expressed itself was my habit of turning in school projects late. Several of my classmates procrastinated until time had nearly run out and then slapped something together to turn in. I certainly did enough of that, but it went further. Frequently I'd ignore a deadline and work on a paper until I felt it was ready, perhaps a month or more late. It was a habit, as one teacher put it, like a crowbar tied to my left leg. I thought that was a stupid analogy, but maybe it wasn't: years later, the image still sticks in my mind.

I tried out for the high school baseball team, and of course, I was soon cut. Why the baseball team? I didn't like the sport and had absolutely no talent. On the other hand, I was a good runner, so why didn't I try out for the track team?

My tendency to pick the least likely road to success sometimes extended even to dating. The Stewart sisters graced the class I was in. About the only thing they had in common was high marks on natural beauty, but even there they differed radically. Alita's long black hair seemed to go with a dark reputation, vastly expanded by male classmates' wishful thinking. She did have a predisposition to be a little free on dates. Her sister, Katherine, had brown hair, attractive enough, but her disinterest in taking advantage of nature's blessings left her looking rather drab. Alita radiated heat; her sister seemed more like a block of ice.

In a local hamburger joint Alita dispensed popcorn and candy. Every tenth sack of popcorn had a special mark; get enough marked sacks, and they were worth a hamburger or a sundae. Every sack of popcorn I got from a smiling Alita had the special mark. I don't think I could have been slow-witted enough not to get the message. But I was stupid enough to ignore the sister who, in retrospect, was the more attractive of the two, by any criterion. Instead, I pursued Katherine—and was rewarded, as might have been predicted, with all the warmth a block of ice can generate.

Why the self-defeating choice of goals. Maybe I didn't like myself. Maybe I embraced defeat because I figured I was going to be defeated anyhow.

Not all of my choices were bad ones. I went out for the school debate team, and achieved some success. (After all, Dad was a successful persuader; I should have inherited something from him.) I also was in the class plays two years. On stage I could legitimately be someone other than who I really was.

While I wasn't consistently a loser, I sure as hell wasn't always determined to win. In fact, lack of consistency was my only reliable characteristic. My treatment of Marian Mason, for example, varied from almost groveling to callous arrogance.

My focus in life was further screwed up by a religious conversion that hit me out of left field. My buddy and I were in a Boy Scout troop, the leader of which, Don, had unusual ideas about being a boy scout. He believed a scout was meant to learn hiking, camping, outdoor cooking, and the like. He wasn't opposed to passing tests to work up in rank or gain merit badges. He just ignored the system in favor of taking us on hiking and camping trips. The result was that we developed some real skills.

Don himself had been rejected for the World War II draft on the basis that his flat feet would make him unable to keep up on long marches. I lost my faith in military physical exams: this leader would take us on hikes where we covered in two days what was supposed to take three. On one hike up a mountainside, we were all pretty exhausted and complaining. One guy announced, "I'll keep going until I can't go another step." The rest of us stood to the side of the trail and waved him on, to which he responded, "I can't go another step." Neither could the rest of us.

After a year we had no one in the troop who had risen in rank far enough to qualify for an assistant troop leader. We stumbled on until Don cut a corner or two in order to bestow the required rank on one of the fellows who was, in fact, clearly a leader.

Don had a lot of charisma. He was also a confirmed member of the Albany Pentecostal Assembly of God Church—which had some strict rules about things you couldn't do, such as dancing and movies, even some things you couldn't eat or drink, like coffee. He got me started going to church. I liked the emotional life in the church. They weren't holy rollers or snake handlers, but from time to time someone would speak in tongues, and they did a good deal of faith healing, especially at revivals. When they sang, they belted those hymns out. Some of my sporadic past churchgoing had been dry as dust and manifestly hypocritical. The Assembly of God services invigorated me, and gave me something to belong to. I truly think those reasons weighed more heavily in keeping me attending than the pastor's pretty blond daughter, whom I got to know pretty well.

Assembly of God people were strongly into saving souls, and Don was no exception. I was a sitting target: Mom was my only relative, I had an unstable background, and so forth. One day, we were sitting on the church steps, killing time after the service. Out of the blue, Don asked, "Ken, where do you want to spend eternity?"

"Huh?"

"You have any idea what real burning heat is, like you'd feel if you stuck your hand in a fire?"

I shrugged. "I guess I've been burned before." I thought of the times I'd stuck a lighted cigarette into my hand or arm, but I didn't bring that up.

"Fire all over your body. And like it was the first time. Only forever." Don was getting kind of intense.

I shook my head.

"That's hell, one choice. But you have another choice: to spend eternity in bliss, with people who love you."

I figured Don must know something. This fit sermons and fragments of conversation I'd been hearing for months.

My imagination went to the preacher's daughter, and to another girl in the church, also blond. Eternal torture versus eternal bliss. It was an easy choice, as long as it didn't cost anything.

"You are full of sin—sinful thoughts and sinful deeds. They will carry you down to hell, if you have no redemption from the One who died on the cross for you. He alone can save you."

Don had me on the "sinful thoughts," and probably on the deeds too, though no recent sins came to mind right then. I didn't say anything.

"Think about it, Ken." He paused. "See you in church next Sunday?"

"Yeah, sure."

Without warning, I had some heavy stuff to sort out. No one was going to help me. Mom would tell me she thought it was all poppycock and leave me to decide for myself. Dad wasn't there. I didn't have friends I could talk to about my salvation, except Don, and he was hardly objective.

I spent a lot of time the next week trying to figure this out, but I got nowhere. I was sixteen; I should have been able to deal with it, but I kept running into dead ends. If what Don said was true, it wasn't logical that God would waste His time on me. If it weren't true, I would be playing a sucker game. Shadowing all this in the back of my mind was a fear of burning in hell for all eternity, while the preacher's daughter enjoyed bliss in clover fields of heaven.

The next Sunday, I sat toward the back in church. The sermon was on heaven and hell and the wisdom of choosing heaven. Our Redeemer was generous and forgiving, but He didn't make the choice for you. You had to choose. Once you accepted Him—really accepted Him—as your personal savior you were home free for all time. (Later, I wondered about the lifetime guarantee: seemed like a person, a backslider, might abuse that. But right then I was in the moment, so I didn't look for fine print.) A little more from the preacher on how good eternal bliss felt and how it took but a moment to gain it, and I was primed.

The preacher went all-out on salvation, like he was warming up for the next big revival. He moved around the small stage a lot, sometimes punching air in my direction. He'd pause for several seconds, so you'd look at him to see what the problem was. Then he'd come out with some heavy sentence, like, "If you are given a chance at Salvation and reject that chance, you have earned more time in the fires of hell than a thief." At times, his movement and dramatic pauses hypnotized me. I'd jerk back to awareness of the church and the people around me.

He cut down on the sinner's options by explaining the difference between earning your way to Heaven through good deeds versus faith. Good deeds without faith wouldn't cut it. If you had faith, you might get away with some bad deeds. The rub was that if you really had faith, you'd stay away from bad deeds. So someone who professed faith, but went to dances, maybe had a few drinks and attempted to seduce a comely young member of the congregation would be dismissed, with righteous pity, as a hypocrite.

Near the end of the sermon, he invited anyone who wanted to accept Jesus Christ that morning to hold up his or her hand. My hand shot up like it was spring-loaded. I'd committed myself. I was called to the altar, where a couple of older church regulars prayed with me.

A week later, I was baptized right after the service. A big part of the congregation waited around. I was a little disappointed because most baptisms were done in clumps at a local swimming pool, but with only one or two at a time, as in my case, they were done right in front of the altar. Church deacons rolled out a tub big enough for at least the minister and one newly saved soul to stand in four or five feet of water. I confirmed my intent to serve the Lord. The minister dunked me under to have my sins washed away. Mere sprinkling, as in some churches, was regarded as inadequate, if not downright blasphemy.

I felt euphoric for the next few days. When that faded to a sense of commitment, I stayed steady on for several months until the end of the school year. I didn't drink, and infrequent smoking with a buddy or two seemed a minor transgression. I still avoided most temptations. It was, alas, easy to remain chaste, what with my ineptness with girls together with lack of opportunity. I was enfolded into the congregation. Somewhat to my surprise, Mom accepted this benign aberration. She even cooperated by not having ketchup or other banned food on the table.

I finished high school with support from Mom, and maybe some, but not much, helpful advice from her. For the past three years Dad contributed nothing. I'd pretty much gone my own way, and often not wisely. I did have, by some miracle, a good academic record. Athletics were a total bust. Debate hadn't gotten underway at Albany High School long enough to produce serious results, but at least it was something I could put on my record.

This survey may give a misleading impression that I was calculating my assets, getting ready for the next step. Actually, I was just blundering on, with no blueprint and no goals.

Mom had determined that I move up the ladder of success. The next rung was to get into a respectable college. I could go along with that. I didn't grasp the idea of moving up anything, but I had no other plan. Much later, I would appreciate Mom's determination and great patience—when it would be too late to tell her.

CHAPTER NINE

Mom and I agreed on a target, Deschutes College, some thirty miles down the valley. Deschutes was a small liberal arts college with delusions of being elite. The school's graduates reinforced the illusion when they did well in business or professional life, and this justified fairly selective entrance standards, which in turn tended to produce more graduates who would be successful even with a mediocre education. I had a few good teachers there, but overall from the get-go, I was aware of a tacit agreement to believe "aren't we great!" rather than to pursue real excellence in academics. My backup school was the State University, also in the valley.

Unfortunately, I was accepted, with a small scholarship, into Deschutes. Mom was more than satisfied. She felt I was on schedule. She believed her Albany teaching job was in jeopardy because she took the wrong side in an acrimonious dispute between teachers and administration in Albany. (I was pleased to see she wasn't entirely unlike Dad: her cause was just.) She moved to a job in Salem. I could live at home, which would cut costs. Money was in short supply.

Three or four of my entering classmates, less naïve and more purposeful than I, would see Deschutes College for what it was. After one year—in one case, after only one semester—they would transfer to State University or elsewhere. Out of inertia more than any other reason, I stayed at Deschutes. Mom figured a school with a decent reputation was better than the unknown, so she was for staying. Besides, she now had a good teaching job in Salem.

So, we moved into an apartment in Salem, not far from the Deschutes campus. Our living quarters were within a block of the railroad tracks, and not on the better side. We had our own bathroom, so it was a step up from places I'd lived before. In Salem, a new phase of life began—at least that's what I told myself.

I wished to make college more productive than high school had been. It takes self-discipline to turn wishes into reality. I didn't have a great supply of that virtue, so I mostly drifted with papers often turned in late. I completed a semester-long project in an accounting course, with aid from a more responsible friend, in one night. The result wasn't pretty: I'd sacrificed quality to meet a deadline, rather than fail the course. So much for self-righteous standards.

My sense of moral failure went beyond grades. A senior professor in my major, Dr. Paulson, was a gentle old fellow who, for some unfathomable reason, was well disposed toward me. Based on my promise to complete a term paper, he gave me a grade in a key course I needed to get into graduate school. I never completed the paper. Even after Paulson died of old age, that incomplete haunted me. I had broken a promise to a person who believed in me.

To many of my friends I appeared to have a cavalier attitude toward courses and grades. Actually, I was mightily concerned with grades, at least with meeting Mom's expectations, but procrastination and other failings of willpower were like a disease for which I could find no cure. Angst at times became almost unbearable.

I began to contemplate suicide as a serious option. Fortunately, the life of a college undergraduate reasonably well integrated into campus life provides lots of distractions—girls, beer, classes, friends, even free reading—and suicide requires, at least in my case, focused attention. I bounced between the amusements and demands of the moment and the despair that didn't become black and sustained enough to do the trick.

The best distractions were girls and beer, often both together. With girls I was both insensitive and intimidated—not a winning combination. In one instance, I finally worked up courage to ask a popular and attractive girl for a date two days hence.

She explained, "I'm going to a party with Joe Bottenmueler that evening. Perhaps some other time?"

"Break the date," I responded. Her rejection threatened me beyond endurance, which might give you some idea of how nutty I was. I hardly knew the girl.

She looked at me more in surprise than anger. "I can't do that, Ken. We've had this date for over a week. He's a good friend."

"Don't you want to go out with me?" I persisted.

"That's not the point."

"I think it is."

That sort of ended the conversation, probably to her relief.

On another occasion, I asked a girl, whom I knew better, to go to a major school dance with me.

"She said, "I think Bill Salver may ask me. So give me a few more days, and I'll let you know."

"Okay," I responded. This girl had no particular attraction beyond her, I thought, probable availability.

As these two examples suggest, not only was I cloddishly insensitive, but I was radically inconsistent in attitude as well as a strategy.

My insensitivity to contexts did cost me a good deal at times, including a near disaster with one girl I dated occasionally, Sherri Swartz.

Sherri was a few years older than me, though I didn't know this at the time. A friend, Ernie, and I were driving around town in his car one evening. We decided to go to Phil's bar. I decided I'd look really studly if I could get a last-minute date, so I suggested we stop by Sherri's house. She was home and invited us in.

After a pass at conversation, I said, "I was thinking you might want to go out for a beer."

After thinking a minute, she decided that sounded good. "But first, I've got to make a phone call. Just take a minute." How naïve was I? I didn't even wonder why she had to make a call at the last minute.

We got into Ernie's car.

"Where to?" he asked.

"Phil's, of course," I said.

Phil's bar had almost mythic status for Deschutes students and many others in Salem. It was a huge room, paneled in rough-cut pine. Phil had made a virtue out of cheap wood, and used the same, a little more finished, for booths, tables, and benches. He had been known to survey his thriving business and remark, "What a dump." His dump clearly brought in a lot of revenue and didn't have much overhead, except for free drinks for female state office workers a night or two a week. The office workers, at least the ones who came in small gangs to Phil's, were young, attractive, and presumably unmarried. They brought in young males, like flies to honey.

"I don't want to go to Phil's," Sherri said.

"Why not?" I asked.

"I want to go someplace else."

"Like where?"

"Just someplace else."

"That's not a good reason," Ernie said. Sherri was in the car, which was moving.

She wasn't exactly sulking, but she didn't have much to say.

Ernie and I were on our second beer at Phil's when three guys, a little older than college undergrads, came in and sat at the table next to us. One of these guys, about five foot eight and built like a fireplug, seemed to be having nonverbal communication with Sherri, even mouthing words back and forth. After two or three beers, I knew I wasn't razor sharp, so I just watched for a few minutes. She seemed disturbed and trying in a friendly way to shut down the conversation. He'd go back to talking to his buddies for a while, but he couldn't let it go.

After another round or two of beer, his persistence got seriously annoying. I said, "Can't you find your own date?"

"I think you should butt out."

This required a comeback from me. "Yeah, I think you should stop making a pest of yourself." That seemed kind of lame, so I added a term of address: "Jerkass."

The conversation went rapidly downhill from there, though I can't remember exactly what was said. In fact, my memories of what happened after that are disconnected bits, sort of like debris bobbing up in a murky sea.

My next impression is following this guy and his two friends across the room weaving among tables, to settle this in the parking lot. I realized, fleetingly, that Ernie was not with me, but I was too wasted to worry. Next, the two of us—the fireplug and me—faced each other, about three feet apart in cool night air. My antagonist's two buddies stood a couple of feet behind him, in case they were needed to finish up.

I wasn't too dim to realize this was a no-win situation for me. But, enough beer, and I plunged ahead without thinking through consequences or alternatives.

In the next moment of sanity that bobs up in my memory, I looked where the enemy had been. They weren't there. The bar owner was in my face, saying, "It's all over. The fight is over." Phil had to repeat himself for it to sink in. I apparently had neither hit anyone nor been hit. I felt relieved, though not as relieved as I should have been, as I later discovered. I couldn't figure out why the opposition had just disappeared.

Then Ernie was at my side. "Come on, get in the car. We're out of here."

"Where's Sherri?"

"In the car."

Indeed, she was. And not entirely happy.

"Where are those other guys?" I asked.

Sherri volunteered an answer. "They went back into the bar." She added, "His car is still here, and you'd better take me home. Now."

Ernie was in total agreement with her request.

Sometimes, when your thinking is muddy, one connection will come into sharp focus. From the back seat, I addressed Sherri sitting on the passenger side of the front seat. "How do you know his car is still in the lot?"

Without turning toward me, she said, "I've been in it. Several times."

"Oh?"

Now she turned toward me. "He thinks I'm his girlfriend. I broke a date with him tonight. When he gets frustrated, he heads for a bar, usually Phil's."

"So that's why you didn't want to go to Phil's," I said, in an aha, slightly accusatory tone.

For several seconds, Sherri was silent, staring straight at me. I'd pissed her off, though I couldn't see why. Then she said, "His name is Pete DeMarco. He was a Golden Gloves boxing champion three years ago, before he turned professional."

We let that sink in a while before Ernie pointed out, "Sherri was trying to save your ass by staying away from Phil's tonight."

"Okay, I appreciate that."

"You damn well should," she said.

"So what happened in the parking lot? I was alone facing those three bruisers. Then they just sort of disappeared."

"You weren't alone," Sherri replied. Ernie hung out in Phil's and other bars a lot more than I did. While I followed Pete and friends out of the bar and squared off outside, he was recruiting among his numerous drinking buddies at the bar. Pete had two backups. Turns out they faced about a half dozen behind me, at which point they threw it in and went back into the bar.

We dropped Sherri at her house. I'd see her again.

Early in my first semester at Deschutes, Mom and I faced an important decision. Should I try to join a fraternity? Later I would find several arguments for the negative, but at this point the only apparent downside was the cost.

Mom said, "I think you need to meet more people, have more social life." From grade school, she'd been concerned, when she paid any attention to me, that I wasn't relating well to my peers. Her concern was only partly justified. I couldn't figure out why anyone would like me, so I tended to withdraw from social groups and to avoid possible friendships rather than risk the pain of rejection. But not often was I totally alone.

"Do we have the money?" I asked. Actually, we didn't, but somehow Mom would manage.

Mom was desperate to attach me to something that would get me moving. A fraternity might work, so she was positive about that. It was okay by me, so I went through "rush" and pledged. This did get me more involved with some other students, but our chief activities were dates and drinking beer. I also attended regular and frequent meetings, participated in decorating the house for Christmas and other major occasions, and supported the brothers when they ran for school office. All this was a drag on time. Late in my junior year, I wondered, why I was screwing around in a fraternity? I think this is a fairly common doubt. About the junior year, many "Greeks," men as well as women, tend to split into two groups on the issue of belonging to a fraternity: the gung ho and the cynical.

Deschutes' hypocrisy extended even to the Greek system, which the administration encouraged mightily, even though it was the crucial time when lots of students, including me, got hooked on drinking and other vices. Deschutes' religious affiliation favored temperance, but the University administration did little to control drinking. One area they did control was smoking, which then was almost universal among students. Smoking was banned on campus, so clumps of students and some faculty would gather on sidewalks at the edge of campus and light up between classes. The ban was enforced in an oddly gender-specific way in living quarters. Girls were forbidden to smoke in sorority houses, even though the buildings were physically a block or two off campus. Boys were allowed to smoke in fraternity houses, even though the buildings were part of an on-campus dorm complex. I suppose I was one of a few students to feel conscious contempt for Deschutes' policies on smoking and drinking.

Even when I tried, I couldn't buy into the idea of achieving the standard markers of success. Mom became so concerned about my continuing lack of ambition that she sought the help of a family acquaintance, a semi-retired psychologist.

Baffled by the case, he had me do major school assignments in his home, so I would have little choice but to succeed. So every weekday I was confined for a couple of hours to his large study, with my books and papers spread out on his desk. He was a sincere old fellow, and I really wanted to do the right thing by him. But I didn't. Was my failure deliberate or something over which I had no control? Was I following in my father's footsteps, as a talented failure? That thought didn't scare me enough to force me to overcome a desultory attitude toward school.

Rather than just sit in mild misery, I explored my benefactor's study. He had a remarkable library. Here I learned, for example, about Salvador Dali—a weird artist then known for painting limp pocket watches. I could relate to Dali's cynical view of success—except for one big difference: he was productive; I wasn't.

The one activity that engaged me was forensics, chiefly debate and oratory, but I ran the whole gamut. This was intercollegiate competition, and while it never approached the importance of athletics, winning did significantly influence a school's standing in the pecking order of perceived excellence. Since reputation dominated Deschutes' value system, a successful debate team was not without value. And we were successful.

A local woman of means also sponsored an intramural oratory contest, with money prizes, every year in late spring. I won in my sophomore and junior years, and the modest cash prizes were welcome. My senior year? Ah, yes, that's an interesting story, an example of the Deschutes ethic.

Deschutes, in keeping with its Christian mission, every week during the school year had a religious assembly, "Chapel," with attendance required for all students, and roll scrupulously taken. To encourage reluctant students, some of whom would rather study or go out for a beer that hour, three unexcused absences and the student was barred from all College related extra-curricula activities.

By this time, my salvation in Albany had lost its luster, but I did go to Chapel—once in a while. Within the first couple of months I would use up my three absences, and therefore, theoretically, be barred from representing the College at forensics tournaments. My, my! What to do? In my freshman year, the Dean of Students and I established the routine: I'd go to him with some half-assed excuse, and I'd be cleared to compete. That script worked through my junior year.

But my senior year was different. Through the last tournament, my excuses worked fine. The annual intramural competition came late in spring semester. When I sent in my entry application, it was rejected. What the hell?! I went to the Dean.

"Why is my application for the Turner contest rejected?"

The Dean looked at me with a why-are-you-asking expression. "Because you have excessive Chapel cuts, of course."

"That hasn't been a problem before now."

"Well, yes." the Dean smiled. "We have been generous with you, Ken, but there does come a time when rules have to be enforced."

"Yeah, when I've used up my eligibility to compete for the College." I paused. "Now for the first time, I'm barred from the Turner competition. I need that money."

"The timing is purely coincidental," the Dean lied.

I didn't call him a sanctimonious bastard, nor did I point out how miserably inconsistent this was with what he'd done in the past. I'd discovered by then that persons with serious moral deficiencies get vindictive when their failings are pointed out. I did give it one more try.

"I've done a lot for Deschutes. Will you reconsider?"

"Rules are not made to be broken, Ken." He smiled. "And we do have to treat all students alike."

His fake-friendly smile—that more than his unfairness— almost drove me over the edge. It boggled my mind that he could know he was lying, really hurting me, and still keep up the façade. That level of hypocrisy can be achieved only with years of practice.

I got out of the room before I commented on his questionable ancestry as well as his pallid morality.

I thought of asking the debate coach, Dr. Hamish, to plead my case. A moment's reflection ruled that out, however. Many people I encountered in my academic career cut me some slack or gave me the benefit of the doubt—sometimes way beyond what I had any right to expect. Hamish was not among these generous people. Rather, he fit the prevailing Deschutes ethos as if he were born to it. That is to say, he was a lying hypocrite and prissily self-satisfied.

My debate partner, Lamont Eddy, adapted to Deschutes far better than I did. Hamish was convinced Eddy was the stronger half of our team, a view not shared by several coaches on the circuit. Hamish regarded me as a lightweight, I guess because he sensed I didn't respect him as a coach. After one big tournament in which Deschutes won second place in sweepstakes, I asked him if he'd be willing to give the large trophy to the squad member who had contributed the most points to the team win.

In his usual supercilious way he said, "Yes, as long as his name isn't Lamont Eddy."

I went through three events in which I'd placed. They added up to more points than Eddy had contributed, "So I guess I qualify to receive the trophy."

Hamish, not to my surprise, changed the subject. I didn't get the trophy.

This, however, was not my main gripe with Hamish. The big prize in debate was representing the region at the National Championship tournament at West Point. Our region—Oregon, Washington, and Idaho—were entitled to send two teams, and one slot had been given to Deschutes in my junior year. Hamish split me from Eddy and teamed him with a senior who had done well in one-man debate.

"We have to do this for the team," Hamish explained, apparently anticipating my complaint.

I didn't say anything.

Hamish knew he'd done wrong, so he started making amends to me. "If we get an invite next year, I'll leave no stone unturned to raise the money for you and Eddy to go, I promise you that." I remember that phrase, "Leave no stone unturned."

So Eddy and the senior went to nationals—and compiled a record of two wins and six losses. But there was next year.

I later heard from a coach on the selection committee that our senior year Eddy and I were given one of the two slots without discussion. They told Hamish the good news.

His reply? "I'm sorry, we'll have to decline. I don't believe we can raise the money for the trip."

"You can't! You're sure? We can name an alternate, and you can give it a try."

Hamish knew, if he asked, the money would be forthcoming from local merchants and alumni.

"No, no, we will decline now," he said. Leave no stone unturned, my ass. Why did Hamish forestall any chance of raising the money? I think he'd tried nationals the year before and had been shot down. The bastard was too lazy to try again.

The other coaches were shocked. They had no choice but to accept his decision. This was the most painful betrayal I have ever experienced.

CHAPTER TEN

Two skills enabled me to avoid academic disaster at Deschutes. I developed a habit of always attending and taking thorough notes in classes, and I had a good short-term memory. I had nothing against textbooks. I just rarely took time to read them. In courses in which exams were based on lectures, I did fine. In other courses, not always so good. Procrastination was a character defect that plagued me. A screw-off student with a little ambition would have avoided, as much as possible, courses which required promptness in turning in papers. I lacked the discipline to be that selective. By my senior year, my transcript was a mess of incompletes and made-up courses that almost defied interpretation.

Mom was as generous with money as she could be. I didn't expect more, but she couldn't meet all my needs. We were poor. This problem became more acute when in my sophomore year I felt an overwhelming need to have a car. I didn't need transportation for work or school. I needed a car because for someone living in the dorms that was the only convenient haven of privacy with a girl.

Double-dating was an unreliable solution: I was always at the mercy of a friend's schedule. Sometimes the pace of progress on a date was uneven between couples, which made at least one person, me for example, too fast or too slow. If congenial "progress" were to occur, my date often had to be pretty adaptable. Sometimes she chose not to adapt, creating an awkward problem not often depicted in romantic movies about college students. On at least one occasion my date insisted on walking home, by herself.

By the time I was eighteen, my need for a car as a social tool became desperate. I persuaded an experienced mechanic to help me select a car. I ended up with a twelve-year-old Chevrolet for $300. I had wheels—and another drain on my slender finances.

I needed money. How to get it?

My summers picking beans ended when I turned seventeen. In my first year in college, I applied for a job at, among other places, Sears Roebuck. I figured my obvious talents would net me a job as a salesman, maybe in men's clothing or hardware. The personnel manager, Lois Mars, assigned me to the Auto Service Center. I never discovered why she did this. At first, I saw this assignment as luck of the draw, but in ensuing months, when she refused to even consider transferring me, I took it personally. Had I offended her? Or was she just another mediocre person who enjoyed using a little power whimsically?

The Auto Center was in a satellite building a couple of hundred yards from the main Sears store. My first day on the job I walked there from my dorm a half-mile away. I was an innocent college student about to expand my understanding of the ways of the world. Shawn Perkins ran the Auto Center as his personal kingdom, free of much oversight from the upper administration.

I approached a kid three or four years older than me, in brown overalls with "auto center" stitched above his chest pocket. He stood under a car raised on a hoist, its tires in two parallel tracks connected to a single shiny column. I knew enough to recognize a rack and a small drum with a catch basin under it. The kid twisted a wide screw on the bottom of the pan under the engine block. Black, gritty oil poured out into the basin and down into the drum. He concentrated on his job, while I watched in silence. When the oil slowed to a trickle and then to drips, he screwed the plug back into the pan. That looked simple enough, and I was sure I could handle it.

The kid then moved the drum on four small rollers over a floor drain between the two racks in the service center. He released the filthy oil, probably from several jobs, into the drain where it accumulated until the worst gunk settled out, and a filtered pipe carried the rest away. I later learned this somewhat less dirty oil was put in barrels and hauled away to be processed into clean oil for reuse. Compared with selling furniture, doing oil changes seemed a very dirty business.

After I stood watching this process for a few minutes, the kid squinted at me. "What do you want?" His tone wasn't surly, but it wasn't friendly either. I don't think he liked his job.

"I'm supposed to see somebody named Perkins."

This kid was a little shorter than me, slender and rat-faced. "What about?" he asked.

I curbed my impulse to ask him what business that was of his. "My name is Ken Bailey. I've come to see him about a job."

"Yeah?" He scratched two or three days growth of dark facial hair.

"Lois Mars in personnel sent me over."

His tone changed, but I don't think his attitude toward me improved. Maybe he thought I was competing for his job—and maybe I was. So far as I was concerned, he was welcome to his crummy job, but I was underage and I needed income.

"He's in the office." He nodded toward a large enclosed part of the building just past three bays for servicing vehicles. The bays could be closed at night with large metal doors that slid down on tracks from overhead.

I strolled over to the enclosed section and through the door. Inside was office space to my right and a large selection of tires and batteries on metal racks to my left. The middle-aged man sitting behind the desk wore a clean white shirt and tie—no overalls for him.

"Mr. Perkins?" I asked him.

"Yeah. What can I do for you?" He gave me his full attention; seemed friendly, like a person who wanted to be helpful. I sensed something hollow behind the friendliness.

"I'm Ken Bailey. Ms. Mars says I'm to work here."

His smile disappeared. "Did she now?"

I waited. So far this wasn't the most welcoming place to work.

"Well, Ken, I decide who works in the Auto Center."

I nodded to show I understood the way it was. I didn't want to get caught in a pissing contest between him and Mars.

"You're here, so let's see how you work out." This told me two things: Perkins was not about to try to buck Mars straight off, and if I screwed up he'd have an excuse to get Mars to fire me. I doubted she'd move me to a job inside the store.

"What experience have you had working on cars?"

"None." I figured his little empire was mainly a tire store—tires, batteries, oil changes, and maybe a few odds and ends, like rearview mirrors. The job didn't require an enormous amount of special training! (It turned out that selling and installing the right tires and batteries wasn't that simple.)

"Well, you might as well go to work. We can take care of the paperwork later." He paused. "You know what a sump pump is?"

"Not really."

"Come on into the service area." He got up and, with an amused smile, headed for the door. I followed him.

He pointed to the grate through which the kid had emptied the small drum of filthy oil. "That's where sludge from the used oil accumulates. The sludge has to be emptied out every few days. Dexter here can show you how." Perkins turned on his heel and walked back into his office.

I glanced at Dexter in his dirty overalls. To make a good first impression, I'd worn clean slacks and dress shirt. I imagined what that sump pump under the grate looked like. I was tempted to say to hell with this and go back to picking beans. But I wasn't going to give Perkins the satisfaction of running me off.

Dexter led me around the corner of the building and opened a door to a storage closet. He took out a bucket and large hand scoop and handed them to me. I tried to hold the bucket away from my pants. They were fairly expensive slacks, at least by my standards, and no way could they be cleaned if this gunk got on them.

He gave me a three-foot length of iron bar with one end bent at a right angle. "You'll need this to lift the grate enough with one hand to get your fingers under the edge and pull it up." With a grin, he added, "We had a guy a year or so ago got his fingers smashed when the grate slipped off the lifter. Pretty messy. So you want to be careful."

"Maybe removing the grate should be a two-person job," I suggested.

"Nah, it's a one-man job. Can't take someone off another job to help, Perkins says so." Dexter went over to the tire-repair mount and lifted a wheel into place. I was sure he'd watch me out of the corner of his eye.

I surveyed my situation and tried to plan. A tentative lift showed the grate was heavy enough to require both my arms to get it started. I could try to hold it up a few inches with one hand while I slipped the other hand under the edge, and then let go the lifter and, with split-second timing, get both hands under the edge. This was clearly inviting disaster, maybe permanent loss of the use of one hand. There had to be another way. Then I realized I could keep both hands on the lifter until I flipped the grate over onto the cement apron.

Dexter must have guessed what I was thinking, probably because that was the way one person usually got the grate off. He walked over to me. "Perkins don't like the grate just flipped onto the apron, says it could crack the cement."

Fuck Perkins, and you too Dexter. "I'll do the job my way, okay." I paused. "You plan to tell Perkins?" I glared right at him.

Dexter turned and walked back to his tire job.

I hooked the lifting bar into the grate and got ready to put all my muscle into moving it.

"What the hell you trying to do?" a voice behind me said.

I looked back. My questioner was over six feet tall and well-muscled, maybe late thirties. He smiled, amused. It was the first genuinely friendly smile I'd encountered on my new job.

"I'm trying to flip this grate over." I paused, anticipating being criticized for endangering the cement floor. "It's the only way I can figure to get it off without risking a smashed hand."

By now, Dexter had slunk over to us. Apparently, repairing the tire had lost its urgency.

"Uh, hi Earl."

"Dexter, didn't you tell this kid removing that grate usually takes two people?"

"Well, it doesn't always."

Earl estimated my physical strength. He turned to Dexter. "Suppose you show him how this is a one-man job."

Dexter studied the grate. I handed him the lifter. He took it, reluctantly, looked back at Earl and mumbled, "He can figure it out."

"Uh huh." Earl grabbed the tool out of Dexter's hand, inserted it near one edge of the cast iron grate, lifted that side a few inches and held it up with one hand while he reached under it with the other hand. With both hands under it, he hoisted one side. The grate flipped back and landed with a loud thud on cement near the edge of a gapping oily black hole. He looked at me. "Don't try this by yourself, understand." He glanced at Dexter. Then he seemed to notice my slacks and dress shirt. "Are you working here?"

"Yes, at least I think so."

"You don't seem dressed for the job."

I didn't know what I'd be doing. I initially reported to Mars. That wasn't completely true; I knew it would be in the Service Center.

"Come on." Earl turned and strode to the office. I followed along, thinking there might be trouble between this guy and Perkins. Inside he stood in front of Perkins' desk. "This kid," he stopped and turned to me. "What's your name, kid?"

"Ken Bailey." As a matter of principal, I never say "Sir" to anyone, even cops. I caught myself before I added the honorific to Earl; he seemed to merit it.

"Ken thinks he's working here. He was about to muck out the sump pump in those nice clean clothes. On your orders."

"I figured he'd know enough to get a set of coveralls out of the cabinet." My new boss lied in his teeth to cover his ass. I knew that, and so did Earl. I'd soon discover that among workers, especially low-level administrators, at Sears this was standard procedure. A few people did not buy into casual lying. Earl was one of them.

A few minutes later, I was in khaki coveralls outside, scooping black, greasy muck into a bucket. Earl, now in his khaki uniform, raised an old Chevy on one of the lifts and started loosening lug nuts on a wheel. Between blasts from his pneumatic wrench, I said, "Thanks."

He glanced at me and shrugged. Then he said, "You'll be doing this before long. Always loosen all the lug nuts before you take any of 'em off. Remember that. You'll be less likely to find yourself flat on your back with a wheel on your chest."

I would remember that and a lot more from my job at Sears. I'd also learn what dickheads and liars some people in a large department store could be.

Earl was the one who went with me to Portland to pick out a used car. At the last minute Dexter decided he wanted to go with us. That was okay. After two or three months, we were all getting along and got to know each other pretty well.

Though Sears provided me a part-time job for nearly three years, Mars sticking me in the Auto Center rather than sales continued to gall me. During a two week or so lull at work, I applied for a job at a Montgomery Ward store and was hired to work in men's clothing. The personnel manager was a helluva lot better person than Mars, but my department head turned out to be a jerk, albeit a pathetic one. All but the most junior salespersons, like me, earned a commission on sales. I was pretty good, and about the third day, when I sold an expensive leather coat, the department head slipped up to me and said, "Put the coat on my sales report. You don't get a commission; I do."

"You want to split the commission?" I asked.

He shook his head. "We can't do that." He paused, and went into a poor imitation of James Cagney. "I can make life good for you, or I can make life bad for you, depends on how you want it." My god! I realized he was serious.

The personnel manager had struck me as a straight-up guy, and I was pretty sure I could get this department head fired or at least chewed out. The jerk was only a few years older than me, married, and with two little kids at home.

So I said, "Yeah, go ahead, put it on your sales sheet."

That afternoon, I resigned my job at Wards. The personnel manager asked me why. "It just didn't work out," I said. That sounded lame. I assured the manager I thought he'd been fair.

As I walked out of the building, I had a twinge of guilt that I hadn't told the manager why I quit. But if I had told him, I'd feel guilty about throwing the hooks to the department head. That fellow wasn't malevolent, just weak, and maybe a little desperate.

Dad was fading in my memory. Once in a while Mom got sappy letters from him, which she rarely showed to me. So far as I know, she never answered them. He lived with his two sisters and sold home protection systems. Even as a near-basket case, he must have retained some of his charm and persuasive powers. I suppose if I admitted it, I was kind of proud of him, at least glad for him.

He could have made at least a pass at helping my college costs rather than leaving the whole load to Mom and me. He didn't help with our finances at all. When I thought about that too much, it made me bitter, maybe a little depressed, like I'd been deserted. I tried to avoid thinking about it. That's just the way it was.

Halfway through my third year in college, Mom got word from my aunts that Dad was going intermittently nuts; sometimes he was hostile even toward them. As they put it, he was dangerous and they could no longer control him. He was committed to the Cook County Hospital for the Mentally Disturbed—*i.e.* the county insane asylum. My aunts had interfered three years before, and now they deserved having to make that decision.

A couple of days after the letter arrived, I saw Mom sitting on the edge of her bed, re-reading the letter. Her eyes were moist. She'd never, that I remembered, been this close to crying. Our eyes met, but neither of us spoke. I backed out into our genteelly impoverished living room.

For a while, I sat on the sofa and experienced an unfamiliar emotion: compassion. For Mom, of course, but more deeply for my father. What grinding frustrations had changed him from the confident man I'd seen in newspaper offices and on our ranch to someone who had to be locked in a loony bin? Did he know where he was, how bad was it? Would the frustration continue unabated, or even get worse?

I'd tuned a lot out in my life, and by God, I could tune my father out also.

During my first year at Deschutes, I worked about twenty hours a week at Sears. That left enough time for partying and what studying I was inclined to do. In the first summer, my hours at Sears didn't go up much, so I had a lot of time and not much money.

Across three hundred yards or so of weed-covered lot and two lines of railroad tracks was a large cannery. How convenient!

I went up four or five wooden steps, across a small, green plank platform, and through a door marked offices. A woman at a reception desk asked me what I wanted. I told her, a job. She pointed down a corridor, "Second door on the left, personnel office." When I stood awkwardly waiting, she added in the same flat tone, "Just go on in."

In the personnel office, an older woman slid a one-page form across a counter and told me to fill it out. In a disinterested voice, she asked me, "How old are you?"

"Eighteen." Okay, so I lied. I would be eighteen by the end of the canning season. During the season, labor was in short supply, and nobody was scrupulously checking age. Anyway, eighteen fit where I was in school.

"Do you have any physical handicaps? If so, list them on your application."

I shook my head. I'd find out later this wasn't a trivial, routine question. Dishonesty here could cost you your life.

"Do you want to join the union?"

I shook my head again.

"Fine," she said.

My choice was okay with personnel. I'd find out it wasn't okay with the Teamsters union. By halfway through the season, I'd be a dues-paying union member.

She was about to dismiss me. I said I wanted the night shift. She glanced up, a little puzzled.

"I have a part-time job I need to keep till next fall."

For the first time, she smiled. "We'll see to it you're on the night shift."

Later, I'd find that shifts were assigned, for summer workers, on a pecking order vaguely based on seniority. Night shift was at the bottom of the pile.

The guys at Sears cut me some slack, and Earl ran interference if things threatened to get ugly, as when a customer complained I hadn't changed his battery fast enough. By the end of the school year, my Sears job seemed little more than an annoying interference with my free time. I expected the cannery job would pull more out of me, and it did.

CHAPTER ELEVEN

The next night a little before eleven, after a six-hour day at Sears Auto Center, supper, and a couple of hours sleep, I showed up at the front entrance of the cannery.

In a big lot near the front of the plant, cannery workers unloaded trucks, mostly sacks of green beans, sometimes cherries and flats of strawberries. I walked from the entrance toward the middle of the canning plant. After spray washers, the beans ran on a wide endless belt past three inspectors. They had the ultimate in boring jobs, it seemed to me: staring at the flow, constantly alert for defective beans. Reputations of brands depended on these workers' vigilance. Cans were filled in the cutters area. A belt with high sides brought a continuous stream of empty cans from a boxcar. The cans clattered as they jostled together, adding a higher pitch to the general din of machine noise.

Within a couple of days, I heard the cautionary story of one seasonal worker minding a machine that, with incredible speed, trimmed and cut green beans into uniform lengths. This guy's attention lapsed for a few seconds. He lost most of his index finger, but being a brave lad he continued at his post until someone noticed the blood. Immediately the whole line—cutters, and machines that measured the proper amount of cut beans into each can and then sealed the lid—shut down. Everybody on the line began to search on the floor, the belts, and the machines for the missing digit.

The kid thought he'd be praised for his courage. Instead, he got holy hell for not immediately notifying the nearest foreman of the accident. The finger had to be found, and not by a customer discovering it in a can of premium green beans. The crew was about to start opening cans already cased, an expensive use of manpower to say nothing of stopping a line all the way to the warehouse. A worker found the missing piece of anatomy caught in a Y joint in a machine near where the accident occurred.

I wondered what happened to the kid. He probably got fired. I doubt if the union would've protected him.

Past the canners, the sealed cans rode belts and dropped into heavy mesh baskets, a couple of dozen cans to a basket. The baskets were loaded onto small railcars on metal wheels, a ton or so to each car. The cars then moved to the cookers, long cast iron tubes sealed at one end. A man could just about stand upright as he pushed the heavy cars on rails back as far as they could go. When the tube filled with seven cars, the front entrance was sealed and steam was turned on. The beans cooked in cans under pressure. At the end of the cooking cycle, the cooker foreman loosened the front door, carefully, and near-boiling water spilled out and into a drain.

A man on the floor would maneuver each car to the beginning of a labeler line. Because a line ran about eleven hundred cases an hour, it took two people at the head of the line to keep a turntable loaded. The first person would flip each basket over onto a turntable and another worker would lift the basket off as cans jostled to begin the trip to get labels glued on.

One line, however, didn't run nearly that fast, maybe four or five hundred cases an hour. A single person, if he moved fast, could both flip the baskets of cans onto the turntable and remove the baskets. I was assigned this job. Every two hours we got a break for a smoke or a meal—

union rules. We'd shut our line down and go past the cookers to the cafeteria. Two hours can be a long time. The motions are repetitive, and I liked that. I couldn't let my mind wander, however, because bad things were likely to happen if I didn't pay attention. I kept the turntable filled. I knew I did a good job though no one said so.

The guy who managed the machine that glued the labels on cans, the labeler, was straw-boss of the crew on that line. He'd load a stack of labels into the machine, and watch to see they got glued on correctly and cases were filled properly. Being straw-boss paid more than base for bottom-level workers. It was the easiest job on the line, if everything went well—which, it seemed, rarely happened for very long. If the labels were going on crooked or jamming, or the casing machine screwed up, he'd have to fix it, at least try. He'd stop the line while he fiddled with the equipment. Too much downtime did not reflect well on him, so, if you say a labeling machine was messing up about every tenth label and it was near the end of his shift, he'd limp through and leave the problem for the next crew. This dodge was not always greeted in a spirit of good will. In extreme altercations, the leader of the next shift crew would decide to mark his displeasure with a knife or fist.

The final man on the crew pulled the cases off the line and stacked them on pallets to be trucked away. Pulling cases off the line was not for a weakling: he had no control over the line's speed and he had to stack each twenty-five-pound case right the first time. There was no time for a second try, much less a short break.

With a mixture of college kids, ex-cons, homeless drifters, and retirees from jobs that required more muscle than brainpower, we had a somewhat volatile work environment. Tight order was maintained by a few year-round foremen, whose word was law. So peace generally prevailed. Personal friction in the ranks was resolved, in most cases, in the parking lot. The rare case of serious violence was likely to be ended with a shuck knife.

These knives enabled a caser to open a bound stack of flat boxes in one stroke, which was often as much time as he had. A shuck knife had a thick, inwardly curved blade about three inches long and razor sharp. Normally, a hostile stroke would leave a shallow gash on an offender's arm, just a warning or reminder. One well-placed stroke, however, could take out a throat or jugular vein.

After a few weeks, the manager of warehouse operations on our shift offered me the labeler position on one of the lines. I'd be a boss before I was even old enough to work legally in the cannery, and my pay would go up modestly. I should have rejoiced. I didn't. The job intimidated me: a lot of things could go wrong on a line, and whatever the problem was I'd have to fix it, or at least improvise my way through until the end of the shift. I knew a few of my fellow workers in the cannery were ex-cons not favorably disposed to smart-ass college kids—like me. But this was an offer I couldn't refuse if I wanted to keep my job, and I did want to keep it.

The next season, I ran one of the faster lines. I made good money between that job seven days a week, overtime, stacking cases in a warehouse, and the hours at Sears. I didn't sleep a lot. If Dad could work the ranch and still job out to neighbors, I could do this. And I didn't have to depend on Dad for spit.

The worst accident didn't happen to me. It occurred one night after my shift started. As I and a couple of friends strolled to the casers, we noticed a half-dozen or so people gathered around the open door of a cooker. When we shifted direction to take a closer look, a year-round employee intercepted us and ordered us to get on to our jobs. Our questions about what was going on brought only a repeat of his order. By the end of our shift, the whole story was all over the cannery.

A college kid, big and hefty, seemed a natural for wrestling loaded cars into the cookers. He didn't want to risk not getting a job, so on his application, he neglected to mention a type of epilepsy that on rare occasions caused him to pass out with little warning. He'd apparently pushed a car near the back of the cooker. Then he passed out. In the half-dark, someone pushing in the next car didn't see him collapsed on the floor of the cooker. The foreman of the cooking stage, the man who opened the door, wasn't keeping close track of his workers. The kid got boiled along with several tons of canned green beans.

When the foreman pulled the door open to drain the cooker, the rushing water carried the body between the car wheels. He swung the door open wide, and there was what was left of his cooked crew member. The foreman was put on tranquillizers and sent home for a couple of days. The work went on. It was the height of the season and beans had to be canned.

That was my last summer at the cannery, but not because of any risks. I'd graduate from Deschutes University.

During my four years, I'd started out in pre-law. Dad's sisters were eager to have a lawyer in the family, and my experience in debate pointed in that direction. Mom was okay with that, and the faculty and support staff at Deschutes sure as hell weren't going to take any initiative in guiding me. So, for a year and a half, I'd vaguely thought of myself as a future lawyer and took appropriate courses in Political Science.

A friend, Victor Sokolov, also went pre-law. One evening, over beers at Phil's bar, he mentioned that his uncle, a successful lawyer, had a heart attack the week before. We started talking about why his uncle, only in his fifties, had a heart attack. Turned out being a successful lawyer takes long hours and hard work, but what apparently nailed Victor's uncle was the stress. I was indecisive for about a week before I switched to Education. I'd be a high school teacher, with short days and long vacations.

I discovered I was short of credits in Education and would have to stay at Deschutes as a teaching assistant in forensics. I had neither affection nor respect for Hamish, but it was a job and the setting was familiar. Since his favorite, Lamont Eddy, had hired on as an assistant debate coach at a neighboring university, Hamish figured I was the best of what was left. He agreed to take me on, but I'd be paid largely in graduate credits—considerably less useful than cash! Hamish really fit Deschutes. The school's philosophy was to screw the students except for those who seemed likely to make a lot of money that they would someday share with their alma mater.

In April, I was about to graduate with an undistinguished academic record and face a dismal future. I lacked both confidence and ambition to try for anything better. Being vaguely depressed when not drinking or debating seemed a normal state of mind. I don't think even Dad went through so much of this walking near- paralysis, but maybe he did. Maybe he could have helped guide me out of it. Mom supported me, but she didn't seem to have much insight, and she had demons of her own to deal with.

I was pretty much on my own and facing a dead-end with mild despair. Some days I'd sit in my dorm room for an hour or more at a time and stare into space.

Out of the blue came a way out. If some of my religious inclinations had survived Deschutes, I'd have to believe I was blest by what came next.

★

CHAPTER TWELVE

Late afternoon in early summer, I was in the Deschutes main library starting to face up to a couple of incompletes I'd promised two profs. Next year in school would be more of the same for me, and that was depressing.

"Hi, Ken." Liz Stillwell slid into a chair next to me.

Liz left Deschutes after her first semester, to go to a real university. I'd admired her courage, but hated to see her go. She had long dark hair and an enthusiastic smile, and I had a crush on her. I hadn't seen her for three years.

"Hi, Liz. What're you doing in these ruins?"

"Researching a paper," Liz replied with more energy than I could have mustered about most research projects. "I'm staying with my parents near here for part of the summer."

"Why? You must have graduated." That was a dumb thing to say. I was really happy to see her.

"Yes, I did. But life doesn't stop, you know. I'm in graduate school at State University, Russian studies. How about you?"

Every once in a while I wished I'd amounted to something. But I hadn't. "I'm staying around here next year. Getting a high school teaching certificate."

"Somehow, I never imagined you as a public school teacher." She smiled in a gloriously friendly way. How could I tell her I was too lazy to go to law school?

"Well, someone has to teach the little creeps."

"Ken, that's not a good attitude!"

I shrugged. "I know. But Education is there for me. Not much else is. Hamish is giving me a little money for helping in debate."

"Hamish is a jerk," she said with conviction. She'd been a debater herself, but at State. I'd gone up against her a couple of times. She was good.

"Interesting that Hamish has that reputation," I said.

She focused those perfect blue eyes on me. "Ken, you do have other choices. You're that good."

Lord, I wished she was right, but I knew better.

"You do know that. . . . Don't you?" she said.

I shrugged.

Her jaw set. "Petroski needs an assistant. Apply for the job."

I wouldn't like persuading her how bad I'd look on an application. I had to cut this off quickly. "My academic record is a mess. Incompletes and other problems."

"Your GPA?"

"It's okay, I guess."

"I'll get Petroski to send you application forms. He'll be more than willing when he finds you're available." She turned her chair to face me and took my right hand in both of hers. "Promise me you'll put your best self forward." She smiled. "We can be in graduate school together." I was glad she hadn't asked me to go through a burning building. For her, I'd try, but I'd probably get burned to death.

In a few days the application forms arrived, and I tried to make the best case for myself. I knew it was hopeless, of course, but I'd promised to give it my best shot.

A week later, Petroski called me and asked me to come down to State University to interview with him and the Dean of the Liberal Arts College.

I hesitated to invest money for a bus ticket. But I figured I'd committed to play this out all the way.

So five days later, I sat in a cozy, book-lined office with Petroski and Dean Clark.

Knowing this wasn't going anywhere left me fairly relaxed. That was a blessing. If I'd known this was actually my chance to escape Deschutes and Hamish, the pressure would have gotten to me.

Petroski let Clark do most of the questioning. I had prepared a somewhat ethical position on debate, how best to motivate students, and so forth. But Clark nailed me on one question I hadn't anticipated. What did I intend to take as a major? I'd never paid much attention to that matter, since, in the absence of goals in life, it didn't seem to make any difference. That omission in my preparation could dash any fantasies of a couple of years dating Liz Stillwell. I stalled.

"I don't know your Liberal Arts College very well. What would you suggest?"

Clark's eyebrows went up a bit. He seemed on the verge of smiling.

Oh damn, I've really blown it.

"What I'd suggest, since you would be working in this Department, is that you major in Speech and Drama."

I nodded affirmatively as if I'd given the matter considerable, if uninformed, thought. Asking for Russian studies would push my luck too far.

"Good," Clark said. "We have some routine procedures to go through. But I think you will get an offer of a graduate assistantship within two weeks." He glanced at the third person in the room. "If that meets with Dr. Petroski's approval."

"Absolutely."

Near the end of the summer, I moved into a dorm at State University. Four students shared a common room for studying and a separate bedroom with bunk beds. My most esoteric roommate, Vishnu Waisimal, had been sent by his father, a tribal chief in the middle of Africa, to get an American education. Vishnu, giving speeches about his quaint culture, was a great hit with local civic organizations and women's clubs. I suspect he didn't talk much about the knife, slender like Vishnu and with a nine-inch blade, that he always carried. He told his roommates his father had to get him out of the country because he'd used the knife once too often. The other three of us figured this was bullshit, but when he claimed the top bunk near the window no one argued.

In the first week of fall semester, I met what was left of last year's debate squad at State. Petroski called the meeting. He would remain the "debate coach," take credit for what the debaters achieved, and accompany the squad at the most significant tournaments. Otherwise, he made no contribution. By the end of first semester, most people on the squad and on the circuit knew I was running the program and coaching debaters to win. People who'd gone out for debate just to add it on their record sloughed off. I was left with a half dozen men and two or three women who meant business and had talent. That part of my life was real work: practice debates at night plus research and discussions, long drives, two- or three-day tournaments that tested endurance for me as well as the debaters.

The program encompassed my life. It probably kept me sane, maybe even alive. Fantasies about Liz Stillwell faded. One of the women on the squad was a beauty queen, and no administrator was much interested in enforcing limits on "appropriate" relationships between students and faculty. Besides, my status was ambiguous: I was a student with more responsibility than many faculties had.

Another student, also attractive, was enormously talented and energetic. We had an affair on and off for two years until she transferred to another university. Too bad, I liked her a lot. Later, I realized her transfer might have been because she'd concluded I was an irresponsible dead-end as prospective husband material.

How irresponsible was I. One aspect of the forensics program was a Speakers' Bureau. I'd take three speakers from the squad for a presentation of divergent opinions on a current topic before a civic club, high school assembly, or some other real audience. We traveled all over the state and often had to stay in motels overnight.

One night, after a presentation, I went for a ride with one of the speakers, Barb Conklin, which, of course, led to parking and so forth. She and I were about the same age. I found a great place to park: a quarry with a maze of roads weaving around pits and great piles of dirt.

Alas, I got the car, provided from the University fleet, stuck in a shallow pit.

Barb and I walked to the highway and to a service station, where I called a taxi to take her back to the motel. That solved her problem. It didn't solve mine. Where do you go for help in a strange town? I couldn't find an open garage that might have a tow truck. The taxi dropped me off at the town police station, which seemed to be manned by one cop sitting at a beat-up office desk.

"I've got a car stuck in your dirt quarry."

The cop stood and eyed me, not really hostile, just wary. "Yeah, so?"

"I can't find a garage. Can you give me a tug to get it out?"

He looked to be early forties, muscular, shirt with badge and gun the only signs of his official status, civilian pants; it seemed to be an informal place. That was good since my problem seemed to call for an informal solution.

"What were you doing in a quarry this time of night?"

It was an obvious question. So far, I'd focused on the next step in dealing with this situation. It dawned on me now that I was in deep trouble. Trying to make out with a student when on official school business was bad enough. Thank God Barb's virtue had triumphed over my seduction skills. Losing a State car would be harder to explain. Dean

Clark seemed, inexplicably, to have a lot of good will toward me, but he wouldn't overlook the careless loss of several thousand dollar's worth of State property.

When in doubt, tell the truth. Besides I could think of no other even vaguely plausible explanation.

"I was parked with a girl. We walked to an all-night store on the highway. I sent her home in a taxi."

He stared at me in silence.

"I'll be glad to pay you twenty dollars for your help."

He frowned at me. "I'm a public servant. We're not allowed to take bribes. What's your name?"

Hell! Just my luck to get a straight-arrow cop!

"Ken Bailey. I don't look at it as a bribe; just thanks to an officer helping a citizen in distress."

"Yeah," he said sarcastically.

I stared at the floor, contrite, feeling helpless.

"Okay, let's go," he ordered.

I jumped to follow him. When we got to his cruiser, I didn't know whether to get in back, like a prisoner, or in front near his pump-action twelve gauge standing upright near the dashboard.

He gestured toward the front door on the passenger side. "Get in."

I swallowed and hoped to heaven I wouldn't mess up the deal, but I had to ask. "Ah, do you have a chain or rope? I think it may need a tug." He was already half into his car.

He glanced at me with disdain, but he started driving toward the entrance to the quarry. "You're not the only dumb kid I've had to haul out of that quarry."

He turned off on a side street for a block or so. "I got to check out a warehouse, been hit a couple times recently. Just take a few minutes."

I kept my mouth shut. This unpredictable small-town cop was my tenuous link to a future at State. At the moment, I had no other prospects for the rest of my life. Even going back to the cannery was not a viable option for a year-round job, though I'd thought of it a few times.

He parked in a large vacant lot back of the warehouse and exited the car. "You stay here." He undid the strap around the butt of his gun and kept his hand on it, but he left it holstered as he entered the cavernous door. I waited alone in the cruiser, just me and the shotgun.

After a few minutes of staring at blackness in the entrance, I checked my watch. My chance for rescue hadn't reappeared. Not good. I'd give him two or three more minutes. Then what?

The shotgun was not locked down. In a flash of rational thought, I decided against taking it. What could I do with it? Maybe come to a face-off with a thief? Blasting someone could be a seriously bad mistake. I was already in far too much trouble. I took out my own weapon, a switchblade with a four-inch blade. The knife wouldn't be much of a weapon against professional criminals, but it made me feel less naked.

After easing out of the car, I went inside the warehouse slowly and quietly.

In a few minutes I saw a light bouncing around the walls near the back of a huge room stacked with boxes. I moved toward it.

The light swung around to frame me. It seemed to be a powerful flashlight, like a cop might have—I hoped.

"Officer?" I said quietly.

The light started moving toward me. "Bailey, what the hell are you doing? I told you to stay in the cruiser."

"I didn't know what happened to you. I thought you might need some help."

He didn't say anything until he caught up and we walked out of the warehouse.

"Just what did you plan to do if I was in trouble? You armed?"

I was holding the knife at my side. Now I flicked it open and brought it up.

The cop looked at it. He shook his head as if staggered by my stupidity. After a pause, he said, "I guess you meant well." He took a close look at the knife. "How long is that blade?"

"Three and a half inches."

He smiled. We got into the cruiser and drove down the highway until he turned into the quarry. We stopped among great piles of dirt and a labyrinth of narrow roads.

"Which way did you go from here?"

Oh hell! I don't remember! With Barb, I'd parked in a shallow pit, careful so someone else coming through with intentions similar to mine would be less likely to see us. I figured I was clever to avoid coming face-to-face with the locals. Now it didn't seem clever at all.

After my second bad call giving directions, he turned to me. "You don't know where the hell your car is, do you."

I shook my head. So close, and now I was stymied.

He flipped the switch for the spotlight on his side of the car and began driving along one of the roads, checking each dip. "This is probably going to piss off some of our local lovers," he remarked.

I felt a surge of relief. This cop has taken it as his personal challenge to find the damn car!

After twenty minutes we'd found nothing.

"If we don't find it tonight, what then?"

"You getting worried?" He sounded almost sympathetic.

"Yeah."

"We'll give it another try, down this road." We were back near the entrance to the quarry. "In daylight, it'll be a lot easier." He paused. "This quarry isn't that big. I'll put the watchman, maybe even a deputy on it. We'll find it, if it's in here."

Yeah, daylight would give us a better shot at finding the car, but it wouldn't be just me and this cop looking.

Others would find out what I'd been up to. Which was worse: the obvious picture of what I, a quasi-faculty member, was doing, or trying to do with a student, or the miserable mess I'd made of the whole attempt? And what if we didn't find the car? What if no one found the car because some local rustics had stolen it? Something in the pit of my stomach churned, close to forcing an exit. I didn't want to ask this cop to stop while I puked beside the road.

"Hey, look."

I looked. The black top of a car showed just above the edge of a pit. My stomach began to settle down. "I think that's it." I'd entered the deep pit from a different angle.

He stopped and we walked to the edge. After a minute surveying the car and pit, he said, "Now, I've got to figure out how to avoid getting stuck while I get you out."

I looked across at the ramp I'd driven down to get into the pit—and silently cursed my stupidity for driving in without thinking about getting out. I swore I would never again let hopeful lust cause me to ignore risk. But I knew this experience probably wouldn't produce a lifetime of caution.

"I came in from that side over there. Maybe you can get closer without getting into loose dirt."

He nodded, and we followed a rough road part way around the rim, turned and went carefully part way down the ramp. We stopped. He opened the trunk, and took out a roll of third-inch cable with a hook in each end.

I stood beside him. "What can I do to help?"

He ignored me while he attached one end of the cable to a power winch on the reinforced front of his cruiser. He walked down to the University car, uncoiling the cable as he went.

He regarded the State plate on the car. "How come you got this car?" In the near dark I sensed him squinting at me. "Don't you have an adult chaperone on this trip?" Bad questions, but not as bad as him assuming the car was stolen.

"Yes, we do." I hesitated. "I'm it."

He snorted. "You really got your tail in a crack!"

"Yeah, I really do. You have no idea how grateful I am that you're helping me."

"We haven't got you out yet." He ducked under the rear bumper and attached the other end of the cable to something, part of the frame or axle I guessed. "I'll back up until the cable goes tight. I'm not sure this winch will drag out your car's dead weight, so you're going to have to get in reverse and help it out. This takes some care."

He looked at me as if he wasn't at all sure I'd have the judgment or skill to do my part. He shrugged as if reconciled to the possibility of disaster. "If you give it too much gas and smack in the front end of my cruiser, I'll have your ass. You got to pay close attention, understand."

I nodded, and prayed I'd have the necessary skill.

He got into the cruiser, while I started the University car. He pulled the cable taut and leaned out his window. "Okay, this is for real."

He got back into his car. I gave the State car a modest amount of gas, like trying to get started in reverse on ice.

My car lurched back and sideways. I gave it more gas. The car began almost stately progress backward out of the loose dirt at the bottom of the pit. When I felt on more solid ground of the ramp, I eased up on the gas. The car now moved under its own power and traction. The cable went slack. I moved a few yards more. I was loath to stop until I'd gained the upper edge, but I was more loath to back into the front end of the car behind me.

The cop disconnected the cable under my car, coiled it as he walked to his car, and disconnected it there. He tossed the cable into his trunk. "I don't want some punk son of a bitch helping himself to my cable."

"Makes sense."

We stood a few moments silently congratulating ourselves on a job well done. I held out the twenty bucks.

He shook his head. "We already been through that. Besides, for straight entertainment, you've made my night."

I followed him out of the quarry. He waved as he turned into the police lot, and I gave a short toot on my horn.

When I got to the motel, my three speakers seemed to be asleep. Good. Though I was a little disappointed Barb didn't wait up to see if I made it to the motel.

I resolved they'd never know how the story played out.

More serious problems faced me when we got back to the University, academic problems.

Incompletes and overdue papers, that's what waited at State University.

CHAPTER THIRTEEN

Near the end of my first year, we'd gone to the last tournament and the last panel discussion before an audience. No more distractions in the one area that gave me a sense I could actually achieve something. My top team qualified for the national debate championship tournament, held in New England. Petroski, of course, took that trip. I stayed home, vaguely aware I'd been screwed. I said nothing. He was teaching me in individual readings courses to bring me up to speed in my major. If I became angry and created a stir, the net result would be only to shoot myself in the foot.

In a desperate search for something academic that would give me a sense of achievement, I tried a crazy range of courses. A course in music, playing the piano, trailed off in lack of discipline to practice; I dropped out before getting a failing grade. Two different courses in creative writing produced little, except another incomplete.

Historiography seemed a worthwhile area: much of my major focused on the historical development of Rhetorical Theory, and great speeches were usually adapted to specific historical contexts. The professor, aptly named Quintius Green, taught a seminar in his home, and he graded us on our contributions to discussions. At one point, when I sought his advice for a paper in another course, he remarked, "When you encounter an important, untranslated source, you take time out to learn that language." I liked Green, but when it came to scholarly effort, we clearly were not on the same page. I finished the course, but ended my pursuit of that minor.

Forays into other studies produced mostly defeat. I was dogged by lack of self-discipline. I seemed unable to force myself to focus and finish. I became more desperate, and more depressed.

Few people can understand this. Most would say, decide what you want and buckle down to the job of getting it done, or go with the flow and enjoy life. I seemed unable to do either. Near the end of my second year at State, my mental condition became untenable. I'd written both parents, now living widely separated lives. Mom responded with predictable assurances and familiar exhortations to do better, mostly the latter. I appreciated her attempts to help, even if they were useless. Dad never answered my letters.

For reasons I don't understand, I wrote my "sister" from bean-picking days, Marian Mason. While I was at Deschutes, she worked in Portland. We'd had a few dates, but hardly a close relationship. Then she moved to California. My letters explained how much I missed her. Was this whining? Probably. But I wasn't thinking straight. A correspondence started. I suppressed awareness that in my letters I was trying to manipulate her. I did successfully bring her around.

Mason gave up a comfortable situation in California and moved to Eugene in the late spring of my second year. Within a few days, she had a job as a legal secretary and a crummy apartment with the shower in a cold basement. We dated quite a bit. Even after what she had done for me, I kept dating other girls. I didn't think about her emotions, much less fairness. Years later, I'd realize what a cruel mistake I'd made, perhaps, as it turned out, more cruel to myself than to her.

One warm evening sitting on the bed in her apartment, she said quietly to me, "Why did you ask me to move to Eugene?"

"You're not happy here?"

She didn't answer directly, maybe because she didn't indulge in self-pity. Her mental toughness made it hard for me to admit, even to myself, how much I was floundering.

"Where is our relationship going?" she asked.

The question caught me off-guard. I didn't take responsibility for any relationship going anywhere. I stalled.

"Where do you want it to go?"

She didn't answer. She just leaned across the bed and kissed me on the cheek, gently like a mother would a child.

We talked about school, in a neutral way, and enough about her job for me to realize it was okay, but not as good as the job she'd left in California. The almost constant rain in the valley, after sunny California, must have depressed her. She didn't complain.

Marian would have helped me, if there were any ways she could, and if she'd known how bad things were in my head. She'd moved to Eugene. How much more could she have done?

In the fall I'd go back to coaching debate, and Petroski would take credit for whatever we accomplished. That poor bastard was taking the fun, for me, out of winning.

I'd be mired, now entering a third year, in a master's program that almost any knucklehead would handle in two years at most. Dean Clark and the rest of the faculty seemed infinitely patient, but that only made it easier to procrastinate. They must have a helluva low opinion of me. When I couldn't ignore how much I'd let them down, the guilt and the frustration with my weaknesses would overwhelm me. I could suppress guilt; I'd been really good at that, but it was getting harder.

One evening I sat at a desk in our common study area in the dorm. Spring finals were over, so the dorm was nearly deserted. There was no one I could talk to. I went outside and walked in cool night air across campus and into a cluster of modest faculty homes.

I found myself staring at a lighted window of my creative writing professor's home. He was a no bullshit, here's how you do it guy. He had several stories in print. At one in the morning I walked onto his porch and rang the doorbell, though I hardly knew the man outside the classroom. That's how desperate I was, for any kind of release from a pain so intense it made my muscles ache.

I waited, breathing in short gasps, beginning to realize what a stupid fool I was about to make of myself. As I turned to slink away, the door opened.

"Mr. Bailey, what can I do for you? The hour is late, you know."

"I know the hour is late," I said impatiently, not bothering to apologize. "I need help, Dr. Manville."

He waited, regarding me the way a biologist might examine an annoying species of beetle. I began to slip out of my messed-up head enough to see this situation from an objective perspective, to see how absurd I appeared. One or two of my profs were able and willing to engage absurdity on its own terms without losing their grounding. Manville wasn't one of them. But he was courteous.

After several seconds, he said, "What seems to be your problem?" He put emphasis on "seems."

"I'm depressed."

He didn't roll his eyes, but his ghost of a smile told me he figured he'd heard this before. I was sure he had no inclination at this late hour to endure another student's dramatic angst. Should I beat a tactful retreat or push on with him?

I truly believed that my condition was not the same feeling as those other poor bastards who'd come to him for help. At least it was more intense, and it sank deeper in my psyche. I gave him a quick description of my pain and confusion

"You're having a deeply emotional experience. You can recall your mental state in a calmer time and use it in your writing, like any other emotional experience."

My "mental state" is unraveling into insanity, and all Manville does is give me standard crap about using emotional experience in writing! Maybe that's all he can do.

"Yes, I'll do that." I thanked him and got out of there before I forced us out of our roles.

About all I'd gained from my awkward adventure with Manville was panic. I was doomed to lose my mind. My only hope was Marian Mason. I'd messed up her life and given nothing in return. She didn't owe me a damn thing.

Earlier, when depression hit with its twin loads of guilt and frustration, I'd massaged the idea of suicide—usually on a sort of theoretical basis to be used if worse came to worse. Now I had to deal with suicide, cashing in, as a practical option. I planned how to go about it. Poison and pills were unreliable: I could throw them up, or they might go only far enough to muck up my mind, turn me into a basket case, without finishing the job. Jumping from a window had the same problems unless I jumped from a very tall building, and having myself smashed all over the pavement wasn't appealing. And so on through other choices: either unsure or very messy. I was determined to get it right the first time.

I'd selected my method: a little messy, but certain and quick if done right. Put a gun in my mouth, tilt the barrel upward and pull the trigger. I had a .22 pistol, but that small caliber left too much chance of an incomplete job. I'd get a twelve-gauge shotgun and double-ought shells, but that was only a minor inconvenience. There are a lot of hunters in this part of the country, and no one would take amiss the purchase of a gun and shells.

I walked dark streets, finally going back to the deserted study room at three in the morning. A plan was in place, but I needed time—a few days at least—to be absolutely sure I wanted to pursue it. I wasn't too insane to realize I had faced a decision neither trivial nor reversible. At times, I seemed to be just playing with the idea of suicide, but I knew I couldn't be certain I was serious until that moment I pulled the trigger.

It seemed schizoid to begin the summer trying to finish up incompletes that I found I couldn't concentrate on, and reconciling myself to a decision to kill myself. Why did I care about the incompletes? They mattered because I'd told profs I'd finish them. Being dead wouldn't exempt me from responsibility—at least that's the way I saw it. I know it was kind of stupid. In deep depression, you confuse priorities.

For a few weeks, Marian Mason pulled me through. As with many people our age, she'd been depressed and she didn't see it as life-threatening. I refused to humiliate myself by trying to convince her how bad it was for me. Just by her being there, she seemed to suggest that somewhere out there might be alternatives to the dark place I was in. We never explored those options, so I was suspended in limbo, without even the debate program to rescue me from abject futility. In the worst moments, when I was on the verge of executing myself, an image of Mason would appear in my mind's eye: dark hair; splendid, slender body; slightly mocking, or maybe just cynical smile. The vision would draw my focus away from walking downtown and buying the shotgun and shells, so I'd sit in a semi-paralyzed state in my dorm room, sometimes for hours. In more rational moments, I knew that sometime the vision of Mason wouldn't be enough to draw me off course. Then I would end it.

- - - -

One afternoon I arrived at my dorm room after a couple of hours of fruitless fiddling in the library stacks. Tommy Duvall handed me a message he'd taken on the communal phone in the hall. He gave it to me personally rather than just putting a note in my mailbox.

"Dean Clark's office called. You're to make an appointment to see him."

The blade was descending on my career at State. I felt curiously relieved. I figured this would get me out from under a load of crap, maybe, just maybe, without blowing my brains all over the ceiling; I was that hopeful. Or maybe I was just curious about the meeting.

Two days later, in early afternoon of a glorious spring day, Dr. Clark opened the door and invited me into his office. He sat down at his desk and pointed me toward a chair across from him—business-like. His friendly smile confused me. I was sure the dean did not enjoy throwing the hooks to students, which he was about to do to me.

"How's your work going, Ken?"

"We're losing top debaters to graduation, but I think we could still have another good season next year." The "we" was presumptuous; I regretted it.

He folded his hands one over the other and rested his chin on them, regarding me for several seconds. He was passing judgment on me, and, of course, I didn't measure up.

"You've done a remarkably effective job with the forensics program."

I stared at him and waited. Yes, I'd done a good job there, but I'd screwed up in every other facet of my career at State.

"Well, it is Dr. Petroski's program."

"Generous of you to say so, Ken." He paused, smiled and added, "Don't you think I know what goes on in that department?"

"I'm sure you do, sir."

"We need to give an official impression that a full-time faculty member is in charge of a major program, for several reasons. For one, some funding for the program comes directly from the legislature. You understand?"

He paused, as if he wanted to be sure I did understand. I nodded.

"Some other faculty members and I are a little puzzled that you never complained about not getting full credit for your work."

Where is Clark going with this? He's criticizing me for not complaining about Petroski?!

"I was paid to do a job, so I did it." I hoped to hell this wasn't a preamble to discuss the mess on my transcript, but it almost certainly was. That will be hard to take. I admired Clark and placed great value on his respect. With conscious effort, I kept my breathing regular.

"I wanted you to know we appreciate what you've done with forensics. But that's not why I asked you to come in."

Now it comes. Friendly praise, then whammo. I waited.

"Our Ph.D. program is not yet in place, so we can't use doctoral candidates to teach undergrad courses. We have a large number of M.A. students, but we've never put them in charge of classes. We feel it's time we explored that resource to help with the freshman speech sections."

I nodded, still confused.

"We want you to take a teaching assistantship next year. Two sections of freshman speech a semester. Department syllabus. Otherwise, you'd be pretty much on your own. It's an experiment for us. We believe you're the most capable graduate student we have."

I stared across his desk, dumbfounded. For several seconds, he watched while I tried to get my mind around what he'd said.

"You want me to teach sections of the regular freshman speech course? On my own? Do I understand you?"

He nodded. "That's what I said."

"And the debaters? What happens to them? Do I continue to handle forensics?" A really efficient person could do both, but I knew I was not that person.

An optimist would leap into double duty and have the self-assurance to carry on unless it became manifestly clear he couldn't handle both jobs. Then he'd deal with that. Maybe he would handle both, partly because he believed he could. My pessimism doomed me to failure from the get-go.

How could I turn down Clark's offer without revealing myself as a sad mess?

"Yes," he continued, "that was a hard decision for us. Your devotion to the forensic program produces gratifying results, but at considerable cost to your academic work."

I chose not to explain that what handicapped my academic progress was beer, women, laziness, and lack of focus. Odd he hadn't picked up on that. I was a fake, but I let it ride. The depression lightened up, at least a little. It did not occur to me I might lack skills and knowledge needed in teaching. My misgivings were all about not having the self-discipline to stay with the job and do the work.

"We believe that teaching, while demanding, will provide clearer parameters on your work for the department." He paused. "Do you think you can give lectures, critique speeches, manage tests and final grades? That, and individual conferences, is about all there is to it."

Relief over not getting canned and not having to deal with suicide right away carried me to an up-beat emotional extreme.

"Yes, I can do those things." Was this confidence actually coming out of my mouth. I shivered, realizing self-confidence was a role I'd slipped into. But I was into it, and by ostentatiously focusing I could stay in it for the duration of this conversation.

The relief, and a bit of confidence, carried over into the first part of the summer. Somewhat to my surprise, I finished a major paper to clear one incomplete off my record. The professor noted the paper was excellent, but then gave me a C on it and a B in the course. This seemed an obvious injustice. Like most students, I judged according to my own lights. But unlike most of my classmates, I hated injustice as a moral evil—or was this self-serving rationalization. No, I really did value justice as in itself a great virtue. My reading in classical rhetoric reinforced this view.

I cornered the professor in his office. "Dr. Adamson, I don't understand my term grade." This, of course, is the standard opening for a complaint.

"What don't you understand?" Standard response.

"I believe all my grades, except for two minor papers and my final paper, were in the A range. Why do I get a B in the course, and why a C on my final paper?"

Adamson sat stiffly behind his desk. He must have seen this coming, and he didn't want to argue about it. I believed he should have judged the final paper on its own merits and given me the grade the paper deserved. The term grade was a separate issue. In this sort of situation, there are people with an appreciation of excellence and there are tight-assed bastards enslaved by rules. I'd often depended on the former to slide through, but Adamson was clearly rule-bound. In a few months, I'd be an extreme version of Adamson, God help me!

"Your papers were always late. For me to ignore that would be unfair to others in the class." The "Always" . . . was an exaggeration: two minor papers were turned in on time. It would be petty to argue on that basis, so I didn't. Besides, he'd nailed me with "unfair to others."

"You did think the final paper was good, an A paper?"

Apparently, he thought he saw a trap (which I did not intend), so he didn't give me a straight answer. I'd worked hard on the project and I just wanted him to give a favorable judgment on the paper. Like many of his kind, he was too paranoid to risk straight honesty.

"Well, Ken, I can't really separate out the lateness from the rest of the paper. It's like an omelet with one rotten egg."

A rotten egg! This seemed strained even as metaphor, but it was nothing compared to his next launch into poetic judgment.

"You should get over procrastination. This habit of getting work in late is like a crowbar tied to your left leg."

It may have been a lousy simile, but the image — dragging along a four-foot crowbar tied with laundry cord just above the knee on my left leg—has never left me. Unfortunately, neither has the tendency to figure tomorrow is soon enough to get to work.

I thanked Adamson for his advice. I was going to say "helpful advice," but I knew sarcasm would show through my voice if I said "helpful."

A couple more incompletes were wiped clean that summer. I resolved that in my up-coming career as faculty member, sort of, I'd turn over a new leaf.

CHAPTER FOURTEEN

I had an office, just as if I were really on the faculty. The room had one desk and an office chair, two sturdy wooden chairs for students in conference, and nearly enough bookcases. It was the smallest faculty office in the department—quite a bit smaller than the debate coach's office I reluctantly abandoned.

Petroski lined up a new graduate assistant, from another school, who as an undergrad had done well in oratory and oral interpretation. This guy apparently figured he'd replaced me because I wasn't up to the job. His misreading of the facts meant he never came to me for advice, and that was fine with me. Most of his coaching seemed for individual events. The heart of any strong forensics program is two-person debate, about which this new coach didn't know squat. A couple of teams left over from the year before used what they knew. They kept the program from looking dismal. Chatting with me in the hall, two debaters said that what they'd learned from me carried them through. I told them I was happy to hear they were doing well. I'm afraid my joy at hearing their report stemmed from a less than admirable reason: they recognized this guy didn't even come close to being as good as I'd been as a debate coach.

Clark made clear I was to keep my distance from the whole program. I missed the adrenaline rush of a two-day tournament, but I did what he'd urged. Handling two classes a semester, plus my own graduate course work, filled my time.

Grading speech outlines became singularly unappealing; I'd rather read whatever was at hand than force myself to grade. I had a couple of books by the philosopher Jean Paul Sartre—short books, about right for my attention span.

Sartre put responsibility for our own behavior squarely on us as individuals, no matter what the circumstances. If someone holds a gun to your head and orders you to betray a friend, you can opt not to obey, and get your head blown off—your choice.

I'd dropped balls right and left all my life. Maybe I blamed Dad or Mom or the University. Sartre made clear that whatever I did, or didn't do, whatever I became, was my responsibility. Acceptance of his premise depressed me, but I did accept a little more responsibility and tried to reform. Only a few years earlier, I'd bought into the Assembly of God religion. That didn't last long, and neither did my acceptance of Sartre's atheistic existentialism—they just lasted long enough to ratchet up my guilt and frustration at my own manifest failings.

Critiquing student speeches is a big part of teaching freshman public speaking. It's so much work some instructors teach only theory, on which students can take multiple-choice tests to be graded by machine. Some faculty rationalize that if students learn theory they can put it into practice on their own. This is bullshit. But it can make the job easier for teachers, who can then teach more students per section. Administrators like greater productivity, so everyone is happy. I never bought into this unspoken conspiracy to keep the work light.

Pure theory is appealing to students who suffer from stage fright—which is most students. Stage fright, or "speech apprehension," can be a source of energy if it's handled right, or a crippling distraction if it's not. Practice is required to learn how to use the added adrenaline to good effect.

In critiquing students' speeches I had trouble finding a middle ground between being a screw-off and being hyper-conscientious. An adequate critique would be to comment on one or two aspects of the speech—confident delivery, for example, or coherent organization. On each speech I'd take a half hour or more, sitting in my office, to write comments on every aspect (most of which would draw, at best, a perfunctory glance from the students). This thoroughness was largely a waste of my time. I hated doing it, but I couldn't escape the compulsion.

I think the cause of my compulsive thoroughness had more to do with grotesquely low self-confidence. If I wrote everything I could think of, perhaps I would do an adequate job.

To dodge responsibility for deciding final course grades, which in many cases are unavoidably subjective, I set up complex numerical formulas. These numerical formulas led to grade decisions that in some cases I believed to be unjust and not in the best interests of the student, but I was determined to be "fair" and apply my formulas consistently. I just couldn't accept the fact that I, and not some mathematical calculation, was responsible for final grades.

The department had a rule that a student had to pass both the theory and the practice parts of the course to get above D as a final grade.

One student gave A-grade speeches, but blew one long part of the final exam. By my algorithm, he failed the final.

This F, in itself, was probably unjust, and it was clearly tight-assed on my part to give him a D in the course.

He complained: "Look, your grades on my speeches show I used the theory, so I must have learned it."

"Yes, you gave good speeches." I countered, "The syllabus, however, is clear. You have to pass the theory. You need to be able to use it in a variety of situations beyond the course."

"I did well enough on other parts of the exam."

"Can you honestly say you deserved a higher grade on the exam, that I graded it unfairly?"

"No, I'm not saying that." He was in a bind: smart enough to know that if he accused me of being unfair, he'd ruin any chance of getting me to change his grade. On the other hand, he couldn't accept the grade.

He shifted to a different appeal: "This D puts me a semester behind in my degree program. The added semester will cost a lot, maybe more money than my parents can come up with. Doesn't that seem a steep penalty for one question on one exam?"

I shrugged. "I don't make the rules." Prof Adamson would have been proud of me—but I doubt if anyone else would have.

Ironically, my "thoroughness" in critiquing, though I knew it to be grossly inefficient and sometimes unfair, impressed senior members of the department favorably as evidence that I was highly conscientious.

The senior faculty's inaccurate impression was one example of something that cropped up fairly often in my life. Even when I acted in ways that signaled serious mental instability, people around me saw my acts as minor aberrations or didn't notice at all. In my senior year at Deschutes, for example, I went through a major tournament, including the awards assembly as Iner Bassinger, an evangelist whose name appealed to me. At the National Speech Conference where I should have been looking for a job, with all the serious self-promotion that is supposed to entail, I introduced myself to the editor of the top journal in the field as Sam Bass. Was I self-destructive? Not consciously—maybe just cynical, or perhaps reluctant to play a game I was not at all sure I could win.

My positive spin on such aberrations is to blame them for my resistance to petty ambitions of the system. This spin can make me appear quite noble—or it would if it were the whole story. Unfortunately, it isn't, and deep down I knew it. I wanted desperately to escape what I was, what I did, my faults and imposed goals. I wanted out of my skin. But I lacked insight and the will to change my character or my situation. So I floundered on.

A small minority of student evaluations of my teaching were discouraging. One student zeroed in on my obsession with numerical scores, and lack of real feeling, by suggesting that I was fitted to teach economics, and not speech. A single negative comment like that would overwhelm a dozen positive comments.

I lived in an emotional wasteland, without even the rushes of debate tournaments. The affair with Marian Mason continued in on-again-off-again dating that was going nowhere. Despite some heavy kissing and groping, Marian could not be seduced. I don't know why. I think she may have actually loved me. She was frustrated by my inability to take control of my life—or, often, to even plan a date—so maybe she waited to see if I'd grow up. Our affair sputtered on until a radical change in my situation occurred near the end of my third year at State. Then I just forgot her, which was the most selfish act I'd ever committed in relationships with women.

My relationship with Marian interwove with other affairs, but only one, with Allison, reached a similarly serious level. Allison was on the debate squad at State, so I coached her. She was a force of nature with boundless self-confidence and energy. We had engaged in full-scale sex shortly after we started dating. I think she saw me as good husband material and she was determined to acquire me. Or maybe she was just promiscuous. At any rate, after two years, she shifted to another university. I lost a fairly reliable lover and a very good debater. Did Allison just give up on me? Or did her parents decide our relationship was unhealthy for her? I scarcely noticed her leaving.

I was too self-centered to empathize with other people. It did not occur to me that my actions could cause other people serious pain. I should be grateful I didn't have to pay a higher price for mindless cruelties.

I bumped along, without insight, doing a cautious dance with black depression. Near the end of my third year at State, three occurrences radically changed my life.

CHAPTER FIFTEEN

One dismal evening in April, my roommate came home to our apartment with an exceptionally beautiful girl. He had a date to take her to a concert on campus, but the event was cancelled. Dave was a geeky graduate student in English, and Victoria was a senior in that department. I never understood how he landed a date with her, but he did.

Blonde, eyes that alone were featured in advertisements, to say nothing of her body, she was Homecoming Queen. She was also the only student that year to survive a senior honors course with a notoriously demanding and irascible professor. She was bright and tenacious.

Dave and Victoria could think of no substitute venue for the date, so they stayed in our apartment. Outside, light rain alternated with sudden, short downpours. I was not inclined to leave them to their privacy, or, more likely, I was too insensitive to even think of it. We had a couple of beers and chatted about school: who'd done what, the promise of the basketball team, and so forth. Turned out Victoria had dated the star of the basketball team, seven feet tall. She said, "He was very polite"—undergrad code for "He didn't try hard to put the make on me." He was probably too intimidated by her to get fresh.

When she asked what I was doing, I said, "Working on a masters," which was nominally true.

"What's your thesis on?" The question indicated polite interest. Now late in my third year, I would certainly have a topic. Right? Actually, no. I'd drifted through several possibilities, including doing a history of rhetorical theory. No one on the faculty, not even Clark, pointed out that this was a nutty idea, unless I intended a five-volume thesis. I can't figure out why I got no guidance. I guess the faculty didn't want to inhibit my floundering about. Maybe they found my naiveté amusing?

At the moment, I'd focused on "premise analysis": reading an orator's true beliefs from the unspoken premises underlying his or her arguments. Victoria picked up on this idea and applied it to speeches by a current candidate for governor. Smart girl—and one who paid attention rather than just drifting through small talk.

We talked about the idiosyncrasies of faculty members, like the one who pronounced th as z, as in "Captain Ahab's personal relationship with ze white whale." We concluded it was an affectation, but that was okay. I fit comfortably in the conversation because I had a minor in Literature.

When Victoria talked about trying to get along with the prof directing her senior thesis, my interest ratcheted up. I had an ongoing affair, more or less, with his daughter. Her nickname on campus was Tiger. I don't remember her real name. With her own mean streak, she was a worthy daughter to her father. She'd go out with some guy a few times, then abruptly cut off the relationship and go on to another fellow. She got away with this repeatedly because she looked really good and had a reputation for a "screw you" attitude—fair warning. In late evenings we'd sit in her father's pickup and drink Olympia beer, tossing the empties into the bed of the truck. I got to first base with her, maybe second base once or twice, but never a home run. That was okay, she was fun.

It didn't occur to me to wonder if these games with Tiger were disloyal to Marian. If I'd thought of that, I doubt it would make any difference. I rarely thought anyone could be pained by anything I said or did. It seemed to be all a game. In my head, I'd isolated myself from the flow of humanity, including persons—Mom, Marian— right around me. Partly, this was what I'd learned growing up: you feel, you get hurt.

The storm lightened up to intermittent showers. Dave took his date home. Before they left, I said to Victoria, "I hope to see you again."

She smiled. I'd done the courteous thing.

"No. I really mean it. I do hope to see you again."

She turned serious. "I guess that's up to you."

That was heady encouragement. When Dave got back, I asked, "Are you going to ask Victoria out again?" I was fairly rigid on unwritten rules like, don't double-cross friends. Rules about being sensitive to other people's feelings, I wasn't so good at.

Dave answered, "No, I don't think so. She was nice enough, but she made it clear there was nothing for me there." He paused. "Why? Are you thinking about asking her for a date?"

I shrugged and gave a non-answer. No point in committing myself to what looked like a long shot. Dave, with his concert tickets, hit it lucky with her. I figured she probably had a line of guys a block long asking her for dates. I later learned I was wrong: Her stellar good looks intimidated fellows, except for the campus studs, and for them her brains and independence made most of them seek easier game.

The next day, late afternoon, I vacillated between not appearing over-eager versus striking while the iron is hot. Finally, I decided to get this likely failure behind me, so I could stop thinking about it. I called the Kappa house. When calling a sorority, it was not uncommon to take a half hour of repeated dialing to get through. To my surprise, I got through on the first try. It took only a minute to bring Victoria to the phone. I'd prepared myself for obstacles and delays that suddenly weren't there. It was like bracing myself to hit hard against a door that suddenly opens. I went sprawling into the conversation.

"Hello, is this Victoria?"

"Yes. Who is this?"

"Ken Bailey. We met last night. Do you remember me?" Dumb!

"Yes, of course." She waited for me to explain why I'd called.

"I was wondering. . . . Would you like to grab a cup of coffee, if you're not busy. I know this is kind of short notice." Some girls I knew would turn me down for any first date on such short notice, just on principle. They'd regard it as "training" me.

"That would be nice," she said. "Do you want to pick me up here or meet at the Student Union cafeteria?"

"Ah, I'll meet you at the Sub."

"In half an hour?"

"Fine. Good." I hung up and stared at the phone on the wall. This seemed unreal. I know how these games are played, and I'd more or less botched this invite. But this gorgeous woman was going out with me! Maybe she was. I had to deal in reality. The odds were better that she'd been offended and decided to teach me a lesson. So, I'd be smart and leave her waiting at a table in the Sub. She'd wait by herself long enough to see that she hadn't made a sucker of me. Then it occurred to me, if she kept the date and I stood her up, I'd be a jerk and totally miss my chance with her. And she was one good-looking woman.

I took a deep breath, sat on a couch in the common room, checked my watch, and started the fifteen-minute walk to the Sub.

The Student Union cafeteria, most of the main floor, is a large, round room with windows creating a periphery of glass surrounded on the outside by a patio. I approached the patio from an angle that enabled me to walk on the outside around half the cafeteria. I covertly peered inside as I strolled to the cafeteria entrance. It seemed unlikely anyone could be lost in the sparse crowd inside.

No Victoria to be seen. Not surprising. For the past fifteen minutes, I'd prepared for this. I'd play this role to the bitter end. The entrance doors beckoned.

Inside I glanced quickly around.

Then I saw her, behind where I'd first started around the margin of glass. She did nothing as gauche as waving, but she did stand up until she was sure I saw her and started toward her.

"Sorry," I said, "I guess I'm a little late."

"No, you're right on time. I got here a few minutes early . . . to be sure I didn't miss you." She smiled, and I fell totally in love, at least for the moment.

"I'll get coffee. Cream?" I was still standing.

"Yes. Need any help?"

I shook my head and made for the counter. Now, what to talk about when I got back?

"What's your honors thesis on?" I asked.

"Light and dark in Melville's <u>Moby Dick</u>. I believe it will give some insight into his personality, at least his emotional predispositions, sort of like your premise analysis."

Over the next three months this first meeting led to a succession of others—house parties, movies, coffee dates that sometimes ended up in my car parked in a secluded spot. The dates got increasingly physical. She wasn't as easily available as Allison had been, but she wasn't as determinedly chaste as Marian.

At the beginning of the summer, Victoria moved from the dorm into an apartment near campus. Did she do this because she liked her job in a local department store here better than a similar job that awaited in her hometown or because, as she later claimed, she wanted to stay near me? We kept up a pretty intense romance, though not always a smooth one.

Victoria's family lived on the other side of the mountains, a hundred miles or so away. A month after we started dating, Victoria invited me to attend a county fair in her hometown. I'd stay over two nights at her parents' home, sleeping, of course, in a separate bedroom.

The fair was small-town and more exciting than I expected. One thrill came when I almost became owner of three prize sheep. I'd reached over to get Victoria's attention, a move the auctioneer interpreted as a bid. After a moment of mild panic, I got off the hook when someone outbid me.

An unusual event, Indian girls' bareback horse race, seemed to draw mainly local Indians. It was wide-open. When one mustang balked near the beginning of the race, the rider leaped off, grabbed the bridle and took a quirt to the horse's neck and fore-shoulders, and leaped back on. The horse got the message and took off like a shot, its determined rider, long black hair streaming behind her, rode to the end of the race. She didn't win, but she impressed me.

At the end of the day Victoria and I went to a local bar for a beer or two. A couple of fellows there knew her, maybe had dated her, and continued the friendship by coming over to our table and getting in a conversation. Victoria seemed agreeable to the conversation; she certainly didn't tell them to get lost. This triggered my jealousy. These fellows were sizeable and worked on local ranches.

I wasn't too smashed to realize that if I tried to push them around, they'd beat the crap out of me. I urged Victoria to leave. These were old friends of hers, and she liked their attention. She elected to stay, arousing my anger to full flame.

I got up, walked out of the bar, got in my car, and drove the hundred miles back over the mountains to State. In retrospect, there were some flaws in my reaction. At least, I didn't kill myself drunk on the road. I was supposed to be Victoria's ride; I never found out how she got back over the mountain. It took her only a few days to forgive my irresponsible snit. I suspect she may have seen some justice in my reaction. Her parents didn't know the whole story; they must have thought me an irresponsible jerk.

The county fair trip was by no means the only rough spot in our relationship. We were both strong-willed and a little selfish; she was more strong-willed, I was more selfish. Somehow, we stayed together during the summer, maybe because she was not into cooking. She depended mainly on my roommate, a very good cook, and me, hamburger steaks and fried potatoes, for her meals.

Victoria finished her honors thesis early in the summer. By then she'd accepted a graduate assistantship teaching in the English department at State. She worried about handling a class that fall. This surprised me. Worrying wasn't her style. I assured her she'd do fine because she was bright, knowledgeable, and fluent. I made close to zero progress on a master's thesis. So what else was new? I'd stayed true to character.

A few times that summer, I visited Mom in her apartment. On one visit, in June, she asked me out of the blue, "Do you think you'll marry that girl Victoria?" I'd not considered marrying her or anyone else. Mom had at times uncanny insight, so this brought me up short. She'd never asked me this about any other girl, not even Marian Mason. She'd seen Victoria twice, once overnight when I brought her over to go to a dance at my old fraternity and she stayed at my mother's place.

I shrugged, "I doubt it, haven't really thought about it. You know, we've only known each other a couple of months. Why do you ask?" We sat across from each other over lunch in her apartment. I thought we were relaxed, just making conversation.

"If you marry her, you're going to have to stay ahead of her." Suddenly, I realized Mom was serious. Her body went kind of rigid and radiated intensity. "She's very ambitious."

"Mom, she's anxious about facing the classes she'll teach in the fall. Her department is doing zilch to help her prepare."

"And you. Are you helping her get ready?" The way she said it seemed to imply I'd be subversive to help Victoria.

"Yeah, I am. I know what it's like to face your first teaching job with no real preparation."

"How's your thesis coming?" This seemed to me a non-sequitur. To my mother, it clearly was relevant.

"Slowly, I suppose. Once I think through a section, it's tedious to write it up."

"So you spend your time helping Victoria?"

"Mom, it's not that much time."

She stared at me, her expression set in stone—which was preferable to her exploding in anger. I changed the subject to comment on the neatness of her apartment. To be able finally to live decently, she'd gone through more than most women could handle. But my relationship with Victoria, or any other woman, was not her concern.

Victoria and I continued our romance, me with an imperfect tendency toward fidelity. I think she liked the hamburger steaks I cooked, so she hung around. We faced the approaching fall semester with our separate anxieties.

Fall began to shape up much differently than we anticipated. The surprises were not always pleasant.

CHAPTER SIXTEEN

Late in the semester I read Edgar Allen Poe's "The Imp of the Perverse." The story didn't solve my problems with procrastination, but it was a comfort to think a great author had also been unable to conquer his demons. Meanwhile, the axe to end my career seemed inevitably falling, maybe before the end of the summer.

To keep my mind away from frustration, guilt, and anxiety, I went out with Victoria whenever she was willing. I don't think she was dating other guys; she just worked hard to finish her honors thesis and prepare to teach. With a supreme effort I could understand and accept her situation.

When Victoria was unavailable because the sadist directing her work set a tight deadline for some rewrites, I would see Marian Mason. My old girlfriend seemed to forgive my switch to Victoria. When I asked her about that, she said, "What you do when you aren't with me isn't important." This should have made me relieved and free. It didn't. I shivered as if surprised by a gust of cold wind.

The week after the semester's end, Dean Clark called me into his office. I braced myself for news my services would not be needed next school year. He asked, "How are you fixed for money?"

"Not too good. I usually borrow some from my mother, but she's running a little low herself." The university didn't pay during the summer unless you had an extra assignment like teaching summer school. In more progressive schools, a nine-month salary could be spread over twelve months. You got less per month, but you didn't starve between June and September. Our State legislators were simple folk and couldn't get their minds around that notion. All they could grasp is that they, by golly, weren't going to pay teachers when they weren't working.

Clark pressed the fingertips of one hand against the fingertips of the other, creating an elegant steeple over which he watched me from across his desk. "I think we may have a way for you to make some money."

Fortunately, I caught myself short of a smart-ass remark, like, "I don't do assassinations." I waited. How could what he would suggest be worse than picking rock or cleaning sump pumps?

"In your classes during the past year, you've done an exceptional job teaching organization as a skill in composition and public speaking."

"Thank you, sir." Why am I calling him 'sir'? It's not my style, but it seems a natural way to address Clark. I tamped down my impulse to ask how he knew what went on in my teaching. Of course, he'd know.

"Organization is not the easiest skill to teach freshmen, and textbooks don't seem able to develop much of a sense of it," he continued. "So they provide formulas and models students can follow."

I nodded in agreement and said, "The formulas are okay, if the students know why they use one rather than another." It's pleasant to be on the same page as Clark. But where the hell is this going?

"We want you to come up with a handout on organizational principles and patterns. We can pay you two thousand dollars for the handout, roughly sixteen pages, and a workshop, one afternoon with our faculty who teach public speaking and whoever else wants to come. Can you do that?"

I took a deep breath. Oh, yes, I could do that! Cicero and Quintilian knew more about organizational strategy than I did, but I was way ahead of current textbook authors.

"How soon is this to happen?" I asked.

Clark eyed me for several seconds. If I had any positive reputation, it wasn't for meeting deadlines. "We'd like to get this done six weeks from now. Can you commit to that? For sure?"

I stopped to think half a minute. This was important to Clark. If I let him down, I'd be on his shit-list—better to turn down the offer now, and take the consequences.

"Yes, I can commit to that. I've thought about organization a lot. I'll get on it right away." Not until later, too late to ask Clark, did I wonder why they wanted this provided to faculty in the middle of summer. That didn't seem a very propitious time. But mine is not to wonder why. I plunged in with uncharacteristic enthusiasm. I will be teaching teachers, maybe even senior faculty.

My enthusiasm abated when I realized Clark wanted the project on organization done by the middle of the summer because I wouldn't be around the beginning of fall term.

Two days before I was to lead my scheduled workshop, tragedy threatened. Most people would regard it as a tragedy. I was curiously unmoved. That's not quite accurate: I was worried that somehow this would interfere with my stellar opportunity to lead a whole department faculty on a topic on which I was actually confident.

In a dorm study room, for at least the fifth time, I searched the outline of my presentation for flaws. Found none. By the time I'd prepared an outline this carefully, I'd memorized it. If the presentation plan is sound the handout is also. I leaned back in my chair: I was ready to go—and with a day to spare. I'd rarely before been this well-prepared.

A knock at the door.

"Come in."

Larry Edwards stood in the doorway. He had an agitated expression.

"What's on your mind, Larry?"

"Telephone for you, downstairs."

"Yeah, okay." I hoisted myself to my feet. "Is it Victoria?"

"It's your mother. She says it's urgent."

I got to the phone in about twenty seconds. "What's up, Mom? You okay?"

"Your father may be dying." Mom was not one for subtle buildups. Her voice was shakier than I would have expected even with this news.

"Who says?" I stared at the pale wall in the telephone room.

"Frances called from Chesterton. Your uncle David was on the phone with her." They were the two sanest relatives I knew in my father's family, not given to games or hysterical reactions.

"What did Frances say exactly? What does 'may be dying' mean?"

"You know he's in a mental institution?"

"Yes, of course."

"He'd been released for a few days, into Frances's custody. She was driving them home, as usual too fast. A state trooper stopped them. Your father got into an argument with him. You can imagine that?"

Oh yes, I could imagine that. Dad could be either charming or aggressively hostile. His mind had been losing ground, so I'd bet on hostile.

"He had a stroke, a bad one. The state trooper got them to the nearest hospital in time to save his life, at least for now."

"For now?"

"Frances doesn't think he'll make it this time. He fades in and out of consciousness, and even when he's awake, it's not clear he's aware of people around him. Frances says the only thing for sure is that he keeps asking for me. She thinks I should come back there, but I don't know. It would be a wasted trip if he never becomes fully conscious."

Sometimes, Mom's determined practicality seemed wrong. "And if he does become conscious, you'd never forgive yourself for not being there."

Mom was silent for half a minute, apparently mulling over what I'd said. I fought down the impulse to ask if he'd said anything about me. Frances had always been on my side, and I was pretty sure if he'd said anything—anything at all—about me my aunt would mention it. Though, if she had, Mom would not necessarily forward it to me. I'd ask about that later. For now, it appeared I'm irrelevant.

"Oh, I could forgive myself," Mom said.

In a flash I understood where my cold-blooded lack of empathy came from. It was not from my father.

Mom continued to think out loud. "But you're right. I suppose I loved him at one time. And I suppose he loved me." I felt awkward. Mom wasn't into talking about love.

"And I'll probably have to get along with his relatives, at least a little." She paused, "Yes, I'll do it, and soon. Now the next question is, what about you?"

"What about me?" You're supposed to be with your dad when he's dying. But in two days I'd be doing my presentation, a big plus in my career. Then I remembered, I probably won't have a career after the next few weeks. But I'd promised. I stalled. "When do you plan to leave for Indiana?"

"Tomorrow. Do you want to go with me?"

"I've got a problem. I'm scheduled to give a very important presentation to the faculty."

I waited to hear her tell me she understood, and I should meet my obligations at State. "He is your father. But it's entirely up to you, whether you go or not."

No help from her. What would she do, were she in my place? She'd give top priority to her job and career. Or would she? I never fully understood her relationship with Dad.

"Did Frances say anything about him asking for me?"

"No, she didn't. She just tried to persuade me I should come back there. She may not have thought you and your Dad were close." She paused, "Were you close with him?"

"No, I suppose not." Mom did what she could to see to that. "Give me a little time to decide. I'll call you back."

"I'm ordering my ticket later today. Call me soon, one way or the other."

So I had a half hour to resolve my relationship with my father. I really could use more time!

I called her a half hour after we hung up. "I think I'll stay here and give the workshop I'm scheduled for." It was a damn lonely decision.

Dad died two days later. I didn't go back for the funeral.

Mom was sure he never became conscious enough to recognize her. She said Frances and the others thought he had and that he'd looked at Mom and smiled. They seemed grateful she'd come back.

They weren't grateful enough to see that Mom inherited any part of the ranch, though she and I were the only relatives who had lived there, with Dad, during the past half century or more, and I was the only one in my generation of Baileys who ever lived there. Mom didn't contest their self-appointed ownership. She had little money to finance a fight, and anyway her in-laws were too well connected for her to have a chance of winning.

Dad had held on to the ranch because he'd been convinced a state park would be built on adjacent land. No one else in the family believed him. My uncle sold the whole property a short time after Dad died.

The park did get built, and the ranch began to be developed in small parcels. It's total value eventually: between three and six million. Dad was finally vindicated. Neither Mom nor I ever saw a penny. Maybe this was justice for me not going back, even to Dad's funeral. My mother deserved better, much better, regardless of their stormy relationship.

It was the middle of the summer, so I had plenty of time to revisit my apparent rejection of my dying father and to indulge in guilty regret. I'd been a lousy son. But then he was hardly a model father, and my mother had frequently denigrated him. Besides, he didn't ask for me.

One hot afternoon shortly after she returned from Indiana, I sat in Mom's living room and watched her search through records to make sure her car and furniture were in her name. She suspected uncle David or another relative might try to reclaim those items as part of Dad's estate. Given some of her in-laws, who would act out of spite rather than need, her precaution was not paranoid.

"Are you glad you went back?" I asked her.

She looked up; her eyebrows raised. Apparently, it never occurred to her to wonder about that. After a minute, she laid aside receipts and other papers. "There, I've taken care of that loose end. They can't touch my stuff." She paused and stared at a discarded pile of papers.

"Yes, I'm glad, because I'd feel wrong if I hadn't." I thought she was going to ask, "How about you? Do you wish you'd gone back?" But she didn't ask.

"Did he say anything about me?"

"I told you, he never regained consciousness while I was there."

"I mean, did Frances or anyone mention that he might have said something?"

She shook her head. For a few seconds, she seemed to look at me with pity, like she was sorry to disappoint me.

We didn't talk about him much after that. A vacancy manifested itself in my soul. I don't think it was grief exactly, just an absence of an important reference point. I did miss having my father out there somewhere. When I'd think about this too much and moisture would fill my eyes, I'd tell myself, this is damn silly.

Frances and some other of Dad's relatives and friends sent me a few mementos—public relations booklets he'd designed, his billfold, his gold and silver cuff links—all of which I treasured, and probably neglected to thank the senders.

One evening a couple of weeks after the funeral, when my roommate was out, I went to a dresser drawer and took out his two pair of cuff links. I shook them in my hand, like dice or like I was weighing them. A thick gloom dropped over me. I set the cuff links on my desk and stared at them while the sky darkened.

I tried to reconstruct Dad's character in my mind, at least to heap the pieces together: charming and persuasive as a newspaper man and as a womanizer, great endurance and courage as a rancher, very smart, often frustrated by the hand he'd been dealt, and in a marriage that as Mom's sister said years later "was unusual even by modern standards." One small piece in this heap of parts was Dad as my father, but it wasn't a missing part, just small. The pieces never seemed to fit together.

Where had he failed? He let other people—his family versus Mom—control too much of his life. He'd drifted, accomplished individual projects splendidly, but he hadn't charted his own course and stayed on it. Attractive women, job opportunities, or saving the ranch drew him into side roads. He ended up a sick man in an insane asylum.

What's the lesson to be learned here. As the trite saying goes, the apple falls not far from the tree.

Drifting. Working very hard at times, but not in any consistent direction. Preoccupied with women. I had to face up to where this led for him. And it might lead there for me. Damn! Fear of absolute failure roiled over and over through my mind.

Could I take charge of my life to chart my own course? This was not an overnight decision. It would be a battle, and I might not win. I needed all the help I could get.

Where could I get help? My experience with Manville's disinterest and obtuseness a few years earlier discouraged me from seeking the help of an instructor.

Victoria? Did I want to submit my self-doubt and cruel selfishness for her judgment? Probably not!

Marian Mason? We were, after all, practically self-anointed siblings. How much had I lost when Victoria came between us? Dates were one thing, entirely different from the relationship with Marian I'd discarded and almost forgotten. I could tell Marion everything, and she'd listen without needing to respond. An overwhelming wave of loneliness caught me by surprise. My eyes watered. It helped not at all to accept that I'd brought this on myself.

The pain of guilty loneliness became scary. I searched my mind for a way out that didn't involve a shotgun. It wasn't so much that I decided to live as that it seemed too much trouble to go downtown and get the shotgun and shells. I felt like a rat in a small cage unable to hide from a constant flow of laser blasts into my skin.

There was one place to seek help—almost as scary as trying to wait out this black depression on my own.

CHAPTER SEVENTEEN

I picked up the phone. It felt heavy in my hand.

I looked around the apartment, the bookcases, the table at which I now sat alone staring at cuff links, the door to a tiny kitchen, back to the cuff links.

Yes, it would be intrusive to bother a busy, important man in the evening. It would be presumptuous to place this call any time, but I had to do it. I swallowed and dialed. The ringing seemed interminable, while I fought down impulses to hang up before the phone was answered.

I recognized the quiet, friendly voice that answered.

"Hello, Dean Clark. This is Ken Bailey." Ohmigod, I haven't planned what to say next.

The silence dragged on several seconds, before Clark responded.

"Yes, Ken, what can I do for you." I guessed that, even in my few words, Clark had sensed something in my voice, or maybe it was the odd time to call. At least, it wasn't the middle of the night, thank God.

"I need to talk to you." About what. I hadn't planned how to go about soliciting Clark's advice or help. What did I want from him, anyway. "It's kind of urgent. Please."

"Can it keep until tomorrow?"

My silence appeared to answer his question.

"I want to get some papers in my office tonight," Clark said. "Can you meet me there in half an hour?"

"I'll be there." In the academic world I knew, Clark was a rare find, a genuinely sympathetic human being. I heard myself saying aloud to myself, "Thank God, thank God."

A light fog had settled over the campus. Mist seemed encouragingly familiar. Clark's office window was a solitary frame of bright yellow on a dark campus. Life may be possible, after all.

I walked up one flight of dimly lighted stairs in the venerable Hall, knocked, and entered.

He waved to a chair across from where he now sat with a few papers spread out on his desk. They looked like application forms for graduate assistantships, perhaps for the slot to replace me.

"Good that you called, Ken. We can start this tonight." He glanced down at the papers on his desk.

His remark almost compelled me to ask what "this" was we were to start tonight, but I caught myself. Time was passing. I wanted to get my problem out before we got into his topic, almost certainly my firing. Still to be discussed were the specific reasons for my dismissal, and that could take time. Maybe life wasn't so impossible after all. Even for Clark, I was damned if I'd rush to cooperate in my own gutting.

I waited.

He asked, "How did your project on organization go? I had to miss the oral presentation, but I heard good reports."

Of course, he already knew how the oral version went, and he had the written version, if he cared to read it. Why was he asking me this?

"The talk went okay. I got some good questions, usually a favorable sign, I think."

He nodded in agreement, but I didn't know whether he referred to my interpretation of what several questions signified or to my own evaluation of the talk. In any case, I saw my opening to get us quickly back on the track I needed to pursue.

"I wasn't at a hundred percent. My dad died that day, and I knew it was happening. I was thoroughly prepared for the talk, but still that was a distraction." Then I realized that was an irrelevant excuse, a cheap shot for pity. I disgusted myself.

Clark stared at me, speechless for several seconds. "You didn't live with your father?" he asked.

"No, not much. My parents split, sort of."

"How long had you been separated from your father?"

"Since high school, six or seven years, I guess. Before that, our family was an on-again off-again thing."

"So you lived with your mother?" The dean seemed to be struggling to get on even keel. My cheap shot for pity had more shock value than I expected.

"Mostly." I paused. "In a way, that's what I want to talk to you about. I've got to talk to someone." I felt relieved when Clark smiled, perhaps amused I'd mildly insulted him: "someone" was better than no one. "I'm afraid of ending up like my father." There, it was out.

Clark's smile faded with the last sentence. He stared at me as if he were evaluating me. Oh God, this is bad!

He pressed his fingertips together, in a gesture that usually made me think of church. I could think of him as a wise and kind-hearted pastor, the way they're supposed to be, but often are not. It would not be easy to talk to anyone, but it would be easier with him than with anyone else I could think of.

He asked, "How did your father end up?"

"Sick and old in his mid-fifties, in a mental institution."

"Could I ask, what was the nature of his mental illness?"

"His sisters, with whom he was living, said he was worn out and depressed. He had manic states that were increasingly hard to control. When his sisters concluded he was dangerous, they had him committed. My mother told me he suffered from advanced syphilis. His sisters denied this."

"Are you worried about ending up in an institution?"

"If I can believe Mom, there's no reason to believe I'm doomed. Syphilis is acquired, not inherited." This was becoming more of a confessional than I wanted. Maybe Clark needed to know all this to help me.

"Do you believe your Mother?"

I shook my head. "I think my father's mental illness was more genetic, though his sisters would probably deny that possibility. There's a lot of mental instability in the family. Much of Dad's life seemed to lack focus. His problems didn't just start in the last few years." I put my elbows on his desk and leaned in more closely. "So far, my life follows his pattern in some ways." No reason to mention the womanizing, nor to remind Clark what a mess my transcript is in.

I spoke slowly. "I do not want to have the same lack of focus, but I can't seem to break away from the pattern." After a pause, "I think I'm getting worse."

Clark seemed to ponder that for several seconds, before he said, "No, you're not getting worse. We have an objective point of comparison: your transcripts as an undergraduate and here. Here looks markedly better."

I didn't see it that way. He seemed to be waiting for my reaction. I decided not to try to convince him how bad a student I now was.

"As to your lack of focus, it may be that you're not being challenged and you don't get enough chances for superior achievement. Especially this year, when you don't coach debate."

"Yeah, there may be some truth in that. But while I did have a bit of success in debate, everything else . . ." I caught myself before I said, ". . . went to hell." Instead I finished the sentence lamely, ". . . didn't measure up."

"So you think of the 'everything else' and take little satisfaction from debate, is that correct?"

I nodded.

"We have a star miler on the track team. His course work is mediocre at best. I don't see much evidence that he broods about his grades." Clark paused. "Maybe you should think more about what you can do well. Think less about how you don't always reach routine standards. Such misgivings tend to feed on themselves. They can handicap you."

Clark allayed some of my guilt and anxiety for the moment. But I knew he had not dealt death to my "imp of the perverse." I wanted his help in rooting that little bastard out.

In an ungracious manner, I returned to the issue. "I don't think debate will get me where I should be professionally, any more than winning mile races will do it for that track star." I was cheating a bit, trusting that Clark didn't know that a few really good debate coaches did make a living mainly from their skills in preparing teams to win tournaments. Many of these successful coaches drank heavily and were somewhat isolated from the rest of the faculty at their schools. They hadn't picked the easiest or most cheerful way to make their mark.

With a small wave of the hand, he dismissed my objection. "Perhaps with more challenge, you'd find yourself focusing better."

I doubted that. In fact, I dreaded more challenges. I wasn't able to handle the ones I faced now.

"You want us to win nationals at West Point?" I asked.

He shook his head. "I want to see what you can do in a more demanding program than we've provided here. An academic program."

I'd pretty much set my own goals so far, and I hadn't met even those.

"A more demanding academic program?"

"I think that, despite your feelings of failure, we've brought you up to speed in rhetoric and public address. Drs. Goldman and Benedict agree. So, now it's time for you to move on."

"Move on?" Move on where? With only a B.A. and some graduate hours in hand, about the only job I could move on to would be a public school teaching job, if that.

"Yes, I think we should put your Master's on hold for the time being and send you into a solid Ph.D. program."

I was having trouble following this, as if someone were giving me directions to drive on a route opposite from what I had anticipated.

Dr. Clark continued, "Are you familiar with the program at Cornell University?"

"Vaguely." I'd heard of it, of course, but as a sort of Mt. Olympus where revered scholars in rhetorical theory and history hung out.

He turned around the papers on his desk and shoved them toward me. I glanced down. They were applications for graduate admission and an assistantship at Cornell. I looked up to come eye-to-eye with Clark who was watching me closely. The silence lasted several seconds while I tried to digest this. I took a deep breath. "Sir, I doubt they'd admit me, with my record of failure."

"You won't know unless you try, will you?" I detected traces of impatience in his voice. He paused. "Why do you think we had you prepare that paper and workshop on organization?" He seemed to reconsider. "We found your project useful for our teachers, of course, but we also had another motive. We wanted to see what you could produce. We supplied your paper to the admission committee at Cornell."

"It's awfully late in the summer. They'd have all their slots filled by now." I was wriggling like a worm on a fishhook. I didn't want to have a big rejection to be the capstone on my academic career.

"Perhaps, Ken, you should let me worry about that." I'd strained his patience, and I didn't want to do that anymore. I gathered up the forms, thanked him, and exited the office.

During the next week, I concentrated on the applications to Cornell.

Other faculty at State cooperated by filling out recommendation letters promptly, though several colleagues looked at me as if I'd lost my mind or at least was having delusions of grandeur. I worked hard to get the applications right, despite the hopeless goal.

The Cornell graduate school required a forty-dollar fee to consider someone for admission. I toyed with the idea of stopping right there to avoid wasting the money. A vision of Dean Clark's likely reaction to that frugality flashed through my mind. I wrote the check.

I got the whole mess in its various parts in two over-sized envelopes addressed to the appropriate offices and walked to the post office with greater relief than I'd feel turning in a term paper.

The post office clerk noticed the addresses on the envelopes. She said, "Good luck. I'm sure you'll be admitted." I caught myself in time to avoid arguing with her about my chances to get into Cornell. I thanked her instead.

With the application project completed, Victoria and I celebrated. I didn't tell her what the occasion was. We went to one of the upscale campus hangouts: courteous waiters, cloth napkins, wine list and eighty labels of beer. We each had a seafood platter, which we figured gave us a right to sit in the booth as long as we wanted. It was summer, so it wasn't crowded. We both realized that in a few weeks, we would have to go our separate ways, and we weren't eager for that to happen. Victoria would move into a graduate dorm at State and start on her assistantship. When we talked about future plans, I faded out on my part of the conversation.

She said, "Maybe you could stay here in graduate school." She stopped and looked wistful for a minute, then smiled. "We could keep on dating."

"Four years of assistantships for a master's? Probably not! I think Dean Clark gave me a clear message that I'm off the payroll, and the faculty's radar, when school starts in September."

She nodded. She might not like it that way, but both of us were realists.

"What will you do?"

I shrugged. "Probably go to some desperate high school on an emergency teaching certificate." I said hopefully, "Maybe not too far from here."

This conversation was becoming depressing. We started talking about movies—important directors like Bergman and Fellini.

On the way home from her apartment, walking across campus through Oregon mist at dusk, I realized I couldn't totally free myself from imagining being accepted at Cornell. Damn wishful thinking!

★ 216 ★

CHAPTER EIGHTEEN

Ten days after I sent off my applications, the first response arrived. Not until I sat in the safety of the most comfortable chair in my apartment did I summon the courage to carefully slit the envelope open. It stated succinctly I was admitted to the Cornell graduate program in Rhetoric and Public Address. I should have been overjoyed, but my pleasure was diluted by apprehension about how I would handle a notoriously difficult program. I'd rarely before wondered if I were smart enough to handle academic demands but here the stakes seemed higher and the competition severe. I was growing up to face the real world—and I didn't like it.

Another ugly shadow of reality fell across the crisp, white, one-page letter. With no mention of an assistantship, I faced the challenge of paying full tuition. No way could I ask Mom to pony up that kind of money, nor could I earn it on my own.

I stared at the letter, telling myself that gaining admission was itself an achievement. That solace didn't help. Unless I could prove the admission decision was deserved, it didn't count. How does a hungry man feel looking through a pane of glass at a steak and trimmings when he knows there is no way for him to reach it? I could now admit how much I wanted, needed, that fresh start.

Only a very few people could provide commiseration. Victoria was too far behind in the story to say much that would really help. I carefully refolded the letter, tucked it inside a light jacket to keep rain off, and started toward the Liberal Arts building.

Clark appeared engrossed in some administrative problem. He didn't ask me to take a seat, so I stood waiting for his full attention. Finally, he looked up. "What is it, Bailey?"

I thrust the letter at him. He took it reluctantly, opened and read it. His mood seemed to become friendlier. "Well, this is good news, Ken. Congratulations." He waited as if there was nothing more to be said.

"Yeah, you could say it's good news. But I don't quite see it that way."

"You don't? Almost any student in the country would be thrilled to get this letter. But you don't see it that way. Why?" I could imagine a faculty advisor asking that in a voice loaded with sarcasm. But Clark asked "Why?" in a tone that seemed genuinely seeking to understand.

"I don't have the financial resources to go, so it's just another frustration."

He glanced over the letter again. "They say nothing about an assistantship, is that it?"

"No, they don't. I figure no mention is bad news."

Clark thought a minute. "Not necessarily. Word on the assistantship will probably come from a different office." He added, with priceless understatement, "They apparently have no sense of urgency."

"I have to respond to the letter of admission. I don't know what to say."

Clark stared into empty space. "Did they give you a deadline for a decision?"

"No, sir." But I' m damned if I want to wait for them to kick me in the groin. I want this finished and done with.

The Dean seemed to try to figure out what was going on at Cornell. He did know a lot more about this sort of thing than I did. I desperately need a fresh start. If he sees any point to it, I can sweat it out a while longer.

"Do you have any idea how long they'll wait?" I couldn't bring myself to ask if he thought there was any chance of a sizable stipend.

"Their fall term starts in about four weeks." He smiled. "So they'll have to put their Freshman Speech faculty together by then."

I didn't smile. "Maybe I should have applied to other graduate programs, less prestigious ones in the Northwest." I had unintentionally implied the Dean had given me bad advice.

He wasn't defensive; he just explained, "No, with your record so far, you almost certainly wouldn't be accepted anywhere else, at least any place you'd want to go."

"I don't understand. How could I be accepted at Cornell and no place else?"

"Most admission committees can't afford to think outside the box. Your record indicates you're not likely to finish a Ph.D. program. Cornell can afford to gamble, to place weight on other factors," he paused, "such as recommendations from people they trust."

"Such as yourself."

Clark shrugged.   "Your chances of getting an assistantship would be enhanced if you were confirmed as a graduate student there. Perhaps you should send in your acceptance right away, so they're not wondering what your decision will be and why you're delaying it."

"And if I get turned down for the assistantship, I'm left holding the bag with no money. I'd have to give up the slot, and I don't think they'd like that."

Clark nodded. "True. You can get a black mark by accepting a slot and then resigning. But it happens. Some applicants will get accepted at three or four schools. They can't go to all of them." He paused. "Cornell can't haul you back in chains."

I tried to smile agreeably.

The Dean sensed my discomfort at misleading a prestigious faculty. "Ken, you tend to be a little on the pessimistic side." He chuckled. He is totally correct, and it isn't funny. "Maybe, you should be optimistic, since otherwise you may kill an exceptional opportunity."

"I'll send in my letter accepting the slot today." And I did. Then I waited antsy as hell for several days, so obsessed with the coming response I couldn't focus on anything else until I got word about the crucial financial support. My natural pessimism ruled out, on a conscious level, any possibility of getting an assistantship. But we can't fully control our subconscious. It sneaks in hope for what we want most strongly. I was surprised to discover how much I wanted to get in Cornell, though I didn't have much of a clue why. Maybe I could prove something to myself.

The letter from the director of Freshman Speech arrived a week after the admission letter. It offered a modest stipend for teaching two sections of the course each semester. On that pay, I could almost survive in the trite role of starving graduate student. That was okay. The big blessing of this stipend was waiver of tuition and fees.

On the day the offer arrived, I sat half an hour in warm afternoon light and stared at the letter, savoring it, marveling. I determined to do a better job in life than I had so far. Hardly thinking, I picked up Dad's cuff links and returned them to a box in a dresser drawer.

I did remember to call Clark, who sounded not so much surprised as relieved. I don't think he was completely confident I'd get in with financial aid. He reminded me to get in my acceptance of the job soon. Could they change their minds and cancel the offer?

Immediately, I sent my response.

Next on the list of people to be called was Victoria. Why Victoria? Why not Mom? I wondered about that. Mom had supported me in important ways, and she was my mother. Somehow, it seemed more natural to tell Victoria first, even though we'd known each other only a few months.

I didn't think of calling Marian Mason. Much later, I'd see this omission as carelessly cruel. She was my "sister."

"Can Victoria call you back? She's at dinner." I was sure the sorority pledge who answered the phone didn't intend to tell Victoria she had a call.

My frustration gave rise to a surge of anger, which it took me several seconds to get under control. There was no point in trying to bully my way past a dumb pledge on phone duty.

"Can you tell her I called with important information?" I gave my name.

"Yeah, okay, I'll tell her."

I figured Victoria would get the message about the time hell froze over. This seemed a good time to call Mom. I really wanted to tell someone.

"Mom, how's it going this summer?"

"Okay. And with you?"

"Dean Clark decided I need to move on. He urged me to apply to Cornell, in upstate New York, didn't give me much choice. I get no more stipends at State."

"That's not fair!"

"No, Mom, it's fair. I've had three years of aid to do a two-year degree."

"Well, they've used you like cheap labor."

"That's the way assistantships work."

"Do you think it's even possible you'd be accepted at Cornell? Anyway, how would you pay for it?"

I couldn't fault Mom for asking about the finances: she'd sunk a lot of hard-earned money in me so far, and she was about tapped out.

"I've been admitted. And offered an assistantship." I took great satisfaction telling her about the offers with the clear implication she'd greatly underestimated me. This was tacky. Why couldn't I thank her for all the help she'd given me and let it go at that?

We talked a little more. When would I leave? How would I get there? She seemed sad to think of me moving three thousand miles away, but, until much later, I ignored her feelings.

The phone rang as I walked into our apartment. I picked it up and heard Victoria's voice. My heart started thumping.

I shifted from foot to foot while talking on the phone, savoring these minutes.

"Patsy said you had something important to tell me."

"Yeah, that's right." I was trying, without much success, to sound casual. "I just got word on my applications to Cornell."

"Cornell!"

"Well, I had to apply somewhere."

There was a long pause. No doubt, Victoria was gearing herself up to console me.

"What did they say?"

I waited long enough for her to feel her own curiosity.

"They admitted me, with an assistantship."

Another long pause, while I guess she tried to digest this news, "Really?"

"Yes, really." I have no faith in myself, so it's unreasonable to expect Victoria to believe in me. Still, it would be nice.

"Congratulations." I could almost hear her shifting gears, and she went in a direction which caught me off guard. "Why did you pick a school about as far from here as you could get?" She said it like an accusation, like I had determined to end our relationship after using her this summer.

She would be dead wrong. Since I never assumed there was any chance of getting admitted, I hadn't considered what this would mean for us. Clark was right: my habitual pessimism had tricked me—in this case into looking like a selfish jerk.

I've got to start thinking ahead, and with more confidence.

Without directly addressing the anger she seemed to feel, I tried to explain Clark set this up and I never intended to move any distance from State. Her silence told me she wasn't buying it.

"Do we have a date to the house dance this weekend?" I asked. We'd never formally agreed to the date, but, like a comfortable couple, we'd just noted the dance was coming and assumed we'd go together. Now, no assumptions were safe.

"Sure. Why not?"

In the next few days, we met a couple times for coffee. These meetings were chaste, strained actually. Nothing more was said about Cornell. We talked about her forthcoming teaching assistantship at State. I think she found the advice from my less-than-vast experience more annoying than helpful. She'd get a far-away, patient stare. At least, it was something safe to talk about.

At eight in the evening, I picked her up at the dorm. She looked as beautiful as ever. We both acted with restraint, almost formally, as if already we were working toward the final split a few weeks hence. I was depressed as hell.

Frenetic, innovative dancers crowded the chapter room, the core of the party. Beer flowed freely from a couple of kegs. Victoria joined enthusiastically in the scene, even danced a couple times with other guys. If she wanted me to understand that when I left she'd be just fine, she was making her point with cruel emphasis. I felt morose, and the energy from the dancers seemed to repel me into a corner.

When in doubt and beset with problems, have another beer. I had several, she not so many. We danced once or twice. I felt clumsy and complained, so we mostly sat at tables on the sidelines. I didn't like her dancing with other guys. She wanted to have some fun, and I wasn't helping at all. When the tension became unbearable, she suggested we take a walk on the grounds outside. Normally, this would be an invite for some serious physical contact, but clearly that was not her intention tonight.

"When do you leave for the East?" She broached the topic for the first time since we'd talked on the phone. We stood near a shadow cast by a giant Elm between us and a full moon. Standing in an open space among landscaped bushes and a few small ponds, I tried to think.

"I haven't checked it out to see when I have to show up. I figure four or five days to drive there."

"You're going to drive it? In four days, that's over seven hundred miles a day four days in a row."

I shrugged. Then I realized I was putting off departing until the last minute because Victoria would be left behind. I looked at her in soft moonlight. It finally hit me: In a few days, our relationship will end —sad, painful for me.

She said, "Let's go back to the dance."

This is awkward! I so want to hold her. But if I do, and she pulls away, rejects me, it will damn near kill me. She looked resolute. Resolute about what?

I took the lead and stared straight ahead in the dark, focused on trying to guess what she was thinking. Splash! That was my first clue, followed quickly by wetness around my right ankle and my pants cuff. I'd lurched forward and regained my balance. I quickly pulled my foot out of a shallow fishpond.

"Are you okay?" The question conveyed modest concern, but she sounded more amused than worried. It was the perfect response to my misstep. Before I answered, I turned to stare at her, an ethereal vision in a soft patch of moonlight.

I cannot live without this woman.

"How would you like to go to Ithaca with me?" In a beer-muddled way, I hoped she'd think of Ithaca as the home of the Greek hero Odysseus and not as a town in upstate New York. As a literature student, she should want to see Ithaca, Greece. That was stupid. Of course, she knew what Ithaca I was inviting her to.

"For what purpose?"

Now I saw myself on a downhill path and losing control. But I had to answer her question.

"I thought you might want to marry me." Oh, that was feeble.

She took only a few seconds to recover full composure.

"Why might I want to do that?"

"Because, Victoria, I don't want to be separated from you."

"And why is that?"

She's going to drag it out of me, so it might as well be now.

"Because I love you." The words just about stuck in my throat, but I got them out.

"So you've thought about this, have you? No doubt you have a ring to offer me."

"Well, no, actually. . . ." I was thinking fast. "I figured you might want to pick one out, so I'd wait to see if you said yes."

"Oh, Ken." She shook her head and grinned. "You are so transparent."

"I'll get down on one knee." I looked around for a nearby soft and dry piece of lawn.

She tried to look serious. "That works only if you have a ring to offer me."

"Look, I mean it. I want to marry you. I do love you." That last sentence came out a little easier second time around.

"Let's both think about it. Monday, if you feel the same way, I'll give you an answer."

"What will your answer be, Victoria?"

She sighed with exaggerated patience. "I'll decide Monday."

I waited in silence.

Finally, she said, "I don't know what my answer would be. I'll think about it."

We walked inside the old fraternity building. She gathered up her light coat, and we departed through the front door. As we drove back to her dorm, I said nothing rather than risk saying a wrong thing. I don't know why she was silent.

CHAPTER NINETEEN

Monday morning, I called Victoria. We decided to meet at a big barn-like coffee house after her last class. She seemed less than eager to meet, so I didn't like my chances.

At three o'clock, I took a seat in a booth near the front of the single huge room. An upstairs balcony was arranged on two sides by more booths. I'd be happier in one of them, but they didn't have good sight lines with the front door. Two or three of the interminable bridge games, as well as conversations, continued at small tables in the central area of the main floor. On an unpadded bench-seat in a downstairs booth, I watched, waited, and twitched.

Ten minutes after I arrived, Victoria came in the door and saw me. She slid into the booth across from me. Having turned down probably a dozen or more proposals from other guys, she seemed cheerful and confident this time around. This was my initial try at proposing. I felt clearly out-classed, and resented her casual control. It isn't a damn contest, so get on with the question.

"Well, what do you think?" I've never been good at small talk.

"Think about what?" she asked, in what I was sure was faked puzzlement. Was she making this difficult because she didn't want to deal with the question or just to torture me?

"A few days ago, I asked you to marry me, remember?" Okay, there was a bit of sarcasm hanging from that last word. Not smart!

"Yes, I remember. I need more time."

I caught myself before confronting her with her "promise" to give an answer today.

"Victoria, I don't have much more time. I've got to be moved in at Cornell and ready to teach two or three weeks from now."

That seemed to catch her by surprise. "I don't see how we can get married on such short notice. My parents need to plan, and I've met your mother only once."

Oh, Christ! We don't have time for all the ritual.

"Victoria, in less than two weeks I leave for Ithaca—with or without you."

At that announcement, she looked as stunned as I felt to hear it come out of my mouth. Without consciously thinking about it, we both understood we couldn't manage a long-distance relationship.

For a full minute we stared at each other. She seemed to believe my ultimatum. I wasn't too sure I could leap off into the future alone. It would be so much more comfortable to stay near State and get a job in the public schools.

No! I rejected the easy way out. I would leave for Cornell very soon, probably alone. That felt like the first decision promising severe unpleasantness I'd ever faced. If we grow through pain, I saw a real growth spurt coming soon.

She looked into her coffee cup as if she expected to see her answer there. She picked up the cup. "I'm getting myself more coffee. How about you?" She stood and reached for my cup.

I watched her stride across the open area to the coffee bar. What was so special about Victoria? Attractive girls were a-dime-a-dozen on this campus. But she was indeed special. For that matter, why should she give me a second thought?

With that question, the bleak version of reality I knew so well descended. I expected her to set the cups on the counter and continue out the door.

She waited at the counter two or three minutes, then turned back with two steaming cups. She set them on the table and slid into the booth across from me. I waited.

"Okay." She smiled and shook her head as if she couldn't believe she was agreeing to this. "But you have to take me over the mountain to tell my folks. And you better not leave me there!"

I curbed my impulse to take her hand; that would be too corny. I wanted to say, "You have made me a very happy man," but that would be so trite and silly she'd be annoyed. I did say, "I promise I'll wait and bring you back after you talk to your parents."

That was a promise not lightly given. Victoria's father was a stern man, a grain merchant who worked with farmers who set a tough standard for honorable behavior. My prior visit to her folk's house had ended more or less disastrously when I abruptly departed in the middle of the night, leaving Victoria stranded. They would not welcome the idea of entrusting their daughter to me.

"When should we get married? As you said, we don't have much time." She said this as if she were asking when we should go to a movie we wanted to see—so much better than getting giggly or scatter-brained with excitement.

I did some quick calculations. "If we got married eight or ten days from now, I think we'd have two or three days for a honeymoon at the coast." I paused. "Mom is visiting her sister in Montana. I'll try to get a word to her."

"I have to tell the English Department here that I won't be taking my assistantship."

I said, "It's short notice. You could be burning a bridge behind you. Are you okay with that?"

Her smile was warm, almost intimate. "I may be burning quite a few bridges. You think you can handle that?"

A full sense of the responsibilities entailed by my proposal, and her acceptance, hit me. Should I retract my proposal? Is there still time?

I nodded. "Yeah, I can handle it." I gulped. Scary!

I studied her in silence several seconds before realizing she was watching me back.

She raised her eyebrows quizzically. "Are you having second thoughts, Ken?"

"No," I said, which was not entirely true. "We don't have time for rethinking. Can you be ready to leave for your folks tomorrow morning?"

"Ten o'clock. We'll get there in plenty of time for dinner."

- - - -

We pulled in at dusk. Her parents were polite, which was at least as much as I could hope for. But they weren't warmly welcoming. Wait 'til they hear our announcement! At least her father didn't strangle me, but dinner was a bit tense.

Near the end of the meal, Victoria laid aside her fork. "Ken has something to say."

All eyes were on me. Her dad's expression was neutral. I'm sure he expected an explanation or apology for my abrupt departure a few weeks earlier. He didn't get it. An apology seemed too defensive a note to start on.

"Mr. Sanderson, I'm asking for your daughter's hand in marriage."

He stared at me. His mouth actually fell open. Silence reigned.

I glanced at Victoria, hoping for support. She smiled at her father, and then me, cheerfully, as if I'd suggested going on a picnic. Her mother looked somewhat confused. At least, she wasn't overtly hostile. Victoria's younger sister, Linda, grinned. She enjoyed the drama. All eyes fell on Mr. Sanderson, who recovered with surprising speed.

Sanderson's right hand, fingers striking in unison rather than sequentially, began beating out a solemn tattoo, perhaps a death march. I was not optimistic about the outcome of this interview. I determined that if I'd again departed from this house abruptly, I'd take Victoria with me.

He took a deep breath and looked pointedly at Victoria. She was now in the pitcher's box.

"Dad, I do want to marry Ken. He has to leave for Cornell in two weeks. I've decided to go with him." She waited for a response.

"What about your commitment to teach in the English Department? What about your career? What will you use for money? Do you have any idea what you're getting yourself into? What do you know about this man? How long have you known him?"

"I will resign my assistantship tomorrow. I can pick up my career, such as it is, in Ithaca. I have a couple thousand dollars from an insurance claim, and I can get a job. I've known Ken for nearly three months. He's kind and smart. Any other questions?"

"And you have a plan for a wedding?" her dad asked.

"We want to get married here, in a week or so, take a couple of days on the coast, and drive back to Ithaca," Victoria said.

Linda attended this conversation closely—perhaps preparing for a time she would have to undergo a similar grilling.

Sanderson squinted at Victoria. "Where here?"

"In the church you attend, of course."

Her father wasn't giving up. "I hardly think there's time left to plan a wedding."

Abruptly her mother spoke up, "Yes, there's time. We will get right on it. You'll be ready to leave for New York." We all stared at her. I junked all the mother-in-law jokes I knew.

Her father seemed to grant weddings were a women's thing, and he knew when to quit.

The wedding was set for ten days hence. One phone call lined up the church and the family minister to perform the ceremony. Her uncle would sing. My roommate at State agreed to be best man. Victoria bought herself a new outfit for the ceremony, gold and brown, business cut—much more practical than a wedding dress. She got a sorority sister to be maid of honor.

When her mother asked Victoria what flowers she wanted for the church, Victoria said it didn't make any difference. Her mother broke into tears and said, "I always knew what flowers I wanted for my wedding." So, not everything went absolutely smoothly, but her mother and friends did a remarkable job of putting together a real wedding ceremony.

Victoria and I got away for a couple of hours. We went to the best jewelry store in town, and she picked out a wedding band, which she paid for. It seemed superfluous for me to wear a ring, so I passed on that. Anyway, I had barely enough money to get us across the country and into an apartment in Ithaca.

On our way home from the jewelry store, as we were congratulating ourselves for lining up all our ducks so quickly, Victoria asked, "What about your mother? Have you reached her yet?"

"No. I can't raise anyone at her sister's place in Malta."

"You have to tell her we're getting married."

"I don't think it would be such a big deal for her. She's traveling. I think Mom would be more annoyed than thrilled to interrupt her trip."

Victoria looked at me for several seconds before she shook her head in apparent dismay. "You're her only child. You really don't understand how parents feel, do you?"

I wanted to say, "You don't understand how my mother feels, or doesn't feel." Actually, even after all these years, I couldn't predict Mom's reaction.

Victoria continued in a tone that didn't invite argument, "There must be some way you can reach her. She should have a choice, at least, of coming to our wedding, . . . even if we have to postpone the wedding."

Postpone the wedding! I became strongly motivated to get a message to Mom. She must be with her sister at her in-laws' ranch in Montana's Judith Basin. I knew no one within a hundred miles of there who had a telephone.

Fear of losing Victoria drove me to be resourceful. I called the switchboard operator in Malta, told her my problem, and asked if she had any ideas. She did. Garnet was a little town in the Basin. State troopers frequently stopped for coffee at a café there, a café with a telephone. She connected me with a waitress, who passed the message on to the first state cop to come by. He passed the word to another trooper. Within forty-eight hours of Victoria's ultimatum, Mom phoned to say she'd be at the wedding with two or three of her friends, and who was this Victoria Sanderson person I was marrying?

A couple of days after Mom returned home to Salem, I visited her. It was a conversation we should have had earlier, before I told her I was getting married. But I'd had too many other things on my mind.

When I reminded Mom she'd met Victoria earlier in the summer, she said, "Oh yes. She seemed like a nice girl, though not as pretty as Marian Mason."

"Yes, she is a nice girl, and she's prettier than Mason."

Mom sniffed at my lack of aesthetic judgment. Otherwise, she appeared tolerant enough. The conversation seemed vaguely off-center, but I didn't have time to worry about Mom's lack of enthusiasm.

The wedding, on a warm late summer afternoon, went off without a hitch. Modest in scale, it had all the requisite parts, including a reception at the Sanderson home. About four o'clock Victoria and I cut out for the coast in my eleven-year-old Ford.

I told Victoria about the bit of conversation with Mom I'd had a few days earlier. It seemed kind of funny, and I thought if she paid any attention at all, my new bride would be mildly pleased with me for defending her superior beauty. Big mistake! Victoria said, "Your mother doesn't like me. I could tell by the way she looked at me at the reception. She really does think you should have married Marian Mason."

"That's crazy!" My reaction was aimed at Victoria rather than Mom. I needed an argument to back that up. "Marian is not perfectly stable emotionally." I could have added Mom certainly would not want me to marry someone with mental baggage, but, in truth, I doubted Mom would give a damn whether I married a nut case. She'd probably figure Marian would fit right in with the rest of the family.

"Let's not talk about it anymore. Okay?" Victoria responded.

Community Presbyterian Church - Redmond, Oregon   Founded November 25, 1906

That was fine with me. I didn't want to start a honeymoon with an argument about Mom, especially about how she felt toward Victoria. I'd need to clear the air between the two of them, but that could wait.

We found the small motel near the beach where a couple of my friends had lined up a room. They'd set out a bottle of champagne with two glasses on a coffee table. That thoughtful gesture gave me courage, which I needed, not knowing exactly how to behave on a wedding night. The evening seemed to call for something special. Though, Victoria and I had been "intimate," as they say, I didn't know how to manage a honeymoon or for that matter any other part of marriage. My parents hadn't provided me a very reliable blueprint.

As I uncorked the champagne and poured two glasses, I concentrated on each physical act and throttled down awareness of the commitments I'd made with Victoria and those that waited for me three thousand miles away. Would I ever find the easy self-confidence that had eluded me for so long?

The trip cross-country was a test of stamina. Each night I drove past midnight. We'd find a motel that looked inexpensive, with a vacancy sign still on, and try to talk the proprietor down in price. Victoria joined in these negotiations, and we congratulated each other when we got a room under the asking price.

One oppressively hot afternoon somewhere in Kansas, I stopped at a roadside parking area, got out of the front seat and into the back and began rummaging in my briefcase.

"Why are we stopping?" Victoria asked.

"I need to find the specific date I'm to show up for my assistantship."

"You mean you started on this trip without knowing when you had to arrive?" she asked, with a note of incredulity.

"I had other things on my mind." I paused while she weighed that admission. "Oh, here it is. I'm not due for five more days, plenty of time to get there and find an apartment, if we don't have car trouble."

Find an apartment?! In a flood of new arrivals in Ithaca, we must have been the only ones who didn't know the importance of reserving ahead, or at least arriving early, at the beginning of fall semester.

CHAPTER TWENTY

At dusk, we drove down the strip of land between two long, narrow lakes and into Ithaca. This country is reputed to be very scenic: deep gorges, trees in fall turning bright yellows and reds, and great hiking trails along the Finger Lakes. Dead tired and staring fixedly ahead along the highway, we noticed little of the natural beauty. Ithaca is a small town. Main Street ran from one hill a couple of miles through town to the foot of Cayuga Lake, high above which, on another hill, stood Cornell University. Three steep hills come together at Ithaca, gorges between hills dividing the town and countryside into distinct parts. Pleasant in summer, but, as I was to learn, hell to drive when snow fell and ice formed on roads in the winter.

I drove along Main Street and up any promising side streets. We encountered only "No Vacancy" signs. The town was over-run with new students and with parents who showed up to make sure their little darlings were well situated, families expected to shell out a lot of money for several years. Over an hour of searching didn't produce a single room. Ithaca was somewhat isolated. The closest city was Syracuse, fifty miles away, and with the new semester beginning at a large university there, it was probably as crowded as Ithaca.

"We can sleep tonight in the car. I saw a sign pointing to a city park at the lower end of Main Street."

"Are you sure that would be safe?" Victoria asked.

"Do you have a better idea?" I had the Colt .22 pistol my father had given me, so I could summon some faith in my ability to protect us.

We drove into the park and elected a quite visible parking lot over a more hidden spot. The back seat was full of our earthly possessions. We were after all starting a new life . . . if we made it through the night. I put the loaded pistol under the front seat, and we settled in to share cramped space with the steering wheel and gearshift.

I was almost asleep, when a tapping on my window startled me to full consciousness. I thought of the weapon within reach, but, by the grace of God, I didn't haul it out. The cop was in uniform, holding his flashlight over his head and shining it in my face. I rolled down the window.

"What are you doing here?"

At that moment, I realized my old Ford could look like a pauper's vehicle.

"We came into Ithaca a couple of hours ago and couldn't find a room in town."

"No, I suppose not," he said, in an agreeable tone. "But you can't stay here."

"Why not?" I tried to keep any trace of belligerence out of my voice.

"It's illegal to stay overnight in a city park. It's also dangerous. Bums could attack you and steal everything you got, maybe worse."

Oh, swell! I looked back across the seat and saw Victoria, exhausted, her face tightly anxious. She was starting to panic. "Look, is there any place we can go that is reasonably safe where we can get a few hours of sleep?"

The cop shook his head. "Sorry, I can't advise you."

"Bastard" was one of the kinder things that ran through my mind. I stared at him in silence. Finally, he said, "Up the road, a few miles, is Interlocken. Might be a hotel room there."

Cross-eyed with fatigue, but fueled by some hope, we drove fifteen miles back the way we'd come. Interlocken made Ithaca look like a metropolis. The one hotel, over a bar, was our oasis. Deserted streets and abandoned buildings around the bar looked like they might swarm with the thugs the cop warned us about.

I found the hotel manager in the bar. Yeah, he had a room, payment in advance. Victoria got out of the car, I locked it, and we followed the manager to their one last room. The manager walked in guided by light from the sign outside. He pulled a string that turned on the single light bulb dangling from the ceiling. The room was big and devoid of furniture, except for an ancient bed, a table and two chairs.

I nodded my approval. Like I had a choice. He and I went back downstairs, where I laid out a five-dollar bill and he handed me a door key. Apparently, signing a guest register was too upscale for this establishment.

I tried the key, and it appeared to really lock the door, so we were safe, at least from an amateur thief passing in the hall. Victoria checked out the bed and found no bed bugs, but she still felt we would do better sleeping on top of the torn and frayed coverlet.

"We're lucky to find this place," I remarked. "Must be a slow night for the prostitutes downstairs."

Victoria ignored my attempt to lighten up. She didn't think I was kidding. Actually, I'm not sure I was.

Not having been murdered in our sleep, we awoke to a sparkly bright morning, ready to find our love nest for the next few years. In Ithaca we found a café, not crowded, where we had breakfast and consulted the local newspaper. Apparently, parents and students were mostly preparing for graduation exercises of various sorts and locations.

Apartments appeared to be more available than overnight lodging was the night before. We felt excited, like well-healed kids in a candy store. We checked out the first three places on our list. The first one, in a basement, walls painted a hideous green, had a maze of pipes low overhead. The second one would require us to share a bathroom with an unknown number of fellow residents. The third one was barely livable, and at an outrageous rent. Our optimism began to wither, but we kept trying.

Across a steep valley from the university, newspaper in hand, we came to a large farmhouse with three cars parked in the yard. We knocked at a kitchen door and were greeted by a stout woman holding a bottle of beer—at eleven in the morning. It was an unpromising start.

She had two upstairs apartments available, both clean, but hardly plush. The smaller one had a distinct kitchen and separate bedroom. Victoria and I agreed the view from our kitchen table down the valley between us and the University was worth the inconvenience of a slightly longer drive to campus. This was, of course, before we faced the challenge of making the drive down into the valley and back up to our apartment every day of a freezing five-month winter.

Victoria asked Beatrice if she could hold the apartment for a day or so while we looked around. That seemed to me rude.

"Look, you're good kids, I'm sure, but this is the week when I rent or not. I can't let a serious offer go by. Sorry."

Victoria and I walked back to our car to confer. We decided to take the plunge. We walked back into her kitchen. I asked Beatrice, "What do we sign?"

"You don't sign anything. Just pay your rent for this month and on the first hereafter."

I counted out the money, over half of what we had. I didn't know how we were going to eat until I got my first check in over a month. For sure, we weren't going to get fat on steak.

Beatrice watched me put the money on the beat-up table. "You kids don't have much money right now, do you?"

"The University starts my pay next month. We'll be good for the rent, don't worry."

Beatrice eyed the money on the table. "Keep that money for now. You can make it up over the next two or three months."

I stared at her. She stared back for a few seconds and turned back to her stove.

That was the closest we came to running out of cash for food, but money was tight most of the time the next few years.

Beatrice Compton frequently polished off two or three beers before noon, but we could not ask for a more generous landlady. She did have a few unusual traits like carrying on two-way conversations with her dog and sensing things for no logical reason. One time when Victoria and I were both swamped with work at school and with no hope of getting enough time before evening meetings to prepare dinner, the phone rang. Beatrice said, "You guys get here in a few minutes. I'll have dinner ready for you." She had never before prepared food for us. Why tonight? We got used to these anomalies with Beatrice and eventually we hardly noticed her weird powers. She didn't seem aware of them.

On the hill above the Compton's house was a tree and brush-strewn plot of two or three hundred acres. When I felt overwhelmed by school, I'd walk all over that lot.

We had to rely on one old car to get us to campus and back. We had lots of company in our economic bracket, which meant we had frequent parties with beer and cheap but potent punch.

After a couple of years, we became frequent chaperones at one fraternity. The routine was standard: we'd be isolated, with one or two members at a time to keep us company, in a remote room in the house. Once every hour or two, we'd wander for a few minutes among the partying students. This seemed enough to salve our conscience. Fortunately, nothing fatal or severely scandalous occurred on our watch.

A few days after we moved in,RoyCompton and I chatted in his yard. He said he wished he was hunting deer with his shotgun. I suggested people usually hunted with a rifle. He said I must not know much about guns. I said I did and, in fact, had a Colt .22 pistol upstairs.

"You got that gun registered?"

"No. Why should I?"

"You can't take that pistol anywhere without a license to carry a concealed weapon."

What kind of crap is Roy feeding me? "Well, I only use it for protection. No criminal enterprises." I laughed.

"Do you ever take it with you in your car?"

"Just on camping trips, stuff like that."

Ray pulled up some stories. An out-of-state jewelry salesman carrying a gun for personal protection got stopped on the Interstate by a trooper. The cop discovered a gun in the glove box and hauled the salesman in. The guy avoided jail, but it wasn't easy.

"Okay, I'll register it. At the city police station?"

"Not that simple. You got to get a respected citizen to vouch for you."

"How about you?"

Ray shook his head. "Sorry Ken, I'm not that respected." He continued on his way to the tool shed.

So that was how I met my advisor, the venerated Professor Herbert A. Wichelns: I went to his office and asked him to vouch for me so I could carry a concealed weapon. Years later, I realized Wichelns must have wondered, what the hell had they hired? The old professor, however, didn't blink an eye. He did stab a letter opener a few times into a chewed-up area of his desk, as, I was to learn, he frequently did when thinking through a response to a student. He said, yes, he could do that. Two weeks later, he took me on as an advisee—I suspect out of curiosity, or maybe to protect the rest of the faculty from a dangerous nut case.

Some of my fellow graduate students felt threatened by the intellectual standards at Cornell. I never did. But the workload overwhelmed me. In a course in theater arts, one assignment was to select, cast, and direct a play for public consumption. One assignment in one course! At State, that would be a whole damn master's thesis. And it was in an undergraduate course. In another course, I wrote a paper every week. In that semester, in addition to teaching, reading for seminars, and all the rest, I turned in over two hundred pages of original material. I marveled at those undergrads' capacity to produce, even though their papers were usually much shorter than mine. They took it all in stride. I didn't. What was my problem? Failure to focus? Laziness?

I couldn't match my goals to departmental requirements. An assignment in an undergraduate film course called for a ten-fifteen-page research paper. I decided to tackle the use of films for persuasion. The topic unraveled in various directions. Who would know, for instance, that during World War Two, the U.S. Navy did an elaborate series of controlled studies on the effects of indoctrination movies. The topic sucked me in until finally I cut it off, past due, at one hundred, thirty-five pages. The professor in the course, an unflappable old-timer, must have thought "what the bloody hell?" but he accepted the paper. He said it was a fine paper in a new area of theory. He gave me a B in the course because my paper was late. Did I learn from this? Not at all! I was disappointed at the injustice of the grade.

My resolve that Cornell would be a new start was crumbling. Incompletes cropped up on my transcript, not as many as at State, but here the faculty was less tolerant of them. I seemed to be running scared most of the time. Fortunately, work piled up too fast to permit time for constant self-lashing with guilt-ridden introspection.

Victoria kept me on the rails. Her job as a secretary in the Dean of Men and Women's Office was way below her skills level, but we needed the money. She managed our meals, ironing, and the rest of the household stuff. Some papers I got in on time only because she would sit on the commode and take dictation from me standing in the shower and then type from her notes.

What did she get out of this? Nothing that I could see. I avoided wondering how much longer she would put up with this one-sided relationship if I didn't start producing. I was getting pretty good at some sorts of repression. I had lots of practice.

I messed around without feeling much necessity to get on with my program. I took piano lessons again, though we had no reason to believe I would ever be a good pianist. The same with a creative writing course I took on a whim. Victoria never asked me, as she well could have, what the hell I thought I was doing taking these courses at the cost of time away from work on my degree. She offered praise when I accomplished something as trivial as a pointed remark at a public discussion of a film or paper. She also read a lot of my work before I turned it in. She became the toughest and most helpful critic I would have in my career.

So it would appear our relationship was blissfully happy? Not so. Tension between us became almost constant, sometimes mild and suppressed, other times erupting in brutal arguments. My childhood gave me a distinct advantage in these onslaughts on each other: practice and a capacity for cruelty that her more sheltered background did not prepare her to deal with or withstand. For weeks at a time, our morning trips to campus were continuations of arguments started at the breakfast table. She sometimes was reduced to tears by the time I let her off for her job in the student affairs building.

What was my problem? It was two or three years into our marriage before I began to sense that mostly I was the one causing tension. I usually let that fact slip out of my field of vision. It was easier to blame circumstance or Victoria or my teachers, anything or anybody but myself. I didn't understand what caused me to be such a miserable bastard, so there wasn't much I could do to change. Both Victoria and I realized lashing me with guilt wasn't productive.

Maybe I was frustrated because I wanted to write fiction—something seemed noble about that excuse. And an examination of my circumstances revealed I did have time to write much more than I produced.

Maybe I felt in a straight jacket of job and marriage. Many of our friends were happily monogamous. I wasn't. Nor did plodding through a routine career excite me. But I lacked confidence or energy or sense of purpose or something to break out. I couldn't focus on a goal. Of course, I loathed myself for that deficiency.

After a couple of years, Victoria got restive and decided to go for a master's degree in English at Cornell on a part-time basis. Some of her favorite teachers warned her she'd never make it. She persisted—and walked into a meat grinder of ruthlessly competitive classmates. She began to get the picture when after contributing the bulk of work to a joint assignment, she watched her partner take most of the credit. Students practiced "cut-throat" academic competition, such as checking out all the books for an assigned project before other students could get to them. As soon as class ended, speedy walking from classroom to library did make a difference. She hung tough and in two or three years completed her course work up to the thesis.

Then she blocked. How supportive was I? Not very. On top of this, she really wanted to have children, and I really didn't. This led to more stress in our marriage. Victoria felt vulnerable because her family was thousands of miles away. If they'd been close by, she probably would have walked out on me.

Victoria's anxiety over her thesis plus my stonewalling on children came to a head for her in our last summer in Ithaca. We took a camping trip to Cape Cod with another couple we knew in graduate school. We had a canvas tent just large enough for two people on air mattresses on the ground and the other two crossways above them on camp cots.   The arrangement was awkwardly crowded, but sufficient for graduate students on the edge of poverty.

We stopped in a village near the campground. Victoria wanted to buy bobby pins in a five-and-dime store while we three went in the opposite direction for provisions at a small market.

We returned to the car with our sacks of groceries. Where was Victoria?

We waited a half hour in vain. It was time to move on to the campground. I said I'd go find her back at the store.

I entered the store and walked up to the cashier. "Excuse me, I'm looking for my wife, a pretty blond, short hair."

The cashier looked stricken. She seemed to hesitate before responding. "Wait here. I'll get the manager."

A middle-aged man, gray suit, rimless glasses hurried from the back of the store. It was hard to read his expression, worried, but relieved. He struck me as a kind man. I was in a hurry to find out what was going on.

"Your wife, I think it must be your wife, is resting on a cot in our storeroom."

He started toward the back of the store. I followed.

"What happened?"

He stopped and turned back toward me. After a few seconds, he said, "Your wife collapsed, fell to the floor up front. We got her back here to a cot. Seemed in shock. We put a blanket and a coat on her. She is conscious." The manager seemed almost pleading for understanding. "We were going to call an ambulance, but she said, no, that you'd come for her."

I rushed into the storeroom, the manager right behind me.

"Victoria!" She lay, pale, shivering, under a coat on a camp cot. "Are you okay?" That was a dumb question. She obviously was not okay.

"Yeah, I'm getting control now." She paused and shook her head. "I don't know what happened. All of a sudden, I got scared. Really terrified. I don't know of what. Then I guess I passed out. Next thing, I'm here." She smiled. A little color was coming back in her face.

She carefully removed the coat and blanket and sat up. "I'm fine. We can get back on the road." She was still pale and shaky.

The manager standing behind me said, "There's a hospital about three blocks from here. Got an emergency room. Maybe . . . None of my business, of course, but you could take her there."

You're right, it's none of your business. Then I realized, even for me, this would be over the top in self-centered lack of empathy.

By now, the other two campers had entered the store and found us. I put the manager's suggestion to them.

We stopped at the hospital. A nurse wanted Victoria to get on a gurney. She said that was ridiculous. I stayed out of it. As a compromise, she got in a wheelchair. I went with her into the doctor's cramped office. He questioned her several minutes, while a nurse wrote up her admission and took vital signs. He concluded, "You had a panic attack, rather severe. I doubt it's your last one. Get this filled down the hall." He wrote a prescription for a strong tranquilizer. As we walked out of his office, he patted Victoria on the shoulder and said, "Try to relax. If these attacks recur, you better see a psychiatrist."

I was annoyed that he'd presumed to pat her shoulder.

Victoria seemed in good spirits during the rest of the camping trip.

At home, she had no more severe panic attacks, but she became almost unable to leave our apartment. She couldn't drive, so we went to the grocery store together. I insisted she stay in charge of the cooking, and I helped very little. Given her mental condition, did this make her better or worse? I have no idea, but it took pressure off me.

Clearly, Victoria was not enjoying perfect mental health; vastly different from the confident and cheerful person I'd married. Our social life fell to almost zero. By what I later saw as a supreme effort of will, she managed to go to her part-time job in a dean's office.

She did see a psychiatrist in Ithaca. He was a hands-on creep, so she didn't go back after one session.

I thought maybe if she started on her thesis, she'd rally, but she couldn't get past her block on that. She seemed to lack the confidence to try. My urging may have been well intentioned, but it didn't help. It was painful to watch her frustration, which repeatedly drove her to tears. I vacillated between concern and irritation.

At my core I remained resolutely self-centered—which would be less absurd if I had any goal driving me. I drifted along toward my Ph.D., working vigorously, sporadically, on short-term projects whether or not they were relevant to any long-term goal.

★ 255 ★

★ 256 ★

CHAPTER TWENTY-ONE

A few weeks after Cape Cod, we sat at a table covered with unwashed dishes from breakfast. We seemed to have nothing to say to each other at the beginning of one more awkward morning. When will this end? And how?

"We've got to talk, face up to your problem. It's getting too much for me to handle," I said.

She nodded. Tears trickling down her cheeks gave way to racking sobs.

I should have taken her hand, maybe gotten out of my chair to put my arm around her shoulders. But I didn't. I plunged ahead, determined to continue this conversation.

"Do you have any idea what's bothering you? Do you want to quit on your master's degree? It's okay if you do."

She shook her head. "I want to have children." More sobs.

This issue had haunted us since we came to Ithaca three or four years ago. Sometimes it was buried so deep I could hope it had gone away, and I think even Victoria was relieved. But the issue always lurked, waiting to erupt in mental bullying or passive aggression. My desperate frustration with my own weakness of will in getting on with a career added steam, which was vented in attacks on her for lack of support. In retrospect, of course, I realize these attacks were often brutally unfair. Victoria, at that time, lacked the tools to defend herself or counter-attack.

We had gone to a marriage counselor. I think Victoria expected the counselor to brand me as perverted or at least wrong. Instead, the middle-aged woman said my position was reasonable, and we should work toward a compromise. The session moved me from perverted to normal, if selfish, so I felt my position strengthened. Neither Victoria nor I could see how a compromise was possible: either you had children or you didn't. We didn't go back for more advice.

A few evenings later we sat in our tiny living room and watched shadows fill up the valley. We felt at peace— at least I thought we did, until Victoria started quietly sniffling. So strong was the mood of the moment that I did not reflexively go on a defensive attack. I did, however, see an opportune time to take another stab at resolving that issue which constantly lay in wait to chop us apart. This time I would be gentle, but I was determined to meet our problem head-on. "You want to have children," I said. "That's what's messing up your mind?"

She nodded. Her weeping ceased for the moment.

Oh, Christ, must I agree to raise a family or suffer a severely depressed wife? Maybe there's a way to get her to give up the family idea?

"That doctor on Cape Cod thought you should see a psychiatrist. I know the guy downtown bombed out. Maybe you should try someone else?"

I waited and let her think it through for a minute or two. She blindsided me. "If you won't have a family with me, I'm going to leave you."

I sat stunned. She was shaky, but I had no doubt she meant it, the culmination of years of tension.

All my options were bad. I feebly tried to keep the issue open. "Let's try to work this out, get a new psychiatrist."

To my surprise, she agreed to give that a try. She said, "I love you. I really don't want to leave you." She gasped out a sob. "But I will, I mean it." The stress on her must have been huge, but I was so wrapped up in my own anxiety at the possibility of being a parent that I was totally insensitive to Victoria's inner turmoil.

She got a name from the Student Affairs office. Dr. Panzer agreed to meet her once a week after hours at his office. He insisted I bring her and wait in the outer office during the session; she was very pretty and he was very cautious. That was okay, since I had to drive her anyway.

As part of her job in Student Affairs, Victoria was assigned to teach a couple of sections of a non-credit orientation course. It should have been low-pressure, but for her it was excruciating—an acid test for her recovery. For the first few weeks I went with her, waited and read in a nearby classroom. Dr. Panzer gave her tranquillizer pills, to be taken "as needed." Panzer revised his voluntary dosage when in the first two nights teaching, she took thirteen pills. I had to practically force her into the classroom, but she managed to do it.

After some weeks, she hadn't improved much. Dr. Panzer was probing into her personal life, when she mentioned that I thought she'd be happier when she got underway on her thesis. As Victoria reported to me, Panzer said, "That's it!"

She said, "I'm desperate to have a family. But maybe my husband is right, that I should settle for a career. I know I have to choose between a family and a career."

"Why choose? Why don't you do both?"

"Do both?"

"Yes, of course. Any sixteen-year-old girl can get pregnant. Very few of them can get an advanced degree from Cornell. You can do both."

When Victoria reported this conversation to me, I had to respond. I would make a serious tactical error if I launched a frontal attack on the compromise Panzer had suggested, so I focused on the thesis side of the deal.

Victoria got back on her thesis and seemed to postpone the children issue. I gave her all the support I could, which was quite a bit since her project drew heavily on a major area of my training.

One insecure member of her committee assigned esoteric and irrelevant reading to impress colleagues on the committee. She saw what he did and why, but she plowed gamely through the material. Apparently, she earned the respect of her committee chair. The next time one of her committee members tried to jerk her around to satisfy some whim, the chair used his status to discourage any more of that nonsense.

I hoped by the time she finished this degree she'd be so committed to a career that thoughts of motherhood would fall by the wayside. I'd massively misread her psychology. Maybe I saw what I wanted to see. We both postponed the issue of having a family.

Victoria continued her job and managed most of the home maintenance while she marched toward her graduate degree. She was impressively disciplined. I wasn't. I managed to meet the obligations of my assistantship and to avoid being overwhelmed by my teaching and courses.

What nearly did me in was guilt that morphed into depression. I watched Victoria forge ahead against greater obstacles than I faced.

I had the uneasy feeling that my wife's new-found determination might stem from her belief that as soon as she knocked off her graduate degree, she could start a family. I had to cross the degree line first, though rationally I couldn't see how that would change the equation on the children issue. I was conflicted between wanting to see her finish her degree because that might move her toward placing career ambition above motherhood, and dread that her completion would clear the decks for her to push for a family.

If I were a strong person, I'd put the whole matter aside for the time being and get on with my own degree, as Victoria was doing. My inability to control mental focus and to suppress anxieties cost me dearly, but I couldn't get out of this straight jacket. My will was betrayed by years of self-indulgent habits.

Despite consistent encouragement from Victoria and Dr. Wichelns, I floundered trying to make progress. My depression turned ferocious. I already knew that a person can't know how close he is to suicide until he's actually doing it. Then it's too late to ask yourself, "Do I really want to do this?" The intensity came in waves, but for weeks on end, even with low intensity, the despair would be there. I drank for relief, but it didn't help much. I'd seen a few full-blown alcoholics, including probably my father. I didn't want to join them. I managed to limit my drinking to evenings, and I rarely came close to loss of control. I guess it was fear that kept me from becoming a total drunk, but fear wasn't enough to force me to take control of hour-by-hour living.

Under the heavy workloads, procrastination was rampant among graduate students, so my lack of focus was easily disguised as normal, except from Victoria.

When pressure got unbearable, I'd go into a short-term catatonic state, staring at, say, a table for hours. I'd tell myself I could move any time I wanted to—except I couldn't. After a few hours, one arm would come free, or a leg, or I could move my head, and in a few minutes I'd be back to what passed for normal. Victoria, of course, noticed these episodes. She urged me to see a psychiatrist. But I clung to my depression, as if I were afraid to try for a cure. Why? Did I sense that if the cure failed, I'd have nowhere to go but down. Or I'd lose my excuse for not facing up to my ambitions and responsibilities. I still don't know answers to those questions. Was I being self-indulgent or was I bravely carrying on despite a crushing handicap. I do know, whatever the answers, that my problem was painful. I didn't mind the pain of depression so much, but the paralysis of it seemed deadly at times. If failure was inevitable, why not point a gun in the roof my mouth and end the pain. I was back to that cop out. Pathetic!

How would Victoria respond to that final solution? I was sure she didn't love me. How could she. My death would be an inconvenient disruption of her plans, but in the long run she'd probably decide it was for the better.

Facing a deep, black ravine I had to make a decision. I teetered on the edge . . . or was I yards safely back. The only way to find out was to take a few steps forward to see if I fell over the edge A shotgun in my mouth would do a much surer job than my .22 pistol.

The pistol was all I had at hand. Should I act on impulse? This was not a trivial choice. Don't rush a decision. With a shotgun, I would have to buy the gun and shells, load the gun, position it correctly, and somehow reach the trigger. I could more easily get close to the edge with the pistol, but with it I'd stand a real chance of messing up, ending up alive but incapacitated—worse than dead. Holding the pistol, its heft and cold metal, could at least make that option more real.

My .22 was not where it was supposed to be in our apartment.

Its absence alarmed me, but not because I was denied an option for ending my life. The gun was one of the very few relics, and the most important, from my father.

After hesitating a few days, not wanting to alarm Victoria, one evening before we went to separate rooms to work, I asked her, "I notice that my pistol seems to have gone missing, or maybe it got misplaced. Do you happen to know where it is?"

"Did you put it away and forget where?" She paused. "Why are you looking for it?"

I shrugged. "It's one of the few things, you know, I have from Dad. Do you have a clue where it is?"

She eyed me oddly, as if she were calculating whether to answer me.

I added, "It's unlikely I'd have misplaced it."

"I hid it," she said, flatly, not defiantly.

"What! Why?" Anger she would presume to hide my gun jarred attention from my reason for finding it. "You had no right to do that."

"I was worried. You seemed depressed a lot of the time. A friend advised me to hide the gun . . . to make sure you wouldn't harm yourself." She spoke softly and looked down, as if she knew she had done wrong and hoped she would be forgiven. "I did it for your sake."

I became kindly and forgiving in tone. But it was an act. "You did the right thing. I'm okay now. You can tell me where the gun is."

Victoria shook her head. She wasn't fooled, and on something really important she could be stubborn as hell. I gritted my teeth. With the gun I would feel empowered to manage my future, or lack of it. I controlled a surge of anger. It wouldn't do for her to see that I'd been trying to con her into betraying the gun's location while I was still depressed. Not trusting myself to continue this charade, I got up and walked to my room where papers waited to be graded. I'd have to consciously avoid taking my frustration out on the students.

So the ultimate solution for the sticky mess in my mind was denied, at least until I went to a gun store. There a purchase would confirm my commitment to a plan. What can I do NOW?

What about Dr. Panzer. Was I that desperate. And could he do any good. Victoria was down to a maintenance schedule of sessions, but even so, Panzer working with both of us could create a messy situation. My attention drifted to several books on rhetoric and history I should soon use for a paper, to a pseudo-Egyptian dagger on my desk, to the clock. In fact, I could focus on nothing.

Victoria was near the end of work on her master's degree, and she hadn't committed to a doctorate. Soon we would again face the offspring question. Victoria made clear my hopes to duck that showdown were wishful thinking. Couldn't she realize facing that decision was making me suicidal.

I tried to envision her coming alone to this apartment night after night, with me lying cold in a grave. I told myself she'd do just fine, not alone for long. In a rare moment of empathy—of remembering our honeymoon on the Oregon coast, the trip cross-country to a crummy hotel room in Interlocken, what followed, her resolute cheer and her patience waiting for a chance at motherhood—I realized what a remarkable woman I'd married. And what a shit she'd married.

I pushed away student papers on my desk. Having tear stains on them would call for an explanation I didn't want to give.

CHAPTER TWENTY-TWO

Sunday morning, six months later, December twenty-fifth, I scrambled eggs with chunks of onion, pepper, and tomato mixed in. Victoria made toast. Me sharing in making a special breakfast seemed feeble consolation for the absence of her family during Christmas holidays. A buyers' orgy of homage to commercial interests was not possible for us. I knew that, but I wished I could afford to get Victoria something really nice, maybe a fur coat, instead of the yellow blouse I'd carefully picked out. I knew she'd like the blouse a lot—not just say she liked it, but really like it because it came from me.

We were three thousand miles away from families, and travel was expensive. We had a small tree and Christmas balls and tinsel, and after breakfast, we'd follow our usual ritual of just the two of us opening presents on Christmas morning. To Victoria, our routine, without her family, must have seemed thin gruel for the special day. Mom and I had been alone for enough Christmases that I was used to making a two-person celebration. I missed Mom a little; she now preferred to spend her holiday with her sister in Montana. Victoria was stuck with just me.

After breakfast, she washed up the dishes and I dried, she put a roast in the oven, and we went into our living room. She'd given me an Agatha Christie hardback, and I'd given her a small group of current magazines—Cosmopolitan, Redbook, and a couple of other women's magazines—so we each had something to read in the long afternoon. This was less than exciting for me, and I suspect it was even more barren for Victoria.

She suggested, "Why don't we take a walk, a short one up to the end of the lane?"

I agreed. We put on heavy jackets and, in case we wanted to venture into the lot past the lane, we put on overshoes.

Halfway up the lane, I stopped and turned to gaze across to the next hill. Three inches of snow had fallen on Christmas Eve, and today not enough traffic had passed to remove it from the roads. The air was crisp and cold, matching the clean white blanket covering so much of our world. For several moments, I waited staring in a sort of rapture, the first peace I'd felt for weeks.

Victoria came beside me and wrapped my arm with hers. "It's beautiful," she said quietly.

"Yes, it is," I whispered, as if even a loud voice would shatter the scene like a dropped glass globe.

After a few minutes, we turned in unison and continued up the hill.

But only for two or three hundred yards.

Victoria stopped, and turned to me. "I want to get pregnant." I felt blindsided. Her statement brought to the surface all the weight of past tension and her frustration and self-denial. She shattered my peaceful optimism, but shreds of past happiness made it impossible for me to rally all my abusive negativity.

"Let's wait until we get back to the apartment to face that question," I stalled.

"It's not a question. We had a deal. I meant what I said then."

We said no more about it. A few minutes later, we turned and headed back down the hill. I felt a surge of anger that she had destroyed the magic we'd salvaged for the day. But she was, I suppose, correct: we had to face that decision sooner or later, and sooner had arrived.

I did venture to nibble around the edges of the dangerous topic. "What does your thesis advisor think of you going all the way for a Ph.D.?" I asked.

"He thinks it can be done. The department graduate committee has to approve my application. I'll know in a couple of weeks."

I said nothing.

"You hope they'll turn me down, don't you?"

"That's not fair. I don't want to see your career frustrated."

That much was true. I did want to see her get something out of the marriage if I ceased to exist in her life.

Should I pop myself off or run away? That edgy question marked a depressing reversal from an hour earlier. Running away would be less drastic, less final. That was the big drawback with running: it would solve nothing. She'd still be out there somewhere. I'd have to relive my decision over and over, and I'd know I'd taken the coward's way out.

I watched from a kitchen chair, while she cut up potatoes and carrots to go with the roast for Christmas dinner. Even whacking up vegetables, she was quick and decisive. It was hard to see her as the same person who'd had a nervous breakdown on Cape Cod. She was beautiful, sweet, competent, helpful. Why would I want to give her up. The answer was, I didn't.

Even on this melancholy day, suicide seemed an unproductive option. Trying to think this dilemma through to a logical decision had long since passed being tenable. Neither of my parents had been keen on raising a child, and I could see a host of reasons why, from changing dirty diapers to having career options curtailed by responsibility to the kid (though I couldn't see that my father was ever so limited).

At this point, I'd have to decide, and then live out my choice.

"Do you want a salad with dinner?"

My choice, and she could and would provide the salad. Tears started to well up. The thought of never again hearing her ask me such a question crushed me.

When I didn't answer, she glanced at me, then turned to appraise me more thoroughly.

"Is that such a hard question, Ken? Salad or not?" she asked smiling, but a bit anxiously.

"Okay."

"Okay, what?"

"Okay, you, . . . we can start a family." I smiled ruefully. "At least, we can try." I was being cautious, but I regretted the sour note.

It seemed to take a minute for that to sink in, understandable after over three years

"You won't change your mind?"

"No."

And I didn't.

I'd like to say, "Nine months later, she gave birth," but it was over ten months, well into Fall semester.

Meanwhile, Victoria was admitted to the Ph.D. program in English and assigned a genial professor as advisor. Her assistantship was deferred, but she took one graduate course to cement her presence in the program.

When we were sure she was pregnant, we had to face the forthcoming end of her income, which with my assistantship was barely enough to keep us float. We had decided that we couldn't, or wouldn't borrow from parents.

I worried a lot about money, to the point of being seriously tempted to cut and run for it. I could work in canneries, probably get on a year-round crew, or maybe sell shoes. I thought of myself as fitting into the general run of people in those jobs, which created a sense of independence.   Alternatives to an academic career enfeebled my motivation to do more than tread water in graduate school.

Leaving Cornell would take more confidence than I could muster, and I suppose in my self-centered way I loved Victoria. So I stayed. But I had to increase my income.

CHAPTER TWENTY-THREE

I sat in front of Professor Herbert A. Wichelns' desk. He had told me to go in, and he'd join me in a few minutes. Mentally, I rehearsed my opening gambit. Normally, conversations with the Professor were relaxed, but I had too much riding on this to be casual.

Wichelns took his seat across from me. "What can I do for you, Ken?" That was genuine: he really did take care of his students.

"Victoria is pregnant."

"Congratulations. That must make you a happy man."

"Actually, at this point in time, it doesn't."

Silence, while he waited for me to explain. I'd already blundered off my planned script. I couldn't try to game my advisor. He was too smart, and too decent. He must have dealt before with grad assistants who'd found themselves in my predicament.

"Victoria and I were barely getting by on our two assistantships. Now, she's giving hers up, as of this fall. So you can see I greet this news with mixed feelings."

He nodded and smiled encouragingly.

"I think I've done a fairly good job teaching freshman speech classes. Now I'd like to be increased to four sections, full-time."

He nodded. "I see." A business-like expression replaced his smile. "I'm glad you came in, Ken. Your job is something we have to talk about."

I had a bad feeling about where this was going.

He continued, "As you may know, we have to move our limited number of teaching assistantships around. We normally set a maximum time limit of three years to complete course work and keep an assistantship. You're near the end of your fourth year. The Department can't keep you on stipend past the end of the present semester."

"You've lost patience with me?" And why wouldn't they!

"Ken, we believe you have enormous potential, but we also have to be fair to other applicants."

"Yeah, I know. I discover I'm going to be responsible for a child, we lose Victoria's income, and I'm fired. Trouble comes in threes." Then I consciously forced myself to smile. Not their bloody fault that I've screwed up and wasted four years. "I think I can get a job teaching at some podunk school."

Wichelns looked at me with disapproval. From him this look carried about the same weight as being backhanded across the face by another faculty member. It hurt!

"I didn't know you were a snob, Ken." He smiled. Thank God. "It may not be necessary for you to subject yourself to such humiliation." His voice grazed over a flavor of irony. "You coached debate at State, correct?"

I nodded.

"You were pretty good?"

"We won a few debates." I figured if he raised the topic he already knew the answer to that question.

"Would you like to coach debaters to win a few more?"

"Yes, I would," I said with more enthusiasm than I'd shown so far in this conversation.

The upshot was my appointment as an instructor, low-level, but still full-time faculty at above what Victoria and I together took in. Wichelns had two stipulations: I was to take no more courses, and the job was for a maximum of two years. "We must get you out of here and on your way." No way was Wichelns going to let me become a professional student.

The next academic year went smoothly. As I had at State, I turned a debate club into a squad. Several talented and experienced freshmen showed up. Some older members dropped out when they realized that this was not a club for exercises in petty politicking. By the time we were well into the contest season, we decided that two- or three-day trips were too much of a grind for Victoria to take in stride every weekend. We both regretted that.

In contest debate, some Ivy League schools were at the top of the pecking order, while others were disdained as dilettantes and amateurs. During that first year, Cornell moved from amateur rank to be accepted among serious schools. I got a lot of satisfaction from that, which made me more comfortable in my skin. There was a downside, however: it became too easy to avoid studying for my comprehensive exams and writing a dissertation. I knew I could coach debate; I was not at all sure I had the discipline required for a Ph.D.

On a dry cold early morning in November, Victoria shook me awake. "I think it's time."

I'd returned late the night before from a twelve-round tournament. "Time for what?" I asked groggily. That is not just a stupid question, but also a damnably insensitive one. But I had only two or three hours of sleep.

"I think the baby is coming." That did jerk me awake. I think most men on the brink of fatherhood for the first time feel somewhat at sea, but few could be as unsure as I was. I'd not looked forward to this event, the result being I avoided classes on birthing. Victoria was in a group where other husbands learned how to talk their wives through labor. I figured I'd have nothing to contribute when the day came, so I skipped the classes. Victoria, who stood by me every step of my Ph.D. work, was the only wife without a husband in attendance at those classes. I don't think she told the other wives her husband was a prick. They could figure that out for themselves.

The one thing I had prepared for was getting to the hospital safely and speedily. Thank God there was no snow or ice on the streets, so I got there without close calls. I drove up to the hospital emergency entrance. Victoria got out and consulted briefly with a nurse on duty. The nurse nodded and ordered a wheelchair. My wife soon disappeared, pushed through the emergency entrance by an orderly. Everything seemed under control, so I drove to the parking lot, reveling in tremendous relief that Victoria and the baby were now the responsibility of someone else, someone competent, not me.

Floodlights in the parking lot dispelled inky darkness. I stopped and looked up, in no hurry to get to the waiting room or do whatever else I was supposed to do. Above me was a cold, starry sky blotted out by the pools of light around the hospital. An eerie, anxious apprehension invaded my mind. I couldn't shake the conviction that this night had great significance—and not necessarily for a good outcome. A wave of sudden fear washed over me. I needed Victoria so much, so very much. Tears streaked my cheeks for a few moments.

I walked quickly across the lot to the hospital. Upstairs, the elderly volunteer woman at the desk in the waiting room for maternity looked up with some alarm at my abrupt request for information about Victoria Bailey's condition and location.

"She has not gone to the delivery room. You're her husband?" I nodded. "She's in room 417, down the hall, first corridor on the left."

When I entered room 417, I felt grateful to see it was a private room. I guess I'd imagined a sort of barracks with a row of beds for women waiting to give birth. Victoria smiled at me from her bed. She looked okay, except for a sheen of perspiration. An older nurse, watching over her and keeping her company, got up from a chair beside the bed and quietly left the room.

"Are you okay?" I said.

"Yes, I'm fine." She winced for a second, and returned to a cheerful smile. "And you, are you okay?" She knew I wasn't fond of hospitals. Why did she ask about me? It's supposed to be the other way around.

"Yeah, I'm doing okay." I sat down and took her hand in mine. Was this a genuine gesture? Or was I playing a role? I didn't know. It was the best I could do. Her hand did feel good. "You don't look like you're having fun." A god-awful attempt at humor.

"Oh, I am having a good time." She winced again and squeezed my hand. "Well, it isn't all fun. But, Ken, I've never been happier."

I stayed with her for a couple of hours, until the nurse, after a routine check, took her to the delivery room and sent me to the waiting room where her doctor would report to me. How long would I be there? No one seemed interested in giving me an estimate. Maybe it was a futile question. I found a New Yorker and set myself the task of reading it from cover to cover, ads and all. I tried to suppress anxieties about a whole smorgasbord of things that could go wrong. Three or four other prospective fathers sat and stared, read, or paced. We acknowledged each other, but obeyed an unspoken rule to leave each other alone.

Windows on one side of the waiting room began to show first daylight when a young doctor came in and asked the room for Ken Bailey. I dropped the magazine onto the floor and rushed toward him.

He grinned. "Your first child, I presume."

"How's my wife?"

"She's fine. Her labor was uncomplicated. The baby boy is fine. In an hour or so, we'll move her into recovery. You can see her then."

"There's a delay. Why?" I asked with some intensity.

He looked at me with labored patience. "We need to wait just a bit to check some bleeding and be sure she's recovering."

"Bleeding?" I remembered my premonition in the parking lot.

The doctor seemed to morph into a fellow human. He put his hand on my shoulder. "Really, she's fine. These are normal precautions."

I returned to the delivery waiting room. Time passed. My anxiety grew. After over an hour, I approached the desk. The volunteer covering the desk knew nothing. Two hours later, I got the same response.

"Where can I find out more?"

"There's a desk inside the entrance to the recovery room."

At that desk, a stern-faced nurse stopped me. I explained I wanted to know what was going on with my wife, Victoria Bailey. The nurse phoned someone in the recovery room. "You can find out yourself. Just don't stay too long."

The recovery room held ten beds, an intimidating beehive of nurses, orderlies, monitors, and electric cords.

I easily spotted Victoria. She was pale. As soon as she saw me, she smiled. Then she looked away. I guess she felt victorious in a lot of different ways. Suddenly, I felt excluded. I didn't begrudge her the victory. In fact, I was glad our struggle about whether to have children was finally over.

As I approached her bed, I asked a nurse if there was a problem.

"Her blood pressure is a little low. We're holding her here until we get it within a normal range."

"Will she be okay?" To my surprise, a catch caught in my throat.

The nurse, a young blond, smiled at my distress. "She'll be fine. She may need a transfusion. It's fairly common."

I sat beside Victoria's bed and tried to stay out of the way.

"Have you seen our baby yet?" she asked.

I shook my head. "The doctor said it was a boy." It never occurred to me to want to see the baby. I guess that was not normal.

"Does that make you happy, it being a boy?" Victoria wanted me to be pleased along with her, but I wasn't elated.

"Yeah, I guess a boy is better than a girl."

She clouded up, almost on the verge of tears.

"Yes, of course, I'm glad for a son. Carry on the family name."

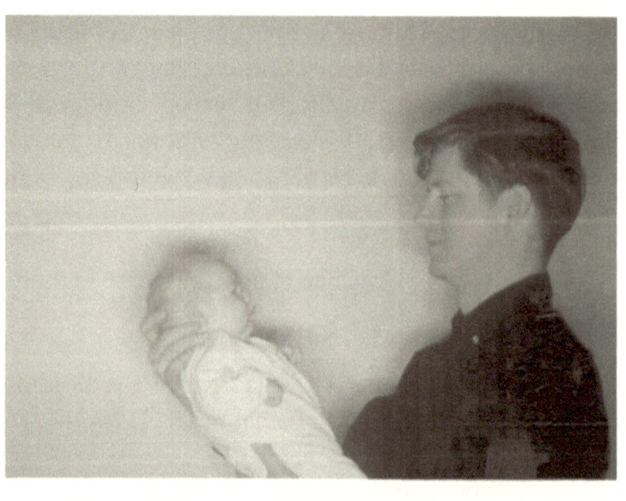

Three days later, I took Victoria home to our apartment. She was tired, but happy. We agreed that raising one kid by himself was not a good idea.

Spring semester, she'd go into school for one course, taking the baby in a carrier or leaving him with me. Now that she'd committed, she was very determined to get a Ph.D.

For the first few months, I was afraid to pick up the baby. I'm not sure why. Afraid I'd drop him. Afraid I'd hold him wrong and snap his neck. I never changed a diaper. Victoria was remarkably tolerant about my hang-ups. She was that glad to have one child and maybe to anticipate another one.

The second year of coaching debate was pretty much a repeat of the first. At the end of many major tournaments, coaches would party with booze and snacks. These began to get tedious for me. I missed Victoria on those weekends. I did not miss Mark, our firstborn—unnatural, I knew, but that's the way it was.

I had only my dissertation to do, but I couldn't get it done in two years. I did lots of research on a topic that at the time seemed esoteric: an application of rhetorical theory to the use of motion pictures to persuade.

Dr. Wichelns hauled me up short after I started writing on the topic. "Your readers will need to know what you mean by rhetorical theory." Readers? Does anyone actually read these things? I did have visions of plowing new and significant ground, so someone might read it.

Over a period of several months, I boiled persuasion from classical sources and modern empirical research down to a tidy one hundred and forty pages. Wichelns read it closely for possible improvements. One evening, about ten o'clock, I was dutifully acting on his comments, when a telephone call came from him.

"How are the revisions going, Ken?"

"Fine, I think. I should have a revised draft in a week or so." I felt guilty that I didn't have the revision done, but then I felt guilty most of the time.

"I think you should move on to your next chapter. You won't need that chapter on persuasion theory after all." What the bloody hell!

It gives an idea of the esteem I, like most other students in the program, had for Wichelns, that I didn't object or complain, at least not to him. Victoria would talk me down from a rage fueled by frustration, not particularly aimed at Wichelns.

He continued, "Perhaps you can write up that chapter as an efficient handbook on persuasion." He was aware he'd frustrated me, as I was aware he wouldn't okay a thesis until he thought it was "right." (A fellow student had a contract from a major publisher for his thesis . . . as soon as Wichelns passed it. Wichelns kept requiring more revision until the student came close to flipping out.)

Other members of my committee said they thought the dissertation did need a brief chapter on the persuasion theory I was applying. I boiled the hundred and forty pages down to forty. I never acted on Wichelns's suggestion to try to publish the chapter as a separate book—one of a host of opportunities I blew off.

A reckoning came midway through my second year of coaching. As with other crunch points in my career, I sat in front of professor Wichelns's desk with him behind it. I glanced out the window, scarcely noticing snow falling through feeble daylight.

"Ken, is this your sixth year at Cornell?"

"Yes."

"Your dissertation work moves slowly." He smiled. "Hardly unusual for my students."

"Yeah, you're right. I can't seem to turn it out."

"Are you distracted— new family, attractive wife, successful debate program?"

Temptation to fix the blame on someone or something else flitted through my mind. "No, sir, it's none of those things. Victoria does a lot of typing and retyping for me. I just can't seem to get into each day's work."

"Perhaps you feel compelled to line up everything for a job rather than just leaping into it. If I asked you to clean my office, for example you might first clean the office next door to be sure no dust would blow in after you cleaned mine. Think there's anything to that?"

I knew damn well there was a lot to Wichelns's point. Why had I built up hundreds of pages of research notes to cover myself on persuasion theory before I began to write a chapter that itself was only peripheral support for the main body of the dissertation. It stemmed, I was sure, from some basic insecurity, some defect that compelled me to cover every angle and to double-check before I hit a project head-on. That defect made me hugely inefficient.

The professor waited for a reply.

I nodded. "There's some truth to that, I suppose, but I don't know what to do about it." I didn't add that past frustration with my slowness had made me depressed enough to consider suicide.

"You have no idea where to begin to change?"

God, I wished I did. It seemed it would be cheating to seek a psychiatrist and take pills, and it probably wouldn't help anyway.

I shrugged. "Not really. I just try to keep it together and moving ahead."

Wichelns smiled. "You're bright and conscientious." He nodded, apparently in response to some internal idea. "Moving ahead, eh? I think we have a next step for you." He paused. "It's time for you to leave the nest and get a regular job. You want to teach, is that right?"

"Yes, sir, at the college level." Without a degree beyond a B.A. Dream on!

He reached into his desk and came out holding a folder with some thirty sheets. "These are jobs available in Rhetoric and Public Address. Pick out four or five and request application materials. Register with our placement center. We'll see that you have letters in your support." He paused. "Ken, get on this . . . now. We're already starting late."

We didn't discuss my options if no university wanted an instructor in Rhetoric with only an undistinguished B.A. in Political Science.

That evening, Victoria and I selected six schools from the job listings. With her kibitzing, I filled out forms. The prospect of moving excited her; me, not so much. Six application packets went out two days later.

True to his word, Wichelns had several of the big guns at Cornell send out letters, which I never saw. The letters must have been good. Within three weeks, I got five interviews. The interviews ranged from straightforward to weirdly oblique. One dean, at a snobbish small liberal arts college, seemed mostly interested in how I'd related to my father—not a promising line of inquiry for me.

Eventually, I got three offers, but not one from the small arts college. I guess my view of my father didn't pass muster! That was fine. The little school was too precious for my taste.

I signed a contract at Rio Grande University in El Paso, Texas. Two of the Speech faculty there were Cornell graduates, so Victoria and I felt we already had some connection.

I intended in a few months to leave behind frustration, inefficiency, depression, and a whole load of other baggage. Amazing how hope springs eternal.

CHAPTER TWENTY-FOUR

Though El Paso is high desert, we drove in during an afternoon downpour that dumped three inches of rain in a few hours. Streets ran like rivers, cars flooded out, and some lower-level homes had several inches of water on ground floors. I kept our car going until we reached the home of a young faculty member from Cornell who, with his family, had offered to take us in while we looked for a place to rent or buy.

After breakfast, Victoria and I left Mark with our host family and started looking at houses. El Paso was a buyers' market. We found one tidy three-bedroom house that seemed almost ideal. As with most houses in this part of town, the backyard was defined by rock walls. The owner gave us a choice: we could buy it, mainly by taking over his mortgage, or he would rent to us. Victoria said it was an obvious choice: buy. But I was reluctant. If my job didn't go well and housing prices tanked in a year or two, we'd have a serious problem. We didn't even have the few hundred dollars to complete the transaction. Victoria said we could borrow it from her father. I knew this was true, and I wasn't really much concerned with the house losing value.

The plain fact of it: I was scared to take on this much responsibility. What if I ended up tied irretrievably to a family and career I might not be willing or even able to handle. Would I in desperation cut and run and leave Victoria holding the bag. I tried to explain this risk to Victoria. She started crying. She refused to consider the possibility I would fall apart and leave her with a child and a big debt. She needed all the optimism she could muster, and I was a jerk for heaping my anxieties on her. I resolved to keep my misgivings about my mental shakiness to myself—if I could manage to keep my mouth shut. But I still was anxious.

On the issue of buying the house, through arguments and stubbornness, I prevailed—unfortunately. We rented the house, and in a few years paid the owner several times over what it would have cost us to buy his mortgage. Victoria was kind enough not to rub in my bad financial decision, very often.

I knew I was cautious to an irrational extreme in money and time commitments, but I figured so long as I stayed clear of paralyzing depression I could manage. Colleagues would from time to time asked me to give a paper at a regional conference or take on some minor administrative chore. Usually, I'd refuse. They may have been irritated by my refusal, but they didn't see my caution as a sign of serious mental distress, so I successfully concealed my tendencies toward clinical depression, except from Victoria.

I was cornered into organizing the freshman speech faculty and designing a uniform basic syllabus the instructors could, at least nominally, agree on. Bringing the faculty together on a plan for the basic course was like trying to herd cats, and it went on for over a year. But I persisted and we did create a better course that teaching assistants, for example, could use.

Success in course design produced enough confidence for me to begin giving papers at local and regional conferences. I based some papers on ridiculously extensive research, and some were controversial enough to excite audiences but, unless a program director asked me, I rarely followed through on the next step of submitting them to journals. My reluctance to make any effort to publish seemed like a commitment to failure.

Lack of confidence, or maybe laziness, caused me to procrastinate on producing course syllabuses. In a grad course, I apologized rather abjectly for not producing a syllabus by halfway through the term. One of the students remarked impatiently, "Dr. Bailey, you're the only person worried about not having a syllabus for this course." That remark should have reduced my guilt, but it just confused me.

Near the end of our second year at Rio Grande University, Mom came to visit us. I was alone when I met her at the airport. This made sense because my wife had to stay home with Mark, but Victoria also was wary of her mother-in-law, though I didn't understand why. Mom and I waited in the small airport for her bag.

"How are you coming with your dissertation?" We'd met less than three minutes earlier.

"It's coming along okay." This wasn't completely true. Except in the summer, I made almost no progress— another rich source of guilt and anxiety. "How was your flight?"

Mom didn't bother to answer my question. "Is Victoria helping you . . . or is she using up too much of your time?"

"Using too much of my time?"

"With housework or her social life."

"Mom, she's very supportive. We don't have much social life, with her taking care of Mark and finishing up her Ph.D. program. Besides, she may be pregnant."

I knew better than to expect Mom to be excited about another grandchild, but I thought she might at least acknowledge it. Her response: "She's completing her Ph.D.?"

"She still has her dissertation to finish."

"And what about you? I warned you she's ambitious. If you let her get ahead of you, you'll never catch up." I dropped the subject.

We showed her the campus and the country around El Paso. Victoria was perfect as a host, and appeared even to like Mom, and Mom was civil, so her three-day visit went more smoothly than I might have expected. Mom did not say when she'd be back, if ever.

As soon as Mom was gone, Victoria went on the attack: What kind of person would ignore her own grandchildren. Was it because she disliked Victoria that she was so cold toward our children, present and future?

"No," I explained, "Mom had a badly messed-up childhood. It's hard for her to feel normal emotions."

"Sort of like your childhood?" Victoria responded. "That's a copout."

I was caught in a crossfire between Mom and Victoria. This was just too damn stupid! I decided to pull back and ignore the whole conflict. This was not the response Victoria wanted.

Mom had made it clear that in her view, I didn't measure up. I'd pretty much come to the same evaluation. At times, my mixture of anxiety and guilt over being so desperately ineffectual in my career overwhelmed me. I wanted to escape the pain. If suicide wasn't an attractive option, I could just go numb. I'd sit frozen in one position for hours at a time, not turning my head or moving fingers. I'd think, "I can always move if I want to." But I never tested that belief until the catatonic-like state lifted, usually in reaction to a question from "outside" or other external stimulus.

I regarded these frozen states as more or less normal defenses to protect a hypersensitive mind. They alarmed Victoria. She saw them as signs of acute depression or some other anomaly. Hard to argue with that! My Colt .22 disappeared again--which was both smart and a sign of a concerned wife. She urged me to seek psychiatric help. I ignored her pleas: I didn't need a shrink to tell me what was wrong with me and what I could do about it; I just needed willpower, and I didn't see how a shrink could provide that.

One thing, I discovered, did distract me from the pain and perhaps develop a little confidence. My father provided a model for my solution. It began at an end of term party in late spring. Victoria's pregnancy caused her to decide against attending, but she urged me to go. A graduate student showed more than a little interest in me. I did go, vaguely aware I was looking for a diversion and ego boost.

CHAPTER TWENTY-FIVE

What would I say to Victoria if she asked me about my early departure from the party. I needn't have worried. When I walked into the living room, I found Victoria cheerfully awaiting my report.

"The party was kind of dull. Not much gossip."

"Probably just as well I didn't go."

"Yeah, probably so."

I began to fear discovery more for the pain and damage it would cause Victoria than for my own sake. I was sure she could take a lot of ill treatment and disappointment and still keep going toward goals she had set for herself. She was probably stronger than I was. But some behaviors would in her view be way out of bounds. She came from a conventional family—husband as stable provider, wife, and children for wife to be concerned about. Spousal infidelity would hit her hard. For me, infidelity, at least by a husband, was normal.

My distress at causing Victoria pain came as a surprise. I had developed a habit of regarding other people as incapable of feeling much mental pain. That's why I could decide it was too inconvenient to go to my dying father, and I could discard Marian Mason without a backward glance.

Passage of time eroded my shield of obtuse arrogance. My cruel treatment of my father and Mason began to haunt me. Guilt slipped in around the edges. I didn't want to add

Victoria to a list of cruelly wrong decisions I would someday regret.

I was thrust back into an old, familiar conflict: wanting to achieve practical, if unimaginative, success to please my mother or live the freer life of my father. I was not inclined to take either parent as a model. My mother's plan oppressed me; my father as my model would fritter away any talents I might have.

There was a further obstacle to using either one as a model. Mom had convinced me Dad suffered from syphilis. My aunts convinced me that Mom, as a result of being assaulted as a child and left dangling helplessly over a deep gorge, was frigid. It was hard to wholeheartedly want to follow in the footsteps of either parent!

Lack of progress on my dissertation depressed me, which made progress even less likely. I was spiraling downward.

Victoria saw enough signs of my distress to guess I was in real trouble. She suggested I see a psychiatrist, and soon.

I told her, "No, it's just a low point. I don't think a shrink would help at all. Besides, I wouldn't know where to start looking for one."

"I'd know." But she backed off on trying to bully me into going to a psychiatrist.

CHAPTER TWENTY-SIX

One chilly, overcast morning in November, I forced myself upright in bed and struggled to get one leg of my pants on. I sat on the edge of the mattress staring at the other pant leg. With focused will I got the other leg into my pants. To keep from throwing up, I'd limit breakfast to dry toast and tea. Was I sick? Not exactly.

I had to avoid sinking into a catatonic fit because a class awaited at nine o'clock. I had promised the students I'd return a set of papers they needed to revise as part of the next step in an assignment. The papers lay unmarked on my desk.

With robotic deliberation of each movement, I got into my car, made it to a parking spot on campus, and started across the quad. Students looked different, more like creatures I observed from a different reality. When I arrived, the students filed in and waited. I could stand up and talk, but with no sure control over what would come out of my mouth. I needed to hold it together for only a few minutes more.

I cleared my throat. "I do not have your papers marked. You may take a walk today. I'll see you Thursday." It took a couple of minutes for what I'd said to sink in. Ninety percent of the students would be happy to take a walk, but some seemed disturbed, confused by my radical departure from my own rigid adherence to the rules.

As they exited, I noticed one student turn back toward the front of the classroom. A classmate grabbed his elbow and said something to him. Together, they left the room. How disheveled did I look?

Somehow, I got to my car and home. Victoria would be gone for hours. I flopped in an easy chair and stared at a wall until she came in the door. She glanced at me, then turned back for a good look.

"I need a psychiatrist," I said flatly.

Urgent concern clouded over her face.

Without discussion, Victoria got on the telephone.

An hour later, she announced in two days hence I had an appointment with a Dr. Jones. "He comes with a good reputation and a waiting list. We were lucky he had a cancellation." I didn't ask how she got me to the top of his waiting list. She can be very persuasive when something really important to her is at stake.

Jones's office was modest, and there was no couch. We sat facing each other across a small desk. He was tall and slender, rimless glasses, mid-forties.

After we introduced ourselves, he came to the point. "Why are you seeking counseling?"

"I'm badly blocked finishing a thesis for a Ph.D."

"Hardly a rare problem."

This guy is apparently not in the business of holding insecure grad students' hands.

"There's a little more to it than that." I told him about last Tuesday.

"Do you experience dissociation or panic often?"

I told him about my self-induced catatonic spells. "Would they qualify?"

He shook his head. "I'm not sure what you mean by self-induced." I wasn't sure either, but I decided not to admit that or try to describe more fully what went on in my head.

"Are you depressed very often?" he asked.

"Yeah, I guess so."

"Do you have suicidal impulses?"

"I suppose they cross my mind."

"How often and how strong? Do you fear doing harm to yourself?"

"I don't think a person knows how close they are to suicide until they do it."

Jones nodded, "And then it's often too late. Right?" He smiled. Cute! Is Jones denigrating my angst, or trying to think along with me? Is there a chance in hell he can help me? Probably not, but he may be the only chance I've got.

I decided to play it straight until I knew more. "My problem is lack of productivity, and I don't know why. Do you think you can help me?"

Dr. Jones thought about that for a minute. "Do you want to be helped?"

I wasn't sure. I didn't want to muddy the waters by trying to figure that out now. "Yes, I want help." That was a simple—and perhaps honest—answer.

"Okay, we'll spend a session or two on background. Then dig down to your deeper problems."

"How long is all this going to take?"

"Maybe two months, once or twice a week. We'll know by the end of that time if I can do you any good."

"Sounds okay."

"Your wife made this appointment for you. Does she manage most of your affairs?"

"No."

"Do you own your home?"

"Yes. Us and the bank."

"Who decided that?"

Was that just a lucky shot? Or did Jones have uncanny insight?

"My wife insisted on it a couple of years ago. I was opposed to getting tied down to a house, but it's worked out okay. The lot backs onto the desert, where I can hike and look for rocks. That helps keep me sane, or close to it."

Jones prescribed an anti-depressant, "just for a few weeks while we get you adjusted. You won't get hooked on pills." Was that a prediction or an order?

We agreed to meet one week hence, and I departed.

My black pessimism faded. Help was at hand. I actually got a little work done on my thesis in the following three or four days.

Then the letter came.

CHAPTER TWENTY-SEVEN

I stared at the return address, "Planning and Zoning Board / City of El Paso." I didn't want to face a threat of major disruption in my life. I couldn't deal with it. But I might be panicking for no reason—my typical pessimism screwing up my thinking. So, with a glimmer of hope, I slit the envelope open.

The message was straightforward. The Board would hold hearings on an application to rezone a parcel of some thirty acres in our neighborhood. Interested parties were invited to appear in City Council chambers March 16 at 10AM. I studied the small map showing the location of the parcel. There could be no mistake. The parcel began right on the other side of our rock-wall fence.

I'd spent ten minutes on a single piece of mail. Victoria asked, "What is it, Ken? Is it bad news?" I must have looked stricken.

"Yes, it's very bad." I paused. "The land right across our fence is up for rezoning."

"Why is that so bad? How can that affect us?"

"If it's rezoned for industrial, we could have a meat-packing plant in our backyard, or a sewage-treatment plant, or maybe an auto-wrecking yard, any damn thing."

"We'd move," she suggested.

Was she naïve, or just trying to make me less anxious. Maybe she knew I was beating myself up over making the decision to buy this place, and she didn't want me to take it out on her.

"Our house would be worth less than we owe on it, probably a lot less, and we'd have to find someone to buy it. I don't know how we could recover from the financial hit. So, we'd be trapped here. That's why I didn't want to buy this house, or any other damn house."

I'd just triggered an emotional argument we'd gone through for years, and it almost split our marriage. Victoria would without doubt come out fighting, accusing me of exaggerating the threat to our finances to put her in the wrong.

But she didn't. She asked quietly, "What can we do?"

"We can oppose the application to rezone," I said.

"Do you know how to do that?"

"Not really. But I can learn."

The next day, I went to the Planning Board's offices. I stood at a counter and watched four men and women in glass-walled cubicles working at computers and drafting tables. A young fellow in shirtsleeves noticed me from his cubicle and came over to the counter. "What can I do for you?"

I showed him the notice we'd received. "What is this about?"

"That parcel of land is up for rezoning from single-family residential to industrial/commercial. All homeowners within six hundred feet of the parcel get a chance to speak their piece."

"Who decides whether it's rezoned?"

He looked at me as if he wondered what planet I came from. "Our staff in Planning reviews the application submitted by the landowner. We send the application with our recommendation and any additional reservations we have to the Planning and Zoning Board. The Board holds a hearing at which the applicant presents his case. Other interested parties respond in support of or opposition to the application. The Board then sends its recommendation on to the City Council, who decide how it will be.

"Do any of these applications ever get turned down?"

The clerk enjoyed being the expert. He also heard the anxiety in my voice and seemed a bit sympathetic.

"It happens, but not often. Most applications are thought through pretty well before they reach the City Council."

"Who's on the Planning Board. How do they get selected?"

He hesitated, maybe deciding how much he wanted to tell me. "Mostly developers. Usually a few other citizens."

"Isn't that kind of cozy, developers deciding on their colleagues' applications?"

"Yeah. But being on the Board takes a good deal of time for two years, so a member has to care enough to make that commitment. He or she should also know something about land values and possible uses."

"I guess you have a lot of power." I didn't know how much power this guy had, but I figured it couldn't hurt to give him a few strokes.

He nodded in agreement.

"What suggestions would you have for homeowners fighting this particular application?"

He shook his head. "We're not allowed to make those sorts of comments." He could read frustration in my face. He had more to add. "The homeowners usually lose because they don't know what they're doing, or they hire a lawyer friend who doesn't know any more than they do. There is one citizen who's come before the Board and won more than once."

I waited expectantly for several seconds.

The clerk shrugged, as if to say, oh well, what the hell? "His name is Charles Fox. He lives up the valley a couple of miles from you."

I thanked the clerk.

Two hours later, I sat in a leather easy chair, with Fox in a matching chair half-facing me. He was tall and lean, a generation older than me, and totally relaxed. His home study quietly suggested wealth, with mementos from all over the world.

I briefly explained what rezoning next door could do to me financially.

Fox nodded and smiled encouragingly. "This rezoning may not lead to a slaughterhouse in your back yard." He paused. "I do agree it's better to nip the possibility in the bud, . . . if you can. You should realize some developers are responsible good citizens, not all are liars or slimy bastards."

"A fellow in the Planning office said you'd beaten the developers more than once. How did you do it?"

"I wish they'd stop telling people that. Folks like you come to me wanting to know the secret formula." He paused. "There is no secret formula. To win a zoning case takes a lot of time, energy, and, sometimes, courage. More effort than many homeowners want to expend."

He waited for me to reply. What does he expect. That I'll say, in that case, I'm not really interested. I said, "I'm ready to put a lot of effort into it, and I think several of my neighbors will feel the same way."

He nodded. "You use a three-pronged attack on the applicant, firm but courteous. The first prong is to get as many signatures in the neighborhood as you can on petitions opposing the application. Second is to get as many bodies as you can to the hearing. Third, line up a team of presenters. They must be efficient; you'll probably have at most twenty minutes for your total presentation. Of these, the second prong is often the most important."

"More important than presenting good arguments?"

"Yes. Presence there shows sincere concern, and bodies vote in local elections."

When Fox saw I was taking notes, he nodded with approval.

"One other thing. Sometimes these zoning deals don't stand the light of day. Get local media at the hearings. They'll usually cover a good fight, if they see it coming."

"Anything else?" I asked.

Fox said, "I assume you're the one trying to organize this."

I nodded. "I guess so."

"Okay. Be prepared for a lot of 'can't beat city hall' and 'let someone who's better do it' copouts." He smiled. "Look for the able and willing. The best you can hope for with many of your neighbors is to get them to the hearing."

I thanked Fox profusely. He wished me luck. "I'll follow your case with interest."

Over dinner I told Victoria what I'd learned. "Tomorrow, we start to mobilize."

"This is going to take a lot of time, isn't it. Away from your dissertation." She's right! I try not to think about that.

The next day I had a meeting with neighbors, one of many we'd hold over the next six weeks. They'd received the same notice I had. Anxious about the future, they were glad to have leadership in an attempt to control rezoning. Over thirty people crowded into our living room. We pulled in every chair or other seat we could find in the house.

We began by tossing out ideas for arguments to be used against the application: heavier traffic on local streets, congestion and noise, crime, overtaxed schools and parks. Our central point was that we have a good quality of life, and a mass of commercial and industrial development next door would wreck it. We see no reason why we should make that sacrifice so a land speculator can turn a profit.

Now we needed to pick people to present these arguments. Fox had warned me not to take just anyone who volunteered. I could end up with a bunch of people just venting anger and fear. We needed a disciplined panel of speakers who could rationally address issues. I steered the group toward two members. Nick Martinez owned a large trucking company; he understood traffic. Sam Brown had lived with his family in the same house more than a generation, and he could not afford to move no matter how bad congestion and crime became. After I promised to help write their speeches and put them through rehearsal, both said yes. A local teacher and Victoria rounded out our panel.

Victoria and the teacher also agreed to organize teams to take petitions to every house in the area. We created a handout stating when and where the hearing would take place and what was at stake.

It took three meetings to get us to the point where we felt organized. We expected everything to go with mechanical perfection from there. It didn't. One problem was people who wanted to participate and express their personal opinions of developers and the damage they cause. These contributions would muddy our central line of attack and eat up our allotted time. I got the delicate task of blocking these people from speaking while still keeping their emotional commitment to the cause.

The two exceptions I allowed to our tight control were Mrs. Muldoon, mother of nine, and our precocious ten-year-old son who had written his own petition stating opposition to the application in simple terms. She read Mark's petition that asserted outside noise would make it hard for children to study or sleep and greater density of cars in the neighborhood would make playing outside dangerous. Mark got over three hundred kids to sign the petition.

With our preparation apparently on track, I took time to keep my fourth appointment with Dr. Jones. I expected he would criticize involvement in this zoning battle as my way to avoid working on my thesis. He didn't criticize; he nodded and said, "I see."

He did ask, "Was this an easy decision for you, to put your time on saving the neighborhood instead of working on your degree?"

"No. And it's still a painful conflict."

"So you elect to go the way your father, and not your mother, would go?"

"I didn't think of it in those terms."

"I do think of it that way," Jones said.

He smiled in his pleasant way. "It's time for you to face your relationship with your father. Your mother told you he had syphilis. Did you ever get confirmation of that, perhaps from your aunts?"

"They sent me some of his papers. They also sent a billfold they claimed contained a letter proving he never had the disease. That was four years ago, shortly after he died."

"What did the letter say?" Jones asked.

"I've never looked at it."

That stopped even Jones for several seconds. "Very interesting," he said finally.

"Why is that interesting?"

"If that letter says he had VD, that would be hard for you to take, but the alternative for you would be worse."

It would be worse news to discover Dad never had VD! What the hell is Jones thinking? I waited for him to continue.

"If he didn't have VD, your mother lied to you. But perhaps more important, if your father's mental difficulties were not due to disease, then they were the outcome of genetic tendencies, genes you would likely inherit."

Oh shit! "I see, so I'd rather not know either way, right?" I said.

"Right. But it's important you do know, if your therapy is to be successful."

"I'll check into the billfold as soon as I have time."

Jones eyed me for several seconds. "How much time will it take to open a billfold?"

"I'll get on it as soon as I get home. Meanwhile, I've a zoning battle to fight."

★ 310 ★

CHAPTER TWENTY-EIGHT

The City Council auditorium was nearly full; I'd estimate well over a hundred people. I hoped most were on our side. We filed in. Our four speakers sat near the front of the auditorium, at a long table facing the Board. Mrs. Muldoon was planted in the audience. Across the aisle, another long table awaited the applicant's team who would also face the Planning Board. That Board would sit on a slightly raised platform facing into the auditorium. The elegant wood paneling and solid furniture added dignity.

I was more nervous than I'd ever been in a debate. Now more was at stake. I glanced at our speakers. Martinez grinned back. Brown looked calm. Victoria and the teacher looked intense. I smiled hoping to relax them, but I don't think it helped.

The Board members straggled in and took seats at their raised table, smiling and speaking quietly to each other. The Board chairman, Joe Barton, seemed impressed with his importance. An officious solemnity seemed to pervade the room, despite quick smiles and a buzz of discreet conversations.

The applicant and his crew were next to arrive. When crossing over to their table, a couple of them exchanged pleasantries with Barton. Now isn't that damn sweet! I glanced over at Martinez. He shrugged fatalistically, but I had no doubt he intended to go down fighting. My speakers appeared closer to unflappable than I was.

I noticed two of the Board members remained aloof from the convivial exchanges of returning colleagues and applicants. Maybe we could hope for a split decision. It would be up to Barton if that happened. He seemed cozier with the applicant than anyone else on the Board.

Planning staff described the application, using a large map on a tripod. I saw for the first time that a major street would cut through our neighborhood to give access to the parcel. Did Martinez pick up on that?

Assuming some minor adjustments for drainage and noise abatement, the Planning staff raised no objections to the application. In effect, they'd recommended acceptance.

The applicant, Raf Melandino, said, "I'm happy to spend money on this project because it will bring more economic activity into this neighborhood." Yeah, for people who want minimum pay jobs in fast food joints or clerking in chain department stores. He smiled like he was giving us a blessing and nodded to one of the lawyers with him. "Mr. Hammond will provide more detail."

The lawyer was not new to zoning cases. He added some implausibly optimistic projections of added jobs. Some on the Board were nodding encouragement. This looked bad.

Hammond took up the noise abatement issue. On a large map of the parcel and surrounding neighborhood, he showed where sound baffles would be placed. "This will be a gain for the citizens by making present streets quieter than they are now."

A couple of Board members were practically cheering, while Barton beamed his approval. This was too much to let slide. I stood up. Barton glanced at me and, with labored patience for this rube, said, "In a few minutes you will have your opportunity for arguments. Until then. . . ."

I interrupted, "I'm not presenting an argument. I'm merely asking for clarification of one of Mr. Hammond's points."

Barton seemed unsure.

I pressed more aggressively. "I assume Mr. Hammond wants to get his points across."

Barton said, "Okay, ask your question." He put the emphasis on question.

"Mr. Hammond, please give an estimate of the total cost of these baffles, for what I'd guess at least three total miles on neighborhood streets. These should be effective sound baffles, not just wooden fences."

Hammond apparently was caught flat-footed, clueless about a price tag they never intended to pay. He turned to one of the engineers on the applicant's team. "Do you have a rough estimate of the cost?"

The engineer shook his head.

Hammond said, "Well, it can't be very much, can it?"

The engineer said, "Three miles? Actually, it could be a substantial cost."

I thanked the engineer and sat.

Barton took over the hearing and rushed through a few positives for the homeowners. He seemed to have some misgivings when he asked if there were anyone wishing to speak in opposition to the application. He realized he was facing a whole roomful of angry opposition, which it would be impolitic to ignore. I guess he hoped to defuse the anger by allowing a few incoherent speakers to argue against the application.

Martinez rose to his feet. In six minutes, using the planning staff's projected figures, he presented a depressing estimate of increased traffic and congestion. He yielded to Brown, who described with dignity and passion his hopes for a secure neighborhood in which to retire. He ended by asking, "Mr. Hammond, can you assure us that crime and violence would not overtake our community?"

"You have police protection now, Mr. Brown. It wouldn't be hard to expand that to meet any needs to maintain your safety and security."

Nice quick answer, Hammond, and you've fallen into a neat trap.

Brown nodded in agreement. "Expanded police protection costs money, paid for by our taxes. So, Mr. Hammond, it appears your proposal would increase our property tax bill while reducing the resale value of our homes. This does not seem to me like a good deal for homeowners. Does it seem to you like a fair deal for us?" Then Brown waited expectantly for Hammond's answer. If Hammond agreed with Brown, he would admit an added economic cost to the homeowners; if he disagreed, he'd be inconsistent with what he'd already said, that is to say he'd be lying. He chose to ignore the question.

Next up was the retired teacher who gave the argument that the change in zoning would open the way for apartment buildings rather than single-family dwellings. Strains on the school system and parks would result. To give the argument bite, she'd tracked down a couple of articles that described how increased population density created lower graduation rates and more urban gangs. Hammond ignored her arguments.

At the applicant's table Melandino looked to Barton to pull this one out of the fire. Hammond wasn't earning his money—but he probably wasn't being paid as much as Barton.

We had only a few minutes left to finish presenting our side of the case. Barton looked to me to make a summation. No reason to meet his expectations.

"I would like the board to hear from one of the citizens who would be impacted by the proposed rezoning. Mrs. Muldoon, please."

She stood up in the audience, holding a sheaf of papers. She was a mother and looked the part, neither glamorous nor frumpy, but confident and straightforward. "We should hear from the young people, who have so much at stake. I have nine children." Instant credibility!

"The children wrote and circulated their own petition. The petition is signed by over three hundred of our youth. It's simple and short. I'd like to read it."

One engineer at the applicant's table smiled. He was amused. The other engineer, the one who'd come up short on the cost of baffles, slumped in his chair, head down in his hands. Barton looked nervously at the reporter in the back of the auditorium.

Mrs. Muldoon didn't wait for Barton's permission to read. "We, the undersigned, oppose this application. More stores and cars and trucks increase traffic on the streets where we walk to school and to friends' homes. Noise will keep us from concentrating on schoolwork and from

sleeping. We gain nothing by rezoning, and we lose a lot."
She sat down as applause swept through the chamber.

Barton huddled with two Board members at the
Council table. The other two Board members seemed
ostentatiously to stay on the margin of the huddle. I
glanced back to see the reporter waiting with pencil poised.
When I looked again to the Board, Barton was watching
the reporter. When he saw me, he returned his attention
to the huddle.

Five minutes later, Barton was ready to announce the
Board's decision. A wave of tense silence swept across the
room.

CHAPTER TWENTY-NINE

Barton cleared his throat. The attention of the entire audience focused on him. He said, "My fellow Board members and I have carefully considered this application. We have a responsibility to consider all requests for changes in zoning to encourage growth in this city."

Yes. Quit covering your ass and get to the point.

"We also must consider the welfare of our citizens, their quality of life. Weighing these considerations, the Board recommends rejection of the application."

It took a few seconds for Barton's words to sink in. Then the auditorium erupted in applause and cheers. The two Board members who had conferred with Barton looked at the applicant's table. They did not share Barton's expansive smile. In fact, they looked decidedly uncomfortable. It occurred to me that if Melandino had spread serious money around the Board, he was going to be very, very angry.

Most of the audience stood and started moving around. They congregated in small groups, savoring victory. I stayed with Joe Martinez and Brown near our table. Martinez said, "We did it, thanks to you, Ken."

"No thanks to me. You guys did this. And you can do it again if need arises." I was already thinking, if we get another rezoning threat, how I could cop out. I'd spent way too much time on this case.

The teacher wandered over toward us. I spotted Victoria near a cluster of people. As I moved over toward her, I passed the teacher and said, "Very nice job." She smiled.

I also wanted to hand out praise to Mrs. Muldoon, but she'd disappeared, presumably to get home and on her job as mother of nine.

Barton and Melandino were off to one side, having what looked like a heated discussion. Victoria stood near them, trying to look casual. Barton noticed her. He silenced Melandino, and the two men then moved off in different directions.

I ambled over to Victoria. She had a broad smile. I said, "You're happy with our victory, I see."

"Yes, but that's not why I'm smiling. Melandino was really reaming Barton out. It appears they had a deal, and the applicant believed he'd been double-crossed. Barton was trying to explain the press was in the audience and he'd lose all credibility in future cases if he made an obviously biased decision."

I said, "I guess we had a strong enough case. And thank god, that reporter made himself known in the audience."

The crowd was thinning out. Victoria and I headed home.

Shortly after we walked in the door, the phone rang.

Charles Fox called to congratulate us. He added, "You know, of course, this probably isn't the end of it. Six or eight months from now, I'd guess, maybe longer, they'll be back. Melandino and Barton weren't prepared for serious opposition. They will be next time. The Children's Petition was inspired, but it's probably good for only one shot, and you've used it. Hammond filled a slot as lawyer, but there are really skillful lawyers for zoning applicants. He's not one of them. Melandino will have a pro next time."

I thanked Fox for calling and especially for the excellent advice he'd provided a few weeks earlier. "But we thought, once a decision is made, that's it. You seem pretty pessimistic."

"No, I'm a realist. That's prime land for commercial development. So you, at best, prepare for the next round."

I hung up the phone and told Victoria what Fox said. "So, I guess the fight isn't over, after all."

"You must be terribly disappointed," she said. She paused and seemed to deliberately avoid my eyes. "You face a tough decision, don't you?"

"I do." Silence for half a minute. "What do you think I should do?"

"I can't make that decision for you."

The conflict between two duties—to my neighbors, versus to myself and Victoria—churned in my stomach. A final deadline was coming up for me to finish my Ph.D. I hated to see ruthless developers get away with rezoning, but I also hated to see my career go down the toilet. I felt close to throwing up.

I couldn't quite define what, but something more basic than whether or not to lead a zoning battle was wrapped up in my choice, and it went way beyond how the land across the fence would be zoned or even whether I'd have a Ph.D. degree or not.

Maybe a compromise was possible. I could advise without getting committed to a drain on my time. I called a meeting of Martinez and Brown and a couple of other veterans of the last battle.

Cheerful in victory, they assembled in my living room. I relayed Fox's warning.

"Damn," Martinez said, "you really know how to rain on a parade!"

"Not if we prepare. I've got some ideas. We let the application slide through the zoning board. Melandino would know what to expect, and he'd be loaded for bear. We'd probably lose. So we fight in City Council. We use the old arguments on quality of life, but our strongest assault is on lack of need. We'd allege harms of over-developing commercial and show pictures of shopping centers occupied way below capacity, thus inviting urban blight. And we'd get to every alderperson individually before the vote. It's a different strategy, one Melandino wouldn't expect."

"Sounds good to me!" Martinez said.

Brown nodded in agreement.

I said, "I'm glad you like the strategy. Because you'll be leading the troops."

Martinez looked at me, his disappointment obvious, but he didn't reproach me.

Brown hesitated. "Maybe you should reconsider. We need strong leadership. This would be a critical juncture." The other two veterans nodded in agreement.

These people had knocked themselves out to stand together for weeks to win this round. How could I explain to them that I decided not to risk my professional career to fight the next round.

Brown said, "We'd lose some advantage without you, no doubt about that." He looked at Martinez, apologetically. "I'm not saying you and I couldn't lead the fight. We'll have to."

The trucker said, "Brownie is right, Ken. You're our leader. We'll do the best we can. You get on with the rest of your life."

I felt like shit.

CHAPTER THIRTY

Three days later, Dr. Jones watched me from across his desk. I reported my decision to turn any new zoning battle over to Martinez. I figured Jones would reassure me that I'd made the best decision, maybe even offer a little praise that I'd actually made a hard choice on my own. Instead, he said nothing for a half a minute.

"How do you feel about that decision?" he finally asked.

"I should feel free to get on with my thesis and my career," I replied without hesitation.

"And how _do_ you feel?"

What the hell is Jones getting at?

"I already told you. I feel free."

"You told me how you think you <u>should</u> feel." He paused and smiled. "How your mother would want you to feel."

Oh Christ, we're back to that!

"What did you find in your father's billfold?"

I hesitated. "I haven't looked into it yet. The zoning case and aftermath kept me busy."

I had a flashback to my undergraduate days when a missed assignment called for an excuse, even a feeble one.

Jones said nothing, but that faint smile told me he wasn't buying it. He offered encouragement for me to get on with my thesis, but it seemed *pro forma*. He was losing interest in my case—at least, until I looked into that billfold.

The next day Victoria went shopping. I was alone in the house. The papers sent by family and friends after Dad's funeral were in a neat stack on a credenza in the den. The billfold, about which I was beginning to have weird misgivings, topped the stack. I'd got the stuff together days ago, and then my nerve or energy gave out.

The kitchen and den didn't give a lot of room for pacing, but about ten trips while breathing heavily were enough for me to feel my head was on straight.

I removed the billfold, set it aside, took a half-inch stack of pamphlets and folders off the top. An easy chair faced out the window. A coffee table beside it would hold the unread documents. I'd turn the ones facedown in another pile as I read them. Even if some of the news to be gleaned was bad, I believed I was comfortable enough to begin.

The first three documents were promotional booklets for small but ambitious tourism centers in the 1920's in Wyoming and Colorado. Dad was listed as editor and on two of them as an author. I recognized one of the centers that had become perhaps the most prestigious destination in Wyoming. I felt a surge of pride that my father was one of the people who opened that area up to tourism and wealthy homes.

The next several documents were newspaper stories, letters, and eulogies about Al Bailey. It became clear that, at least in Western Colorado, he was highly respected as a newspaperman. One letter from an editor of a newspaper from which he'd just resigned gave him a glowing recommendation, praising his character and skills. Praising his character? This was indeed odd, but I could detect no signs of insincerity. This pattern continued into his final years. He also had a love of life and was a great charmer, according to this pile of documents from diverse sources.

I began to see my father as radically different from what my mother had told me. He was guilty of the transgressions and failures of which she accused him, no doubt about that. I'd seen ample evidence of that, but her view of the man, I now realized, was woefully incomplete. I should have seen that years ago. I now saw a deeply frustrated man. As the years piled up, his chances of escaping the conflict between domineering family and inviting career faded. Perhaps that was why he drank so much and went nuts in his final years.

Or was I cutting him too much slack? He was after all, a man who ended his career selling fire extinguishers and as a womanizer. Mom tried to protect me from urges I might have to imitate him. But did she have to destroy my chance to respect him?

A couple of eulogies by people who knew him in those last few years commented that he was very good at selling door to door. I could take little pride in that. It was a pathetic way to end his career. I was surprised by an unexpected surge of sympathy for a father Mom had caused me to hate so much that even when he was dying, I rejected him. He didn't deserve that. I was one of the few last things he could finally point to with some degree of pride. My aunts told me he was indeed proud of me. I'd avoided him even at the end. It was too late now to do anything about that. I was damned if I'd weep. Neither one of my parents wept, at least not in front of me.

My chair faced out onto the desert, now growing dark. I'd fought to protect our piece of land, just as my father had fought to save the family ranch. Dad had set a model that, as Mom would be the first to point out, would be catastrophic for me to imitate. Or would it? She seemed to have evidence for her view that came from his life. And she had her own plan for what my life should be.

My eyes fell on the billfold. I couldn't duck it any longer. I reached over, picked it up, and opened it. The envelope, with a single sheet of paper in it was pressed flat from being carried for years. I unfolded the sheet of paper. The message was short:

After performing all appropriate tests, I can say with confidence that Albert Bailey does not have, nor has he ever had syphilis. To my knowledge, he has no record of any other venereal disease.

I stared at the letter as the desert grew darker. Mom had lied to me. And she knew she lied. She had messed up my relationship with my father. _Why_? There could be only one answer: she wanted to control my life. I didn't fault her for this. She believed her husband had failed in life, and she wanted to keep me from doing the same. But she didn't understand her husband—or me. She intended for me to play it safe, and God knows I tried.

Verbal combat made me come alive. It was true in debate and in my "scholarly" presentations. It was even more true in the zoning battle. No doubt, more such battles would come at me in the future, and I could duck them or not.

Mom had really believed I would be satisfied to, as she put it, climb the ladder of success to a comfortable and secure life. With enough smug self-satisfaction, I could avoid seeing that goal was another version of greed or cowardice.

I could no longer avoid choices between merely grubbing out a safe living versus taking chances in service to what I believed to be good and true. It would often not be an easy choice, sometimes not or even a clear choice. I knew that. But now I'd discovered my path. My father, flawed as he was, became my model.

Mom and I had been through so much together, and she had done so much to support my schooling that it seemed cruelly unjust to abandon her values. My eyes watered. Much as I respected, even admired her, I was my father's son.

The desert turned fully dark, with only a silhouette of the hill outlined against the sky.

I dialed Martinez. "Joe, Ken Bailey here. When the next zoning battle comes, I will join the fight. We will win again."

And we did win again and again. We saved the dessert. It took several more summers to finish my Ph.D. dissertation.

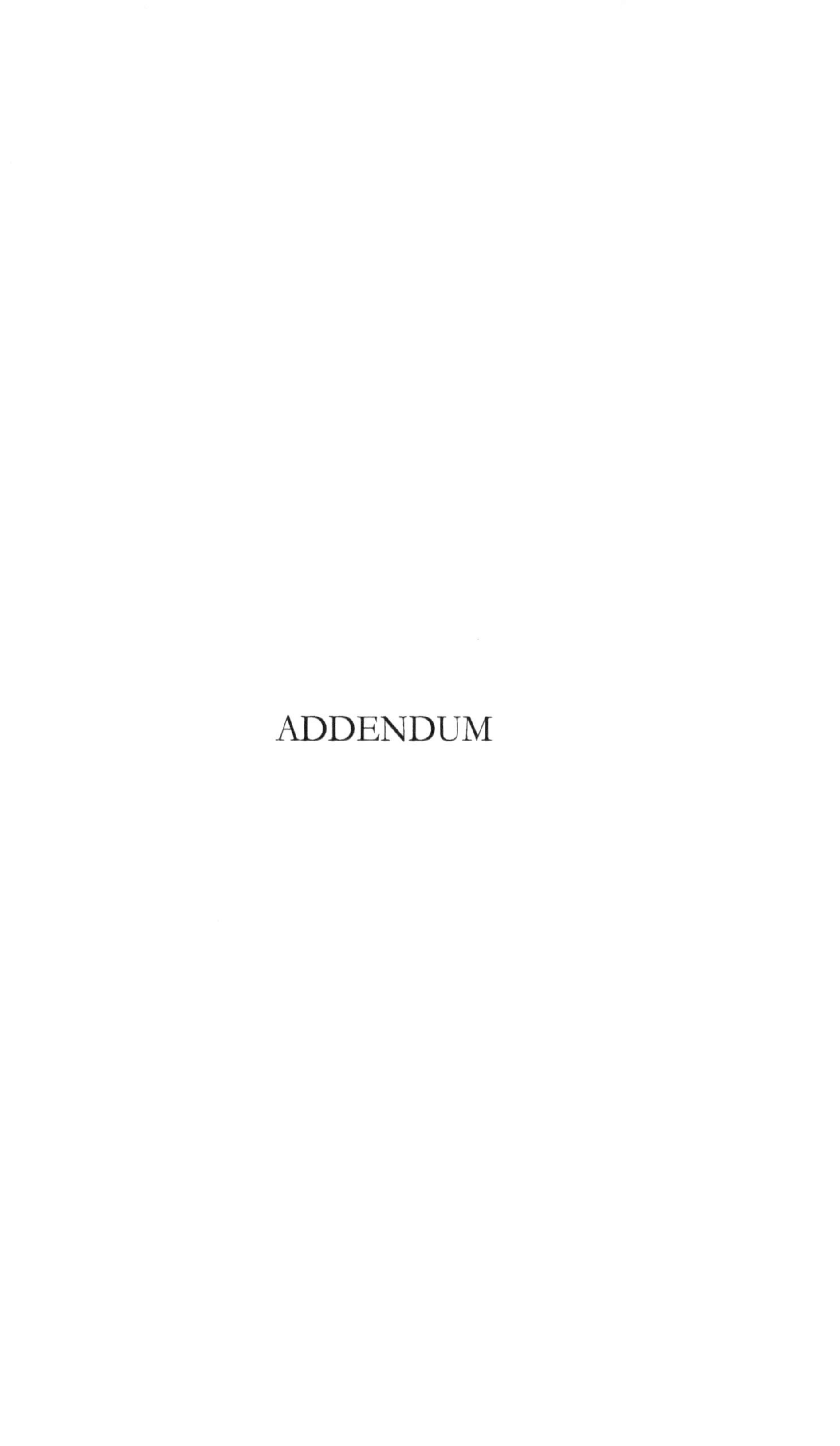

ADDENDUM

When Ken's mother died he disappeared into his study for two days to write. Then he ordered a simple burial for her, with Victoria and a few friends standing around her grave as he read what he had written:

REMARKS AT THE GRAVE OF MY MOTHER, MARCH 3, 1978

As my mother passes from this world, it may be that, as if from a mountain top, she can see her life traced out below.It would appear as a long journey, for much of her life was truly a wandering from place to place. Now she no longer needs be concerned with each step in that journey. Now we also can perhaps catch some glimpse of the totality of her life, some understanding of what it meant.

Her journey begins in harsh mining camps in the Colorado mountains; it traces past the schools where, while still in her teens, she began teaching in order to care for a younger brother and sister; and for a generation it wanders through an alternation of small rural schools and bleak ranch life. Through much of this earlier and larger part of her life my mother felt very much alone, her only constant source of support was a sister, a great many miles distant. Later, her only constant companion a child for whom she felt keenly the awesome responsibility only a mother knows.

What she asked for herself from life was little enough————a home in which her own graciousness could bloom and in which she could at last feel some tangible stability. In her aging years in Salem, Oregon she did at last have this home and this graceful life. She could be content also that, though they were far distant from her, she had a family, with grandchildren in whom she took great pleasure and pride. These few final years of peace seem a modest reward for many years of hard, sometimes desperate struggle and a turmoil which was not conformable to her nature. Still she was satisfied. She asked for nothing more.

Finally, in recent months even that serenity was disturbed, and she was moved to this city. This last stage of her journey was perhaps the hardest, for she knew she was walking into a final dark valley. Yet to her very final day, even this she accepted with a fundamental dignity and grace that only now we can appreciate. Fortunately, her way was eased by the compassionate friendship of those she came to know in this last place. For these friendships she felt a deep and genuine gratitude that often she found difficult or impossible to express.

In all her journey Marie Wood had one unfailing guide: her duty to those persons around her and for whom she was given responsibility. No matter how difficult the journey, she never abandoned that duty. It was through that duty that she expressed her love for her fellow beings. She was a teacher. In her most characteristic and cheerful conversation, she would sometimes tell how she had helped this pupil overcome an obstacle to learning, how she had helped parents to understand and love another pupil, how some pupil who had come to her regarded as a slow learner had eventually graduated from law school with a Doctor of Jurisprudence, how she would let another child work with her after school hours so that child could increase his or her own sense of being accepted and having personal worth. She did really love those children as separate and individual people she could reach and help. That is how love and duty for her came together.

My mother was not a religious person. She did not acknowledge a love of God. This matter, at this time, must be faced. There may be those who fear for her on this account. Many years ago, she gave me a poem to read, a poem that she perhaps long ago forgot as suitable only for a child. But as an adult I read it now.

Abou Ben Adhem[1]

Awoke one night from a deep dream of peace,
And saw, within the moonlight in his room,
An angel writing in a book of gold.

To the presence in the room Ben Adhem said,
"What writest thou?" The vision raised its head,
And answered, "The names of those who love the Lord."
"And is mine one?" said Abou. "Nay, not so,"
Replied the angel. Abou spoke more low,
And said, "I pray thee, then,
Write me as one that loves his fellow men."

The angel wrote, and vanished. The next night
It came again with a great wakening light,
And showed the names whom love of God had blest,
And lo! Ben Adhem's name led all the rest.

The people among whom she worked recognized her gifts of love and skill.

When she retired from teaching, unusual honors were bestowed on her at a special ceremony of parents and past students. Their standing applause gave her happiness, but more important to her were individual parents' private expressions of gratitude. And most important were from the children she had taught. As she went through life she kept few tangible objects, but a letter was found among her last possessions. It is from a girl who had been a student of hers three years earlier. When my mother retired from a teaching career that lasted a half century, this was perhaps her most valued reward.

Dear Mrs. Wood,

I am real sorry you cannot teach anymore. I know how you like teaching. I said to my brother, "Mrs. Wood is a very good teacher, she is very nice. I know you would be in her room next year." After I heard you're not going to be here, I felt sick. Mrs. Wood, I don't want you to go, but I'm glad so many people feel the way I do and I'm sure my brother feels the same as I do. We'll miss you very much!

(Now in Sixth Grade)
One of Your Students
Myrna R. Bumanlag

My mother's journey has come to an end. As she looks down over that journey, she will see not only we who stand here. She will see the hundreds upon hundreds of men and women whose lives as children she touched with love and gentleness and concern. Through her gifts those lives were altered, and through those altered lives her essential being still prevails.

Let us commit the tangible sign of her physical being to this plot of ground.

Let us commit her soul to our memories, secure in our faith of her immortality.

- - - -

The funeral director who was in attendance told Victoria he had been to many final ceremonies, but he had never heard one as meaningful as the one Ken had written.

---

1. *Adapted from "Abou Ben Adhem" by James Henry Leigh Hunt.*

AFTERWORD

Some time ago, and maybe today as well, the notion that a "defining moment" can at times redirect the course of one's life became believed and popular. Reading the "truth" about his father in the letter in the billfold and saving his beloved desert from the developers were, by this definition, "defining moments" for the author. After those events he could then more easily focus on his chosen career and the rest of his life. In this book, he used the fictional names of Ken and Victoria to make it less painful to write about his early life.

He completed his Ph.D. degree at a distinguished university and then pursued his chosen career as a professor in Speech and Drama. In his 45-year career, he coached debate, published a college textbook, and taught several thousand students at the undergraduate and graduate levels at six well-regarded universities in subjects that included Public Speaking, Organizational Communication, Modern and Classical Rhetoric, Film Studies, and Film Making.

At the age of 66 he embarked on a second career writing fiction. He enjoyed attending writer's conferences. He wrote several short stories and four novels, this being his final effort.

He was the father of three sons. Despite his early reluctance, he very early came to admire his sons. He gave them good counsel, and he was, despite his initial misgivings, a proud, good father.

True to his profession, his three sons, David Webster, Sam Chatham, and Joe Tullius, carry middle names borrowed from distinguished orators.

Then, in turn, he named the main characters in three of his novels for each of his three sons: David Webster in

"The Odd One," is named after Daniel Webster, the American orator; Sam Chatham in "Broken Options" is named after Lord Chatham, Pitt the Elder, the British orator; and Joe Tullius in "The System Eliminator" is named after the classical orator Marcus Tullius Cicero.

As for me, I stayed by his side "in sickness and in health," as promised, for 61 years. I dearly miss him.

Nancy V. Wood

www.ingramcontent.com/pod-product-compliance
Lightning Source LLC
Chambersburg PA
CBHW020311160726
47992CB00004B/1479